The Rotinonshonni

The Iroquois and Their Neighbors
Christopher Vecsey, *Series Editor*

Other titles in the Iroquois and Their Neighbors series:

The Rotinonshonni

A Traditional Iroquoian History through the Eyes of Teharonhia:wako and Sawiskera

BRIAN RICE

SYRACUSE UNIVERSITY PRESS

First Paperback Edition 2016
22 23 24 25 6 5 4 3 2

For a listing of books published and distributed by Syracuse University Press,
visit https://press.syr.edu.

ISBN: 978-0-8156-1067-0 (paper)
978-0-8156-1021-2 (cloth)
978-0-8156-5227-4 (e-book)

Library of Congress has cataloged the hardcover edition as follows:

Rice, Brian, 1955–
The Rotinonshonni : a traditional Iroquoian history through the eyes of
Teharonhia:wako and Sawiskera / Brian Rice.
p. cm.
Includes bibliographical references.
ISBN 978-0-8156-1021-2 (cloth : alk. paper) 1. Iroquois mythology. 2. Iroquois
Indians—Folklore. 3. Iroquois Indians—History. I. Title.
E99.I7R525 2013
398.2089'9755—dc23 2013018101

Contents

Illustrations

Preface

Most history written about the Rotinonshonni, by either Indigenous or non–Indigenous persons, is written as a chronology of events of what are perceived to be facts related to the past. They are based on the assumption that history can be written without taking into account the worldview of the people who are being written about. *The Rotinonshonni: A Traditional Iroquoian History through the Eyes of Teharonhia:wako and Sawiskera* is a history written from the worldview of the Rotinonshonni, or People of the Longhouse, to explain why events have occurred in their society in the way that they have. It almost exclusively uses oral traditions to explain the events in that history. The philosophical understanding within the Rotinonshonni worldview is just as important in compiling this history as is the use of the oral traditions. Without that understanding it cannot be considered a complete Rotinonshonni history. That worldview has its expression in the creation story. From a Rotinonshonni perspective, the events that occurred during the time of creation have an effect on what is happening today. They may not be relevant to any other society; however, they are completely relevant to the members of the Rotinonshonni. Without that cultural understanding, the members of the society are left with few answers as to why events have played out and continue to play out as they have. There is, then, little chance of the culture continuing to exist and thrive into the future. If that happens, the Rotinonshonni members will have become fully integrated into a history that is not of their own making. Once that occurs, they will be left with few opportunities to transform themselves, based on their own cultural values and teachings, into the future. This work explains the process of oral history by way of the written word from a Rotinonshonni worldview. But it also teaches the lessons that members should adhere to in order to continue moving forward. These are first pointed out in the creation story; then the *Kayeneren:kowa*; and finally the *Kari:wio*. My own journey in first walking the path of the Peacemaker before writing this work is a contemporary reflective look at what is occurring in Rotinonshonni territory today, as well as a reminding others that, if the three above are no longer adhered to as being an integral part of the Rotinonshonni philosophy and belief systems, the culture itself will stagnate, and the *Rotinonshonni* as a unique people, who have evolved through the intervention of the creator, will cease to do so. As this work shows, the responsibility from the beginning of time lies with the *onkwe:honwe,* real human beings, of the Rotinonshonni People of the Longhouse.

Acknowledgments

Many depths of gratitude are owing to persons. I would first like to express my gratitude to Oneida Traditionalist and Academic, Pamela Apela Colorado, my doctoral program supervisor, for holding the door open and pointing the way, so that this work could get done. As well, to Cayuga *royaner* Jake *Hadajigerenhtah* Thomas for showing me what was inside the door and how to view it. I would also like to thank Mohawk Traditional elder Skokwenionkwas Tom Porter from Kanatsiohareke for giving the original work its needed traditional sanction. I would like to thank the late Tekaronioneken Jake Swamp from Akwesasne for continuing to help with the recitals of the *Kayeneren:kowa* after the passing of Jake Thomas. I would like to thank Norma General and Winnie Thomas from Six Nations for giving this work its purpose by continuing the Journeys of the Peacemaker. Also, thanks to Mohawk historian Darren Bonaparte for valuing this work on his website, The Wampum Chronicles (http://www.wampumchronicles.com/). Due to publishing considerations, Darren has graciously had it removed. I would also like to thank Kimberly Wilde for going over the manuscript and helping with the formatting and some editing. Most of all I would like to thank Kanhotonkwas Yvonne Thomas for keeping the door of knowledge open so that we could learn.

The Rotinonshonni

Introduction

The Rotinonshonni: A Traditional Iroquoian History through the Eyes of Teha-ronhia:wako and Sawiskera is based on the oral interpretation of history about the Rotinonshonni, People of the Longhouse, also known as the Iroquois. The events of the story take place in what are now known as the Mississippi River Valley, upper New York State, Southern Quebec, and Ontario. My goal was to put down as much of that tradition on paper as possible. The purpose was to create from oral traditions a history that could inform the reader not only about events that had taken place in the past but inform how those events have shaped and are still transforming Rotinonshonni society today.[1]

To best achieve this goal, this work had to be written from the cultural perspective of the Rotinonshonni reflected in the story of the twin brothers in the creation story. It is through their actions and intervention that most of this story is given its perspective. However, before this work could be written, its writer would have to embark on a life-transforming journey that would inspire him to tell this story in a way that would reach the most people. That journey began in 1992, two years after the Oka Crisis in Quebec that pitted the Canadian Armed Forces against the Kenienké:haka (Mohawk) communities of Kahnawaké and Kanehsatake over the building of a golf course on a Mohawk burial site.

During the 1990 Oka Crisis, I was involved in an Indigenous teachers training program sponsored by McGill University. The program included Mohawk, Cree, and Algonquin students. As the crisis progressed, there were variances about the understanding of tradition, particularly in interpretations about the origins and meaning of the *Kayeneren:kowa*—Great Law of Peace, also known as the Great Way of Peace—among the Kenienké teachers. This piqued my interest and inspired me to want to explore this subject further. It eventually led me to the door of Kaokwa:haka *royaner,* peace chief, Jacob Thomas Hadajigerenhtah and his wife, Yvonne Kanhotonkwas, at Six Nations territory where I stayed briefly doing some clerical work for them. In return, I was given the privilege of listening to Jacob Thomas speaking about various aspects of oral tradition.

It was thanks to Jacob Thomas and his wife, Yvonne, who first facilitated nine-day Journeys of the Peacemaker in 1991 and 1992 by van that allowed me the knowledge of the places situated in the *Kayeneren:kowa* and enabled me to complete my own walking journey.

Included in the 1992 trip was Onontaka:haka (Onondaga) Clan Mother, Alice Papineau *Tewasentah. Royaner* Jacob Thomas recited the *Kayeneren:kowa* as we drove to the places included in the oral tradition. The late *Kenienké* Elder Jacob Swamp Tekaronieneken recited the *Kayeneren:kowa* on subsequent journeys I made with members from Six Nations and elsewhere after this work was completed.

It was during that same year that Jacob Thomas recited the *Kayeneren:kowa* for nine days at Six Nations territory, which I attended. Each morning there was a tobacco burning ceremony that took place as the Sun began to rise. The recitation was extremely intensive with Jacob Thomas beginning at 9:00 in the morning and finishing at 5:00 in the afternoon. I continued to attend subsequent sessions held each year including a twelve-day session that began with the creation story. In 1994, I was fortunate to travel by car with Jake Thomas to Oneida Wisconsin where he did a five-day recital of the *Kayeneren:kowa.* The last recital that I attended was in 1996. During the sessions I sometimes took notes and other times simply listened trying to absorb as much as I could.

In 1994 I entered an all Native American Doctoral Program. In order to keep a position I held in Native Studies it was required I pursue my doctorate. Previously, I had been in a doctoral program in education at McGill University; however, the only Indigenous courses available were in the department of anthropology. I wanted something more culturally authentic. The Traditional Knowledge Program emphasized culturally specific research methodologies over standard qualitative and quantitative methodologies and was based more on participatory and experiential research.

1. Ceremonial sweatlodge before embarking on my life-transforming journey. Jake Thomas cooked medicines all day. Photograph courtesy of author.

Interesting enough, most Native Studies Programs have reverted back to standard anthropological research methods with anthropology courses now being referred to as Native Studies courses. This is what our program had tried so hard to avoid.

During my studies in Traditional Knowledge, I traveled to several countries where I was taught by Indigenous Elders. However, the Traditional Knowledge Program emphasized that one's work should be based on one's own traditions and not on those of someone else. Before pursuing my own work, I believed that in order to fulfill the mandate of a traditional methodology, it would mean that I had to earn the right to write about Rotinonshonni traditional knowledge. This would require a personal month-long journey of nearly seven hundred miles walking through Rotinonshonni territory, following the path of the Peacemaker.

It also meant going through a ceremonial process, in this case a sweatlodge ceremony and the passing of three beads of wampum, facilitated by the late *royaner* Jacob Thomas. There has been debate as to whether the sweatlodge was even a part of Rotinonshonni tradition. Jacob Thomas was adamant that it was and was beginning to reconstitute it back into the practices of the people at Six Nations.

The original doctoral work consisted of a chapter solely on the walk. However, due to the length of this work, I can only delve briefly here on the walk in this section.

I began my walk in Tyendinaga, a Mohawk community on the Bay of Quinté in Ontario, Canada. There I visited Eagle Hill where the Peacemaker was born and stayed for several hours until a thunderstorm arrived. It took me several days to reach Kingston, Ontario, where I then crossed over to Wolf Island and then crossed over once again before entering New York State.

While walking along Lake Ontario, I had one spiritual experience that had to do with a dream. It consisted of a radiance of light trying to get through the door of the room I was staying in. I tried, but failed, to hold the light back. My director for my doctoral program, Apela Colorado, told me later on, that she believed it to be the Peacemaker. I also had to deal with pain in a leg I had badly bruised a month before. I was afraid that I would have to quit partway through the walk.

I headed east at Port Ontario, New York, walking to Fort Stanwix, in Rome, New York. It was there where several treaties were signed between the Rotinonshonni, with first the British in 1768 and then the Americans in 1784. In both treaties Rotinonshonni land was lost. I crossed into Oneota:haka (Oneida) territory at Woods Creek and came to Oriskany battlefield.

I must mention that each day before walking I burned tobacco and prayed. I consider Oriskany to be one of the most important places that I visited. It was there that Kenienké:haka (Mohawk) and Sonontowa:haka (Seneca) fought against Oneota:haka (Oneida) during the American Revolutionary War. It is the place where the covenant that bound all *onkwe:honwe*, real people, to the Great Law of Peace was broken.

I promised that I would return to this place one day with other *onkwe:honwe* to help heal the wounds that were rooted in this land, where weapons were taken up when brother fought against brother. I was given that opportunity a year after my journey, when I was asked by

2. Eagle Hill, birthplace of the Peacemaker. Photograph courtesy of author.

Sonontowa:haka (Seneca) Elder Norma General of Six Nations Territory to help facilitate a journey back to the homeland. Along with representatives of the five original Rotinonshonni Nations, we held a tobacco burning ceremony conducted by Kenienké Elder Jake Swamp. Some *onkwe:honwe* had powerful visions at this place as we walked in, and then out of, the shadow of Rotinonshonni history. I would subsequently be asked to help facilitate several journeys after as well. And what was more important for me, my doctoral work would contribute to spreading knowledge of the stories and traditions to others.[2]

Traveling east, at Little Falls I met some people who lived in the mountains overlooking the Mohawk valley. They took me to some Mohawk burial mounds where we burned tobacco. I then walked past Molly Brant's place, the Kenienké wife of Sir William Johnson, and sister to Joseph Brant, the Kenienké war chief who led many *onkwe:honwe* to Six Nations Territory after the American Revolutionary War.

I then passed through Canajoharie, the village where the Kenien-ké:haka of Six Nations originally came from. There were also several

Kenienké sites along the way such as the village where the Jesuit priest Isaac Jogues was reported to have been martyred years before. I also passed Fort Hunter where the Kenienké of Tyendinaga originated. Finally, I reached Cohoes Falls, the place where the Peacemaker was tested by the Kenienké war chiefs and then made them into *royaner*, peace chiefs. This included the Peacemaker's spokesman, Ayenwatha (Hiawatha), who, with the Peacemaker and Tsakonsasé, would formulate the *Kayeneren:kowa*, Great Law of Peace. It is this very aspect—war chiefs being transformed into peace chiefs—that Jacob Thomas believed some *onkwe:honwe* miss in the formulating of the Great Law of Peace. According to him, the Peacemaker abolished war chiefs by making them good minded. Therefore the words "war chief" are an oxymoron in a society whose oral constitution is based on the concept of peace.

From Cohoes Falls, I walked west, visiting William Johnson's place at Johnson Hall where many councils were held with the British. From there I proceeded west until I reached old Kahnawaké. This was one of the Kenienké villages of my ancestors. In truth, the original Kahnawaké is about three miles away from the site.

After visiting Kahnawaké, I made my way to Kenienké Elder Tom Porter's home. I was really nervous about visiting him; I wondered whether I would be criticized for making this trip. Tom graciously took me in, and with his family he fed me and gave me bedding for the night. Tom would later be a signatory to my dissertation. This was on the recommendation of my director Apela Colorado, who felt that he was the perfect person to be the traditional Elder required for my committee.

I then traveled to Oneida, New York, where I stayed with a friend. The name Oneida or *Oneota:haka* comes from a standing stone that was sacred to them and was said to follow them wherever they traveled. I wondered if the wounds from the revolution could ever be healed in the various dispersed *onkwe:honwe* communities. At Oneida is the standing stone that the people were named after. From Oneida, I began to walk to Onondaga. As soon as I reached the border of the territories of the two nations, I was met with a ferocious thunderstorm. These storms were referred to as the Flying Heads by my people and were seen as both dangerous and powerful with the ability to heal. In fact, one man was killed that day. I placed my

3. Cohoes Falls, where the Peacemaker was tested by the Kenienké war chiefs. Photograph courtesy of author.

tobacco down and was immediately refreshed by the thunder spirits cool rains and walked without fear to Onontaka community, the central fire of the confederacy where the Onontaka:haka, People of the Hills, lived.

The next day, I was supposed to meet Jacob Thomas and Bill Woodworth at Onontaka. Unfortunately they missed me by several hours. Onontaka was the place of the central fire of the confederacy where the Great Tree of Peace was planted. Like the Kaokwa:haka next to them, the Onontaka:haka were forced west to live with the Sonontowa:haka after been dispersed by Americans soldiers during the Sullivan campaigns of 1779, when many of the Rotinonshonni were ethnically cleansed from their lands. In 1794, a treaty was made between them and the United States, allowing the Onontaka:haka to move back to their lands on the condition that they did not ally with the Ohio tribes during their wars with the Americans. Not far from Onontaka is the stone where Atotarhoh, the great war chief and shaman sat while waiting for the Peacemaker. As the Peacemaker and Ayenwatha—later known as Hiawatha—were heading west to bring the message of peace, he would yell *Asokannee*, "is it

4. Six Nations Confederacy Longhouse at Onontaka:haka (Onondaga). Photograph courtesy of author.

time," knowing a transformation was about to occur that would affect him and his people for ever.

I then traveled south to Tully Lake, where Ayenwatha saw ducks fly off and on the lakebed found shells for wampum. From there, I decided that I would travel east and head for Cayuga country. The Onontaka country was the hardest country to walk. The country was reflective of their name, People of the Hills.

Finally, I reached Cayuga Lake after more thunderstorms passed through. On the north bank of the lake is a stretch of marshes. In fact the Kaokwa:haka are sometimes referred to as the Mucky Lake People and is reflected in their real name Kaokwa:haka.

From Cayuga Lake, I entered the last stretch of my walk. I passed by Seneca Lake where a large Sonontowa:haka village was once situated. I then finished my walk at the seventeenth-century Sonontowa:haka site, Ganondagan. Here, Pete Jemmison, a Sonontowa:haka, had kept the memory of his ancestors alive. He was in the process of building a traditional longhouse. Pete showed me where he thought Tsakonsasé, the mother of nations, once resided. Because she was a member of the neutral nation called Kakwakoes, he wondered why her dwelling would be located near a seventeenth-century Seneca village.

5. Author sitting on Atotarhoh's phallic-shaped stone in Syracuse, N.Y. Photograph courtesy of author.

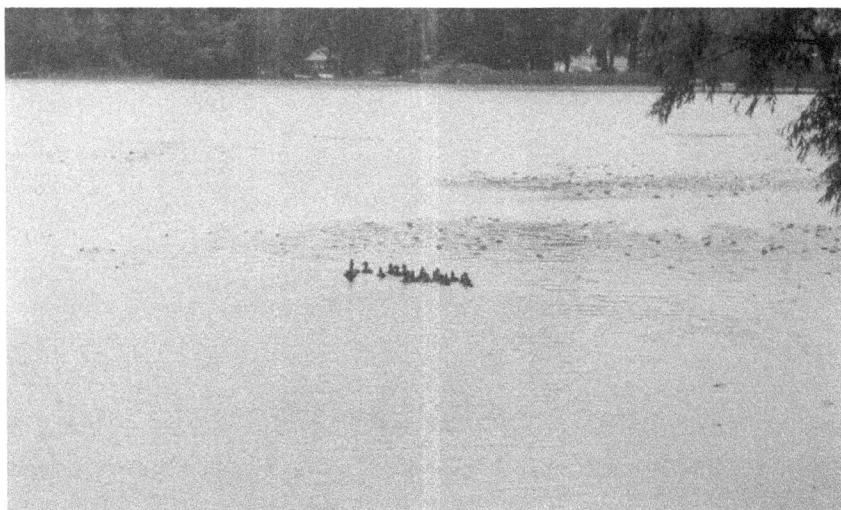

6. Tully Lake, where Ayenwatha (Hiawatha) discovered wampum. Photograph courtesy of author.

7. Marshy Upper Cayuga Lake. Photograph courtesy of author.

8. Ganondagan, where the author finished his 650-mile walk. Photograph courtesy of author.

9. Tsakonsasé's War Trail. Photograph courtesy of author.

The fact is, there were many Tsakonsasés who lived. Hers was a title passed on like that of a *royaner*. She was chosen to keep the peace by all of the surrounding nations. After the Peacemaker visited her, she was given the duty of helping to choose the remaining *royaner*, Good Minded Leaders of the Five Nations, and to be a guide to future Clan Mothers in how to administer the peace. Her original settlement before the advent of the Kayeneren:kowa, Great Law, was near Niagara Falls, at Lewiston, New York, where the Tuscarora people now resided. They had entered the Rotinonshonni confederacy, becoming its sixth nation in 1722, after being displaced by English settlers in North Carolina.

Bill Woodworth and I would, after some inquiry, find the path where her lodge was situated. The Seneca incorporated most of the neutrals during the seventeenth century, including Tsakonsasé's title. In fact, there was a mostly neutral populated village close to Ganondagan during this period of time. It was at Ganondagan that I finished my walk. I would only see Jake Thomas one more time before he passed away. He had just finished another reciting of the Great Law of Peace at Ganondagan. Jake told Bill that when people take your picture it takes a little time out of your life. During the recital Jake had a lot pictures taken, but told Bill it was fine, as the work had to get done before he left. I ended my chapter on my walk with Jacob Thomas's passing not long after his self-prophetic words came true. Now I had found the validation and knowledge to write my dissertation.

There were several problems faced while writing this work. The first had to do with translating concepts that come from an oral tradition into the written English language. Kaokwa:haka *royaner* Jacob Thomas Hadaji-grenhtah had always believed that a great deal was being lost whenever he recited the traditions in English, but especially when he translated them into the written English language. There were certain concepts that couldn't be expressed because of the differences in the understanding of European languages and the Indigenous languages, such as that of the Rotinonshonni. Nonetheless, with the loss of Elders, he also believed that it was important that what was left be passed on, even if it meant being passed on in the English language. Perhaps at some time in the future, this could then be reproduced back into the Indigenous language. In fact, before he passed on, Jacob Thomas was about to make a final recitation in the Kaokwa:haka language.

A narrative approach to writing this work in English was chosen as the best means of expressing what was meant in the oral tradition.

Although many academic works are written using a style rooted in Western academic tradition, this work blends the academic and the Indigenous oral traditions. Oral tradition, by its very nature, uses dialogue as a method to express concepts and information. Because of the uniqueness of what I set out to put down on paper and because it is important to remain true to the oral tradition of the Rotinonshonni, this document follows this traditional way of expression as closely as possible. Therefore, you, the reader are in for a special experience as many may not have had the opportunity to be exposed to an Indigenous Turtle Island, North American, epistemology and way of learning.

The oral traditions are the stories that were spoken about by the Elders from time immemorial. However, in the recent past, many of these stories have been broken up, so that most listeners learn only segments of the story. I wanted to provide a comprehensive understanding of the oral tradition, as well as an understanding of the worldview that formed those traditions. So I have attempted to create a more complete history for the reader through some of these stories. The reader would then be able to see how those events played out in various forms and at different times in Rotinonshonni society, often repeating themselves during times of crises. During those moments of crises, the Rotinonshonni would go through a process of renewal, from the spiritual understandings given to them by the Creator in order to meet the changes that were taking place.

In the recent past, most of what had been written down about the Rotinonshonni traditional stories had been passed on by European Christian clergy or non-Indigenous academics that were influenced by their Christian beliefs. This was especially true from the time of contact up to the early twentieth century. In the case of the Christian clergy, they noted events as they were in the process of converting Indigenous people into becoming Christian. Sometimes, one can find elements of the culture in these writings.

With the beginning of the social sciences in the mid-nineteenth century, most were more interested in taking down the myths for posterity's sake because they believed they were seeing a dying culture that would disappear. Unlike the Tanakh[3] of the Jews—which has been a source of inspiration for millions of non-Jewish Christians as the Old Testament and could also be classified as myth if one used the same standards given to Rotinonshonni beliefs—most writers of the Rotinonshonni traditions up to the mid-nineteenth century, and even later on, never believed there to be anything spiritually significant in the traditional stories of the Rotinonshonni. However the Tanakh is viewed as a chronology of divinely inspired historical events occurring to the descendants of the Jewish people and then passed on to the non-Jewish Christians in a covenant between them and Jesus Christ, whom they believe to be the son of God.

Often, early non-Indigenous writers took down these stories without having any comprehension of the deeply rooted spirituality that was in these traditions. In fact, most of these writers who were Christian did not consider the spiritual stories of any other peoples as being valid unless they were Christian. They had come from a world that believed that Adam and Eve were the first man and woman and that all of humanity derived from these two beings, in spite of the fact that they were descendants of the Jewish people and not European. In fact, as late as the nineteenth century, Christians believed the world had its beginnings around six thousand years ago.

As Darwin's[4] theory of evolution began to gain prominence in the mid-to late nineteenth century, it resulted in the beginning of the social sciences, such as anthropology. The racist views of men like Lewis Henry Morgan,[5] the first writer on Rotinonshonni culture and society, saw humanity as a series of stages of evolution, with the European peoples at the head. The Rotinonshonni were classified by him, along with people of other non-European societies, as being socially and even physically inferior to European peoples. Even the Christian religion was considered a part of the social advancement that European peoples had made toward a better, more socially just, civilized society.

Today, writers who write about the Rotinonshonni, such as those in the field of ethnohistory, are trying to insert a more unbiased and favorable interpretation of the Rotinonshonni culture into their works. However, they haven't deviated from the writing methods that their predecessors used. Most of the ethnohistorians are non-Indigenous with the exception of a few, such as Dr. George Sioui,[6] a Wendat Huron, who believes that we must begin to write our histories from our own cultural perspectives in order for them to be true histories that represent our people. Another is Darren Bonaparte, a Mohawk writer who is writing Mohawk history from his peoples' perspective and was the first to acknowledge this work on his website the Wampum Chronicles.

Other non-Indigenous ethnohistorians have attempted to understand the motivations of the cultures they were writing about by better interpreting the works of their predecessors. However, few have ever spoken to a traditional Elder or have been witnesses to contemporary expressions of North American Indigenous culture that still to some degree retain the worldview they are trying to reflect in their writings. The exception of this being William Fenton,[7] along with a few others who have witnessed Rotinonshonni culture firsthand. Even writings such as his offer little into the deeper spiritual insights of the culture and how from those traditions one may interpret the motivations of the people who represent that culture. They cannot do so, because they interpret things from their Euro-Western understanding; therefore, the spirituality has no meaning for them. However, the writer believes that not writing from an insider's perspective means that they cannot claim to be writing Indigenous history. Instead, they are trying to find a place for Indigenous people in their own cultural construct of what history is.

This is not to say that the writer believes that the histories and stories these people wrote down about the Rotinonshonni have no value. In fact, they make excellent secondary sources and can be used to enhance Indigenous history. The speech by Kiasaton, in the *Jesuit Relations*,[8] for instance, or an even more contemporary work such as William Fenton's *The Great Law and the Longhouse*[9] offer a few examples of Indigenous expressions of culture that have been useful to the writer.

Although Fenton's work has few specifics about the *Kayeneren:kowa*, Great Law of Peace,[10] some aspects of tradition that Fenton learned could be used as reference points to the oral tradition of the Great Law of Peace by Rotinonshonni orators such as Jacob Thomas. If he hadn't put down some of these details, elements of these stories might have become lost. Some of these stories and histories have also been helpful in allowing the writer to find out when certain events in the oral traditions might have occurred, an example being the wars between the Anishnaabe and the Kenienké:haka that are a part of the oral tradition of both groups.

For example, we know from European historical tradition that there were Iroquoian people living along the St. Lawrence River when Jacques Cartier arrived in 1534 and that within a seventy-year period they disappeared. From the oral traditions of the Anishnaabe, we can learn that they migrated and displaced a people they referred to as Muntua, People of Spirit, and then Natowaug, Snakes, around that time. Then from archeological digs, we know that a culture referred to as the Point Peninsula[11] cultures were in the process of a migration from the east coast around that time period. By using all this information, along with various oral traditional sources, the writer was able to surmise when an event might best have occurred that became a part of the Rotinonshonni oral tradition.

It is important to note that, although the writer has read dozens of books on history about the Rotinonshonni, none have allowed him a deeper understanding of the integration of the cultural history and spirituality than have the recitation of the *Kayeneren:kowa,* Great Law of Peace, by traditional orator Jacob Thomas and conversations with someone of his knowledge and insights.

Nonetheless, some of the historical writings have been helpful. In fact, when Jacob Thomas was alive, he would ask me whether I had found something that was written down in the past that could corroborate his knowledge of the oral tradition. If the event had occurred in postcolonial times, the writer would always find the corroboration that Jacob was looking for. A case in point was Jacob Thomas's oral tradition about the loss of many Oneota:haka men to their clans during warfare and the need to replace them with Kenienké:haka men. This traditional story was found in *Jesuit Relations* and occurred somewhere around the 1620s or before. Another example was the ascendancy of the war chiefs over the *royaner,* before and around the time of the Revolutionary War.[12] There is a lot of evidence that the writer found and put down to corroborate this oral tradition.

One of the most important things that Jacob Thomas taught was to look at the creation story if one wanted to understand how events shaped the history and the culture of the Rotinonshonni. He would say that within the creation story exist all the elements that have influenced Rotinonshonni society to this present time. When reading it, the reader will find not only the essential values that tie the Rotinonshonni to their environment but also how as human beings people are supposed to conduct themselves in their relationships with non-human beings.

With this idea in mind, I decided to write my book from the context of the creation story. In doing so, the creation story that best exemplified the Rotinonshonni worldview to its fullest extent had to be found. "The Myth of the Earth Grasper"[13] by John Arthur Gibson, as well as what I had learned about creation from Jacob Thomas were therefore chosen as the bases to the rest of the story. Jacob Thomas's oral recitation of the creation story follows Gibson's recitation, but with less detail. The creation story reminded the writer of the silver covenant chain, an agreement between the Rotinonshonni and the British, that over time would become encrusted with rust. It had to be continually polished before the beauty and the full extent of its meaning could come to the forefront. This was the process that the writer had to take when setting down this story. It had to be continually worked.

Once this was done, the creation story was divided into sections, based on its length and based on the dramatic changes that occurred that have had a profound affect on the world and on the *onkwe:honwe*, real people, themselves. The same was done with the second chapter that consists of two main events in the history of the *onkwe:honwe*. The two main events were the establishing of the clan system and the migration.

In chapter 3, the oral tradition of the *Kayeneren:kowa*, Great Law of Peace, told by Jacob Thomas is used as the main source, although with the writer's own innovations to the wording. The recitations took place over a period of years, most of which I attended. With the passing of many of the Elders involved, the writer believes that he is passing on a tradition in this work in the same manner that it was received. That is to further educate *onkwe:honwe* and others into the understanding of the Rotinonshonni spirituality, culture and history.

All the other chapters are written as one piece in the way they were written or told with sections that I have included, but with the added addition from the perspective of the twins in creation. Only in chapter 4 are historical sources outside the oral traditions used. However, the recorded voice of the person speaking during an event that transpired and that had a bearing on the history of the Rotinonshonni is used. In a few places, the voice of what a speaker might have said during a certain historical event has been embellished. This is to keep it in line with the rest of the story and tradition.

This book and the way it was put together beg an important ethical question: Who owns the right to the stories that the writer has put down? It is believed by the writer that first and foremost the Rotinonshonni own collectively the stories that are put down and not the present writer, or ethnologists, anthropologists, or even traditional Elders before him. The ideas in the story belong to no one person, including the present writer, Jacob Thomas, or John Arthur Gibson. They in fact belong to the society from which they derived. In fact, one can find an abundance of stories from various sources on particular aspects of oral tradition in the library or even on the Internet. However, all these individuals had their own unique way of telling an oral tradition that exclusively belonged to them. This is what made the attendance of a recital of the *Kayeneren:kowa* by Jacob Thomas so invaluable. It was as much about who was telling the oral tradition as it was the tradition itself.

However, the way those stories are presented belong to the oral reciter of the stories, and they deserve the credit. The writer of this story claims only his interpretation of those stories, as this is his exclusive domain. That is what gives this present work its uniqueness. In fact, Jacob Thomas had told the writer that each person has his or her way of telling a story, and that is what makes it unique. In former times, people used to compare stories and learn from one another. No one person owned a particular story. Therefore, the writer has worked out a process so that Yvonne Thomas, the wife of the late Jacob Thomas and founder of the Jake Thomas Learning Centre, will be in part a beneficiary of this work. Without her contribution to the teachings of tradition, this work could never have gotten done, as it was Yvonne who facilitated the first Journeys of the Peacemaker in 1991 and 1992 and the recitals of the Great Law of Peace, sometimes at great cost to both herself and Jacob. The rest of the proceeds from this work will go to the Haudenosaune Promise Fund at Syracuse University to benefit Iroquois students in furthering their education.

Because Gibson's creation story had been simply regurgitated to a writer before in the 1920s in an old form of English, this writer had to delve deeply to interpret every word and meaning in the story so that they would be comprehensible to the reader and reflect the Rotinonshonni worldview, based in a deeply understood relationship with the rest of the creation. Therefore, the writer added elements such as traditional star knowledge to the story and used concepts of the culture that he gleaned from Jacob, as well as his own experiences with other indigenous peoples in interpreting and writing the creation story.

Chapter 5, the *Kari:wio*,[14] may have been the most challenging because of the variety of opinions as to its validity within contemporary Rotinonshonni society. The writer believes that it is as important to the continuance of the culture as the coming of the clans and the Great Law of Peace was. The writer chose to use the oldest version that he could find, which was written down in 1851, in Lewis Henry Morgan's *League of the Ho-de-no-sau-nee*[15] during a recitation by Shokentjo:wane. Although there may be elements that Shokentjo:wane left out that occurs in later versions, the writer believes that this version was put forth in its most pure form. That was before *Kari:wio* became replaced by dogma.

The writer wanted to avoid the versions that were written down at a later date, such as those by Arthur Parker that are still in use today that serve to perpetuate various agendas. The writer used the story of the Kenienké man who first had the visions and then disappeared, cited in Fenton's book,[16] *The Great Law and the Longhouse*. It is the story of the man who has visions and dies in the valley that is a part of some of the *Kari:wio* traditions. These visions were then passed on to Skanyiatar:io. The writer also tried to explain that this came during a specific time period, when the *onkwe:honwe* were once again in a perilous situation. The result being that what has been passed on today in terms of ceremonies and culture is due in no small part to the effort of Skanyiatar:io's visions. However, the writer believes that these visions have been subjected to outside influences in how they have been interpreted, which has caused division among contemporary traditionalists. The writer hopes that his interpretation of this section is just that, and that he is not adding to the controversy.

The writer did not want to make personal judgments about why this occurred, although from the readers' point of view, it may appear that he does. However, it should be pointed out that anything that appears to be a point of view, about events occurring, is only his interpretation of how Teharonhia:wako and his brother Sawiskera vie for control of the creation. It is from this cultural context that the writer chose to write this work in the way that he did. There may be those who may differ by what has been written as they may have their own interpretation; however the writer didn't want to have to compromise anything in this work by trying to be sensitive to the feelings of others but rather wanted to ensure that the twins remain a focus of this story.

The main point and conclusion of this work is this: a covenant occurred between the Creator and the *onkwe:honwe* and, if the *onkwe:honwe* are to survive as Rotinonshonni, they must keep their part of the covenant. That is, they must continue to practice the four ceremonies, the seasonal festivals, the Great Law of Peace, and the Good Message of Skanyiatar:io with both one another and with other nations, so that sin will discontinue among them. To clarify, sin is those things that have infiltrated from the outside by disrupting the balance within Rotinonshonni society, culture, and belief. In the story, Teharonhia:wako, the Creator, continually warns the *onkwe:honwe* that his brother will try any means to disrupt the creation and the *onkwe:honwe's* relationship within it.

The history also tells us that sometimes the *onkwe:honwe* break their part of the covenant, and, when that occurs, the Creator is merciful to the *onkwe:honwe* and restores the covenant in some new manner with them.

It should be noted that this is what the writer perceived and thought about during his walk, and it is his own contribution to the story. In fact, this was the traditional component that the writer undertook, to bring validation to his work on tradition and to give him the inspiration to write the previous chapters. It is hoped that the story will bear witness to those who follow the traditions, so that even if many of the *onkwe:honwe* no longer live in Rotinonshonni territory, the spiritual places will not be lost as long as the stories remain with them. It is hoped also that this work will continue to encourage other *onkwe:honwe* to make their own journeys, to further discover their own traditional homelands, history, and traditions, and to keep up the covenant that they have been given by the Creator. Although these pages are filled with some pain, there is still a wonderful story and lessons within them that need not be lost, as well as a territory that needs to be rediscovered, especially by the young who are so diligently searching to find themselves.

At the conclusion of the writer's walking journey inspired by the first Journeys of the Peacemaker facilitated by Yvonne and Jake Thomas in 2001 and 2002, traditional *onkwe:honwe* of the Six Nations Reserve in Ontario, Canada, were preparing a trip back to Rotinonshonni territory to make their own journeys of healing and renewal. They sent messages to all *onkwe:honwe* in other communities to come and join them.

Community member and Clan Mother Norma General called the writer on the telephone and told him that she and Winnie Thomas planned to arrange a trip by vehicle to follow the path of the Peacemaker.

A draft of the work was sent to her to examine in order for her to have access to more information about the writer's journey. She then asked him to do a presentation and help facilitate the journey that they were planning as he might have specific information that would help guide them. This journey of the *onkwe:honwe* to their homeland took place from June 5 to 13, 1999. There were five subsequent journeys, with the writer attending the last journey of the Peacemaker, in 2004 where he was honored with a gift from community members.

A recommendation is to assist in the recovery of knowledge for the Rotinonshonni youth by providing similar trips with Elders to provide a solid footing for them with which to walk in two worlds with confidence. In the future, these journeys could be incorporated with other learning activities.

Now, I invite you to take a journey of words with me through the history of the Rotinonshonni.

1

The Creation Story

The Sky World and the First Cosmological Beings

A long time before the world on the back of a turtle came into existence there was another world that preceded it, existing in the firmament in the sky situated on a celestial plane above the Earth. It was inhabited by a group of beings whose numbers were few and who were becoming destitute of the light-giving energies called *orenta*.[1] To exist in safety, these beings required this light-giving force to protect them from the malevolent forces that surrounded them. In times past, their world had been in a state of balance between the light-giving *orenta* and the freezing dark energy known as *otkon*.[2] Recently, the balance had shifted toward the *otkon* energy, and the people were becoming fearful. The light of their world was dimming, and there was little *orenta* left to protect them from the forces that could be used against them by those who chose to do so. If it continued, as was now occurring, the light would go out in the Sky World, and only darkness and cold would remain.

An Elder of the people named Akatuni:heno, the Ancient Uncle, knew that there was a way that the balance could be restored. He knew that there was a way of getting the *orenta* energies of the universe to help protect them and bring back the light into the world that was slowly disappearing. To do this, the people would have to find a young person pure of heart who had never had a child. The Ancient Uncle knew that children were brought into the world in a state of purity, and, by the time they reached the age of puberty, their light energies were at their peak. This is because children had not yet been released into the world. Those who had a child had given up part of their energy during the procreative

22

process, which weakened their light-giving energy. Children could also bring brightness to the world, as they had yet to be corrupted by the vices that had plagued the older members of the society.

Most notable were children born with a caul over their face, which means they were born still swimming in the waters of the womb. These children were believed to have special gifts, for they had been born by way of the Sky World and not through a physical act.[3]

During the time of puberty, children would be placed in seclusion for a period of time in which their own light energies could become focused. By doing this, they would be able to acquire the *orenta* that was beneficial to all the other beings in the Sky World. It would be up to the community to make sure that the youth had the proper upbringing so that the power that they received would be properly channeled. When youth were put into seclusion, it was referred to as being hidden under the husk, in reference to the protective husk surrounding the fresh corncob.[4] During this time the children would be protected. Once there, the youth would learn proper conduct to prepare them for adulthood and in this way there would be no misuse of the powers that existed within these energies. These powerful energies put under the control of someone with the wrong moral upbringing could bring darkness to the Sky World. There were some children who were more gifted than others. These special children could learn to tap into the light-giving forces of the universe, and, if they weren't taught the proper conduct, they could end up dimming the inner light that existed in other beings, as well as the outer light of the Sky World. The result of that would mean the end of the Sky World.

Akatuni:heno was also the uncle of his sister's two children, one a boy and the other a girl. As was the custom in the villages of the Sky World, the first brother of his sister's children was always considered the adviser in the upbringing of her children.[5] Akatuni:heno knew that his sister's children were gifted as they had been born with a caul. They were now at the age where they could be put into seclusion. It would be up to him to tell the two children that they would have to be concealed and that no other human beings but their mother and he would be able to see them until they had passed into adulthood. He would oversee the boy, while his sister would oversee the girl. If they did what they were told, the children would remain pure and be relieved of any potential negative energy that may try to enter them. They would have acquired enough of the much needed *orenta* that would protect their inner light from harm. Once the *orenta* was acquired, the children could never be harmed.

Before their instruction, the uncle spoke to the children and said to them, "Children, by the time you are finished your learning in seclusion, I will have left the sky world and you will never see me again. I have been afflicted by the dark freezing forces of *otkon*, which have made me ill."

As each day passed, Akatuni:heno's own inner light dimmed until there was only a flicker of light left in him. After telling the children what was happening to him, he said to them, "My children, after I pass from this world, look for the Great White Celestial Pine Tree that exists at the center of the world and carry me to its top."[6]

He knew that only those who were pure of nature could make it to the top of this tree, the tallest in the sky realm. Once placed on top of the tree, he would be protected from any malevolent forces that may try to further harm him. The top of the tree was situated in a higher world than even the Sky World, and he could oversee the children. This tree connected the different worlds of light. In each of these worlds, there existed a different living energy field that gave light to each world. Some of these worlds were more subtle in nature than others. The higher the world, the more pure was the light energy that inhabited it. The Sky World in which they lived was losing its light-giving energy and beginning to dim.[7]

The uncle said to the children as he was passing from the Sky World, "My children, if you ever need to speak to me, call out my name three times, and I will hear you the third time."[8]

That was because the number three was a mystical number whose sound, at the third attempt, could be heard at the higher levels. Akatuni:heno would always be there to watch over the children and help them if he were needed.

Upon hearing his words, his niece began to weep. She said to her uncle, "How will I ever communicate with you if you are placed so high up in the Great Pine Tree that centers our world."

Akatuni:heno replied, "Remember, as long as you remain pure in your heart, you will always be able to communicate with me."

That was because the heart was where each person's light force emanated from.[9]

Before he departed from the Sky World, Akatuni:heno said to his sister, "Always treat your children well, because if you don't something could one day happen to them."

He continued to tell her, "Once I am separated from you, I will not see you again until the time comes when a great change occurs in the Sky World. Something is about to happen, but I cannot explain to you what that is. When it does occur, you will hear my voice once again."

Akatuni:heno's voice could make the world shake above and below. He would sometime make his appearance through the thunders.

It was not long after that Akatuni:heno's inner light dimmed until it finally went out for good, and he passed from the sky world. His sister wondered what should be done with the body. She asked her children, "What should we do with your uncle now that he has left this world?"

Her son replied, "We should follow uncle's wishes and place him on top of the highest tree we can find."

He continued, "The tallest tree stands at the center of the world and is the Great White Pine. I will climb to the top of the tree and place uncle's body there as he had asked."[10]

The boy's mother then began to prepare a casing for the body out of elm bark; the second greatest tree in the Sky World.[11] After it was finished, her son took the casing on his shoulder and journeyed to where the Great White Pine Tree stood and began climbing it. He carried it as instructed to the top, passing from the Sky World into a higher realm, with the body strapped over his back.[12] After finishing his task, the boy went home to be placed in seclusion once again so that he could continue the process of gaining more *orenta* and growing into adulthood. Meanwhile, Akatuni:heno lay on top of the tree where he looked down at the events unfolding beneath him. From there he could offer advice and protection to the children below.

It was not long after this occurred when a messenger appeared at the lodge of the children's mother. He asked, "Where is the rest of your family?"

She explained to him, "They are absent for the time being and will return when they have completed their lessons into adulthood."

The messenger then said, "The reason I have come is to tell you that something is about to occur that will affect everyone who lives in the Sky World."

He continued to say, "I have been sent by Teharonwetsia:wako, He Who Grasps the Earth, also known as Rotea:he, the Keeper of the Standing Tree of Light, whose blossoms give light to the Sky World. He has asked me to speak to all the beings who inhabit the Sky World. The owner told me to tell you that you must go to him at once, as he has something important to tell you."

He continued, "Once you arrive, the keeper of the tree will decide when he will tell you what he has to say, and then you will be able to return to your lodge. At that time, the owner will reveal to you that something is about to happen that will have grave consequences for everyone in the Sky World. However, this event will occur only if he can't find someone to decipher the meaning of a dream that he is about to reveal to you and the others."

Dreams were of importance in the Sky World and later on to the *Rotinonshonni* on Earth, and not to have them fulfilled could result in grave consequences. As he was the keeper of the Tree of Light, what happened to Rotea:he could affect others as well.[13]

The woman asked the messenger, "What can I possibly do? My brother lies on top of the Great Celestial Pine Tree, and my children are hidden under the husk and being prepared for their responsibilities in life."

The messenger replied, "Your children are to be included in the event that is about to occur, and you should bring them with you when you travel to the keeper of the Tree of Lights place." The messenger then departed back from where he came.

After being told by her mother what had happened, the female child began to weep. She asked her mother, "What are we going to do? I am still young and do not want to be a part of such great responsibilities."

Her mother replied, "Maybe you should visit your uncle on top of the Great White Pine Tree. Remember, he promised if he were ever needed by you he would help you and your brother."

As the daughter didn't think she had enough *orenta* to make it to the top she replied, "I don't think I am capable of making such a great climb, as the tree is very high."

Her brother turned to her and said, "Don't worry, I will help you make it." He then picked up his sister and put her over his shoulder as he had done with his uncle before. He walked to the tree and began climbing until they reached the top where their uncle lay. The niece looked at her dead uncle and suddenly a great peace came over her, as she knew everything was going to be all right. She then descended the tree with her brother, and they walked home.

Soon after, the messenger arrived once again, asking the mother, "Why are you and your children the only ones who have not yet visited the keeper of the Tree of Light?"

At the keeper's place stood a Chestnut Tree, whose blooming buds gave light to the world. It was situated at the entrance of the owner's house where he was giving a feast for all who visited him. This was in accordance with the custom that all visitors were to be fed whenever they visited someone.

The messenger continued, "Even if only one of your children visits him, the keeper of the Tree of Light will be pleased."

The mother asked the messenger, "Who else has visited him?"

He replied, "I think it would be a good idea if you went and spoke to the keeper of the standing Tree of Light first, before I answer any more of your questions."

She agreed and said to the messenger, "I will leave with you and find out what he wants." The woman and the messenger left together for the place where the Tree of Light was situated.

Once they had arrived at the place where the Tree of Light stood, the messenger entered a lodge and said to the keeper of the Tree of Light, "I have brought the person that you sent for. However, she is alone and her children are not with her."

The keeper of the Tree then went outside and introduced himself. He said to the woman, "Why did you not come before when I asked? Everyone else has visited me except for you and your children."

He continued, "I believe that you and your children have the answer to a question that I am seeking. This question has me perplexed and haunts me, right into the inner recesses of my soul."

The woman then asked the keeper of the Tree of Light, "Who are the other beings that have visited this place before me?"

The keeper of the tree replied, "All other beings that inhabit this Sky World have already visited. That includes the Sun, the Moon, the star, the tree, the bush, the animals, the birds, the water, the cloud, the corn, the bean, the squash, the tobacco, the light, the darkness, the Thunder, the Meteor Fire Dragon, and the air. 'Besides your children, only the wind has not yet arrived.'"

He continued telling her, "I had hoped that someone would be able to guess what has been haunting me in a dream that I had."

He explained, "Due to their failure in interpreting my dream, I plan to throw all the other beings of the world through an abyss in the floor of this Sky World. They have all failed to help me in my time of need. Perhaps they would be better off as new living beings springing up below where they would not be subject to the malevolent forces that are depleting the energies of the light from this world. The world we now live in will then be transformed, and new beings will be born out of those who existed previously; then one day they will in turn renew the light of this world. These new beings would be the primal beings of the new world below that will come into existence. They will then pass from that world and be reborn and bring light once again into this world."

The women replied, "When my children become adults, perhaps they will be the ones who can give you the answer that you are seeking."

Rotea:he, the keeper of the Tree, replied, "I will wait for that time."

He then pointed and said to her, "Look at the standing Tree of Light where the blossoms are blooming. When the time comes that all the blossoms have fallen from the tree, that is when the feast will be over."

He continued, "Changes are already beginning to occur. As you can see, the light of the Tree of Light is becoming dim. The only reason that things in this world still remain in order at the present time is because there are still some who are enjoying themselves here, and they give me pleasure watching them."

The malevolent energy that he was talking about was able to put out the light from the buds of the Tree of Light. Cold and darkness would then result. This energy had to be balanced because, if left unattended, it could disrupt the creation in the Sky World. Like the light-giving energy of *orenta*, the energy of freezing and darkness permeated all things and had to be kept in check.

The woman told the keeper of the Tree, "I will return home, and when my children are ready they will make an attempt to visit you."

After she returned to her lodge, she heard her two children talking with one another. She heard her son telling his sister, "Uncle needs you, and you must go to him immediately."

She asked her brother, "What do you think he wants?"

He replied, "I am not sure; only he can tell you."

She replied, "Maybe, it's for the best. I will visit him alone and find out what it is about."

Once again, he said to her, "Go quickly, it seems very important."

The girl left the lodge and went to the place where the Great Celestial Pine Tree stood. She was now strong enough to make it to the top, as she had acquired enough *orenta* during her puberty fast; she began to climb. Once she reached the top of the tree, she saw her uncle lying there.

She then knelt down and asked him, "Is it true that you needed to see me?"

He replied, "It is so." He continued, "The time has come for you to fulfill your destiny in life. You are to go where the owner of the Tree of Light lives and tell him who you are and that you have come to help him in his quest. Once you arrive there, the owner of the Tree of Light will ask you where you have come from. You are to answer that you have come from where the tallest Pine Tree stands, where your uncle, the ancient being who arrives with the thunders, lies. The owner will then ask you the reason that you have come. You will answer that you have come because you had been informed you were needed for a reason that you still don't know."

Her uncle went on, "The owner of the Tree of Light will then ask for your name. You will reply that your name is Otsi:tsia, Mature Flowers of the Fertile Earth. You will tell him that you have the power to bring new brightness to the blossoms that light up the Sky World and are situated on the Tree of Light. The owner will then thank you for coming and will say that you are the reason that he had given the feast in the first place. He will ask that both you and he watch over all things that have been thrown out of this world and are coming to life in the world below. I have to warn you that you must be careful when he offers you his mat to sleep on. However, I cannot tell you why."

The uncle knew that, once the procreative process began, great changes would take place in the Sky World and the world below. As light renewed itself below, darkness and freezing would occur in the Sky World. Only when the light began to dim in the world below would light renew itself in the Sky World. Rotea:he knew that Otsi:tsia was the potential for all this, and he wanted her light to remain in the Sky World.

Her uncle continued to tell her, "Upon arriving, the first thing the keeper of the Tree will ask from you is that you prepare him some mush made from chestnuts. While you are cooking, the mush will begin to sputter out and stick to your body. Remember, you are not to cry out that it is too hot. The owner of the Tree of Light will call out his two white dog servants, and they will lick the mush from your body and wipe it away. During that time, if you remain calm and don't cry, you will have passed through the ordeal."

Her uncle believed that his niece had enough *orenta* to make it through the test and that her inner light could not be dimmed. In order for her to be strong enough to reside at the owner's place, she would have to be further cleansed from any impurities. This required going through a great trial to see if she had the ability to bring light to the buds of the chestnut tree. Only women had the ability for renewal of light that brought brightness to the world.[14]

Her uncle continued, "The next thing you have to watch out for will be when the keeper of the Tree of Light tells you that he had a dream that his tree has been uprooted. Otsi:tsia, this is the tree that bears his name, whose blossoms bring light to the world. There, you will see a large assembly of beings as you approach the owner's lodge. They will be standing, surrounding him. This will take place where the world has broken through and where you and Rotea:he will be seated looking down at the world below. Your feet will be hanging over the edge of the opening. Do not be afraid when these things occur, as you will always be protected no matter what happens. That is because your light-giving powers will always renew themselves."

All these things her uncle was telling her baffled Otsi:tsia. Nonetheless she would heed what he was saying. After her uncle was finished, Otsi:tsia descended from the Great Pine Tree.

Once she arrived back at her mother's lodge, she said to her brother, "*Okweta:seh*, my brother, it is time for me to leave. I have to go to the place where Rotea:he, the keeper of the Tree of Light, is giving his feast."

Okweta:seh replied, "I think that you are doing the right thing. I believe that one day you will leave this Sky World. When that happens, remember, whenever you think of me, something will occur in the world below that you will bring light to. It will begin to shake, making all the living beings who live there aware of what has occurred in your thoughts."

Seeing each other for the last time, Otsi:tsia departed toward where the keeper of the Tree of Light had his lodge and where the feast was being held. Once she arrived, she looked around and saw the Tree of Light and its mass of blossoms. She approached the keeper's lodge to tell him of her arrival. "Rotea:he," she called out, "I have come as you have requested of me."

Rotea:he replied, "Who are you and where do you come from?"

She answered, "I have come from the place where the Great Celestial White Pine Tree stands and where my uncle's body was placed after he had passed from this world into the next."

He then asked, "What brings you to my lodge?"

She replied, "I have come because I heard that you were giving a feast."

He then asked, "Tell me, what is your name?"

She answered, "My name is Otsi:tsia, Mature Flowers."

Once the keeper of the Tree of Light heard her name, he knew that she was the one he was waiting for.

He told her, "I am thankful that you have arrived, because you are the reason that I am giving this feast in the first place."

He continued, "Many persons have already visited me, and I have thrown them through the chasm by my tree into the world below. Once there, they will be transformed. A purification will take place in this world, as well as a renewal of light in the world below."

He then pointed toward the Tree of Light and said, "Look at the Tree of Light, my standing tree blossoms are dimming and beginning to die out. You are the only hope of bringing back light to the Tree and this world."

He then assigned her a mat for a bed, whereupon she seated herself.

He then told her, "Prepare me some mush from these chestnuts." He then handed some nuts to her. He continued. "When you are finished, we will eat them together?"

She asked him, "What can I use to cook them with?"

He pointed and answered, "Everything you need is behind that door."

Otsi:tsia then entered the place behind the door and found what she needed. She began to boil the water until it reached the boiling point. She then cut and grated chestnuts and put them into the boiled water. They began to sputter out of the cooking vessel, and the hot mush began to stick to her body. Even though she was badly burned and her flesh peeled off, she never cried out, remaining steadfast in her duty and remembering what her uncle had told her.

When the mush was cooked, she removed the vessel from the fire and yelled to Rotea:he, "The mush is ready!"

Rotea:he, looked at her in shock and asked, "Why are you are so burned?"

She explained, "When I was cooking the hot mush, it began to sputter out all over me, and it burned my skin."

He then told Otsi:tsia, "I will send for my two dog servants to lick the mush off you."

Not long after, two white dogs appeared and began to lick off the mush, even though it was extremely painful. They seemed to heal her burned flesh with their tongues, and it was as if Otsi:tsia were being remade; she became even brighter than before. During the ordeal, Otsi:tsia did not wince once.[15]

When it was over, the owner said to her, "Now you are ready to be here, and we can eat."

Otsi:tsia's light remained bright in spite of all that had happened to her. She had been remade, so that her *orenta* was at its peak; she could now participate in Rotea:he's world by helping to bring light to the Tree of Light. Whenever someone wanted to enter the place of the Tree of Light, they would have their flesh removed and then be remade so that they were spiritually prepared to enter its abode.

The *onkwe:honwe*, who would one day live on the Earth, would prepare the bodies of the departed in this way. They would wait until the flesh of the bodies of the deceased had gone back into the Earth, bringing new life to it. Some of them would then remove the bones and place them together in a burial so that the community would not only be restored in the Sky World but in the Mother Earth World as well.

When they had finished eating, the owner said to her, "There is a large group who are about to amuse themselves by playing the Creator's game. Let us go watch, as this will help divert my mind from my problems. Make sure when we are there that you don't speak to any of the players if they approach you."[16]

After they arrived, the game began, and when the different players came over to speak to Otsi:tsia, she did not reply. The players then left her alone to resume the game.

Once the game had finished, the owner told her, "We will come back tomorrow. The players will return and resume their game at this same place, and we will watch them again."

The next day, a large body of beings of every kind arrived at the field to play the game. Once again, they resumed playing the Creator's game.

During the game Rotea:he asked Otsi:tsia, "There is a spring nearby. Could you bring me back some water, because I am thirsty?"

She walked past the players and came to a cliff where she saw the outflowing of fresh water. She then dipped up the water in a wooden ladle she was carrying. On her way back one of the players approached her and asked, "Could I have a drink?"

"Here, have some," she replied. She then poured the water for him to drink.

"Thanks! You are so kind," he told her.

She said, "Not at all, I am only doing what I think is the right thing to do."

Suddenly she realized what had happened. She threw the rest of the water away and returned to the spring for more water. She then started back toward Rotea:he's place, and when she entered his lodge, Rotea:he was angry and chastised her.

He said to her, "You have done exactly the thing that I had forbidden you to do."

Otsi:tsia replied, "Give me another chance; I will promise never to do it again."

He told her, "Go back home and tell your mother what has happened since you arrived here. Tell her that I had given you only one condition that you were to abide by in order for you to stay and that you had failed in doing it."

She told him, "I will go back and confess to my mother. I will tell her that I had made a mistake and would not do it again if given another chance."

Rotea:he continued, "You are also to ask your mother to visit me once again because I have something important to request from her."

Otsi:tsia then returned home not knowing that there were those who would always try to tempt her from her path and that this time she had failed. Next time she would be much stronger.

Upon arriving home, Otsi:tsia told her mother what had happened at the spring during the game.

She said, "Mother, I have failed my first test, and the only way I can make amends is to confess to you about what I have done."

She then said, "Rotea:he wants to know why you have not come to confirm our relationship, as this would consecrate the union between us."

Rotea:he knew he could not marry Otsi:tsia without her mother's consent. The marriage would be a bond that could not be broken by two beings unless they decided to end it themselves, even if they separated from one another.[17]

Otsi:tsia's mother agreed and said, "My daughter, this visit is long overdue, and I will go to the owner of the Tree of Light to confirm the marriage between you both."

She then prepared a basket of bread and mixed huckleberries and proceeded to leave for Rotea:he's place.

She left her daughter at home and just before leaving told her, "My daughter, I am very weak. However, the unification of both of you in marriage is very important, and so I will go and confirm the union."

Upon leaving, she carried items on a forestrap tied to her head; this consisted of a basket with marriage bread inside.

After arriving at Rotea:he's place, she explained to him, "I have come and brought the things that will confirm your marriage to my daughter. I have decided to consent to it."

She then set the basket down in front of Rotea:he.

Rotea:he took the bread and said to her, "Now things have been done in the proper manner. All the beings who live in this world have been waiting a long time for this moment to arrive. We will all share the bread together after our marriage."[18]

Continuing on, he told her, "Ever since you left the last time, your daughter did not conduct herself in a proper manner while visiting me. When you go back, you are to tell your daughter to come at once, and this time to make no detours. When you arrive at your home, I will have prepared a basket of dried meat to take to her. You will then share the meat with all the beings who live amongst you as a symbol of rejoicing."

At the end of the meeting, both Rotea:he and Otsi:tsia's mother were happy with the way it had gone between them.

Upon returning home with her basket of meat, she said to her daughter, "Everything has been settled. You are to leave at once for Rotea:he's place."

Otsi:tsia then prepared herself for her journey. She knew this time that there would be those who would not want her to succeed and that she would have to make sure that there were no distractions while on her journey. She knew that her orenta would have to be strong, if she were going to succeed in fulfilling her destiny.[19]

She had not gone very far on her journey when she met a male being that resembled her husband.

He told her, "I have come to meet you on your way."

Otsi:tsia knew that she had to go on and that it may be a trick, so she did not stop to answer. When she looked up, he transformed himself into a fox and then ran off down the trail.

She had not gone very far when she met another male being on the side of the road.

This male being said to her, "I have come to meet you."

She did not answer and continued on. Upon looking up, she noticed the male being transforming himself into a wolf, and he also then ran off.

Once again, she had not gone very far when she saw another male being coming toward her. This one she recognized; for a moment she was certain that it was her spouse, Rotea:he.

He said to her, "Otsi:tsia, I was concerned about your well-being and have come to meet you and bring you home."

In spite of what she thought, Otsi:tsia did not answer or stop. She looked at him and saw that he had transformed himself into a bear, and then he ran off.

Not being swayed on her journey was central to Otsi:tsia's purpose, as she knew that there would be those who would come and try to divert her from her path. She had fasted in seclusion for this very reason, that is, to gain strength so that she would be able to handle any situations that may try to lead her away from her purpose of bringing light to the world.

She continued on her journey and approached the Tree of Light, announcing her arrival to Rotea:he. "I have arrived," she said.

Rotea:he, upon seeing her, replied, "My dear Otsi:tsia, I am so happy that you passed the test this time and remained faithful to me."

She answered, "I have been on a long journey to get here. Is there any place that I can get some rest?"

Rotea:he then led her into his lodge and pointed at some furs he had spread out.

He said to her, "Lie here and rest; I will join you later."

She took a rest and later he joined her. They then both fell asleep with their feet touching each other's.

Upon awakening, as they went to get up, their breath came together. Suddenly, Otsi:tsia began to show signs of being pregnant. This happened very quickly, and when it was almost time for her to give birth Rotea:he spoke to her.

"Otsi:tsia, I had a dream that I believe has come from the inner depths of my soul. I challenge anyone to come and guess the dream so that balance may be restored within me."

Rotea:he then gave another feast for the remaining inhabitants of the Sky World and informed them that the contest to guess his dream was now on once again.

These inhabitants were the ancient ones who had remained behind in the Sky World some of whom had given form to the beings below. In later years, they could only be communicated with by way of the medicine societies and with real tobacco.

Soon after, the ancient beings who were left in the Sky World made the attempt to guess and interpret the dream. At that moment, the Meteor Fire Dragon passed by, and they were momentarily blinded by his light and prevented from succeeding.

Then the Meteor Fire Dragon, whose body was a brilliant white light and had a tail at the end, arrived saying, "Let me try and make the attempt to interpret the dream."

He then told Rotea:he the meaning of his dream. He said, "The Tree of Light has to be uprooted in order for your dream to be fulfilled."

Rotea:he replied, "Thank you, for you have revealed the purpose behind my dream." He then explained to everyone, "In my dream I did see the tree uprooted, and there was an opening through the ground. I also saw my wife and me sitting at the edge of the chasm created by the uprooted tree. I noticed that her feet were hanging over the edge. We had two kinds of food, and we were able to see all the things that were happening in the world below."

As Rotea:he was explaining about his dream, a group of sky beings were listening, and they decided to try and make Rotea:he's dream come true so that he would be satisfied inside. They went to the Tree of Light and once again uprooted it, creating a great chasm in the Sky World. This was much like a womb that opened up the Sky World to the world below.

When Rotea:he saw this, he told everyone. "Now that the dream has been fulfilled, the flowers of the Tree of Light are almost out. This means that a great transformation is about to occur, and all the things that exist in the Sky World will undergo a change. Everything that ever existed will become renewed in the world below."

He then called his wife, "Come! Let us sit at the edge of the chasm and eat the two kinds of food that you cooked, just as it was prophesied in my dream."

Otsi:tsia set the food aside and then seated herself beside the chasm.

She then said to Rotea:he, "Now that all the suggestions in your dream have been fulfilled, you should be content now."

Rotea:he replied, "Now that the dream has come true, we should eat the food that I have brought. From now on, all the things which reside in the world below will always remember this event."

Then suddenly, he grabbed Otsi:tsia, and he threw her into the chasm, where the sky had broken through. She disappeared, falling to the Earth below.

Rotea:he believed that Otsi:tsia had been unfaithful to him once again. He thought that was the reason why the Fire Dragon had been able to interpret his dream. He thought she must have informed him of the answer to the dream he had. By throwing her into the chasm he believed it was the only way that he could fulfill that which had troubled him in his dream.

In fact, it was the Meteor Fire Dragon who had influenced him to think in this way. After that, whenever the Great Meteor Fire Dragon would be seen in the air, those below would know that there would be changes arriving shortly and the Earth mother was about to go through a transformation.[20]

With the falling of Otsi:tsia, Mature Flowers, the light of the Sky World went out, and a new light was about to begin in the world below. What Rotea:he didn't know was that the uprooting of the tree in his dream meant a renewal of the world was about to take place and that the Sky World as he knew it was coming to an end. Otsi:tsia had broken through the womb in the sky and her life giving essence poured down to the Earth, resulting in the birth of life in the world below.[21]

This event would always be remembered by the beings who would be born in the world below. They would also learn that gossip and jealousy can destroy worlds while the life-giving powers of the female could create worlds. Otsi:tsia had been faithful to her husband and, because Rotea:he believed in the gossip that began with the Meteor Fire Dragon, he became jealous. This resulted in the light of the sky going out. If the male beings who would inhabit the world below wanted their world to continue, they would have to trust and listen to the female beings and not gossip and learn the lessons of what happened in the Sky World, for it is through the women that the inner light of the beings of the world is renewed and they must be cherished for this always.

Later, when the *onkwe:honwe* were born into the world below, they would call the men who would represent their people Big Trees of Equal Height. Whenever one of the Big Trees would be uprooted, he would be replaced by another, chosen from the life-giving powers of the women. Then the life of the Big Tree would be renewed, just as the Earth World was renewed when the ancient woman was thrown down from the Sky World.

The Floating Island and the Second Cosmological Beings

As Otsi:tsia was floating downward, she saw the Fire Dragon, whose body was white coming toward her. He seized her and asked, "Otsi:tsia, why are you leaving your home?"

She replied, "My consort has thrown me out of the Sky World, and I do not know why."

The Fire Dragon replied, "Do not worry; I will always be there to look after you when you begin your new life in the world below."

He then explained to her, "You were thrown out of the Sky World because your husband believes that you were unfaithful. I have brought you some things that you will need to survive once you arrive there. That is because I care for you the most."

He then took out some dried corn, beans, squash, tobacco, and straw-berries and placed them in her lap. He told her, "I will accompany you halfway down below and then I will have to turn back.[22]

"Whenever there will be changes in the world below, look up and you will see me pass by in the sky. This will mean that a great event is about to take place which may result in a renewal of the world below."

He finished by saying, "Let there be a lesson for those who will reside in the new world that is coming into existence; jealousy can bring darkness to worlds."

The meeting of the Meteor Fire Dragon and Otsi:tsia was the beginning of a new world that was about to evolve. The things that she had been given would spread and always be held in reverence by the beings that would spring up below. She was the potential that would give the new world life, and, with the coming together of the Meteor Fire Dragon as she fell, he had initiated the process.

Swimming in the waters below were the waterfowl. They were among the first beings that Rotea:he had thrown down when he was looking for the answer to his dream. These beings were unique in that they could survive on land, air, or water. They were of the first order of creation in the new world and the ones with the greatest abilities.

Loon could see something that appeared to be coming up from the depths of the water. He had the habit of always having his head looking down into the water. In the water, he could see the reflection of the woman falling from the sky. He thought she was coming from the depths of the water.

He said to the other waterfowl, "Look into the water and see what is coming to the surface."

There was much confusion as the waterfowl did not know who it was or what they should do about it. At the same time, as the waterfowl were looking in the water, Heron had his eyes looking toward the sky.

He yelled to the other waterfowl, "Don't look down; look up toward the sky." Since this occurred, he has forever after received the name, He Who Keeps Looking at the Sky Kentsiokwas. All the waterfowl looked up and saw the woman, Otsi:tsia, Mature Flowers of the Fertile Earth, falling toward them.[23]

Loon assembled all the waterfowl together to discuss what was taking place. He said to them, "I think we should use our gifts of flight to help this female being so that she can survive. It was Heron who was the first to see her. He should make a plan on how we can save her and find the best spot to place her on." All the waterfowl agreed.

Heron replied, "Perhaps, we can find a way to bring her down safely."

The waterfowl looked up and, seeing the woman falling down toward them, decided that this was good advice and that they should help her. They then flew into the air to meet her. While hovering in the air, they joined their bodies together, creating a cushion. They then flew under her, allowing her to settle upon them.

Slowly, downward they flew, until they hovered just above the surface of the water, and there they circled. They realized they had not prepared a place to put her down. They decided they had to come up with a plan where to place her, but they couldn't come to any agreement with one another on how it could be done.

Loon made a proposition to the second order of beings thrust into the world. They were the animals who could inhabit both land and water and would become known as the Earth divers. However, unlike the waterfowl, they did not have the ability to fly.

Loon asked them, "Animal divers, try and attempt to find some Earth so that the woman who fell from the sky will have a place to settle upon."

Otter yelled out, "Let me try. I am the quickest." He then dove into the depths of the water and when he returned he was empty-handed.

Next, Beaver yelled out, "Let me have a try; I think I can do it because I am the strongest." Beaver dove down and he also failed in his attempt.

Next, all the other Earth divers tried, but none could succeed. There was one Earth diver left, Muskrat. He was the weakest of the Earth diving beings, and none of the others believed that he had a chance to succeed.

Muskrat said to them, "You have all had your chance, and now it is my turn to make the attempt at fetching the Earth from the bottom of the water. If I succeed, we will be very lucky."

At that time, Otsi:tsia's creative powers were weakening. There was only one way they could be strengthened and that was by having a place where the gifts that had been given to her by the Meteor Fire Dragon could grow and flourish. Muskrat was the last hope of the diving beings to save the woman who fell from the sky. He went under the water and remained there for a long time. By the time he surfaced, he was long dead.

Beaver said to them, "I will give it one more try, but before I dive let us search Muskrat first." As he was looking over Muskrat, he noticed that his paws were holding some dirt and that there was some dirt in his mouth as well. They now had the Earth they needed; this would allow the gifts that the sky woman had with her to grow and spread. They were still missing a place to put the Earth on so that Otsi:tsia could have a place to live. They had all laughed at Muskrat because he was supposed to be the weakest of them all. Muskrat had taught them never to underestimate anyone's abilities. Those who look the weakest are sometimes the most capable.

Muskrat had given his life in sacrifice so that Otsi:tsia would have a place to live and grow. In the future, the *onkwe:honwe, real people*, who would inhabit the Earth would always be thankful to the animals for sacrificing their bodies so that their children could continue to live and flourish. Even when they hunted, upon killing an animal, they would give thanks and make an offering to it for giving its life so that they could have clothes and food.

Beaver asked the others, "What should we do now?"

Loon answered, "Someone should volunteer to hold up the Earth that was found so that it is possible to place Sky Women upon it; otherwise, the Earth will sink into the water once again."

Beaver said to the others, "I will try to hold up the Earth as I am the strongest of us all."

The Earth divers then placed the dirt that Muskrat had brought up to the surface onto Beaver's back.

Beaver cried out, "This is too much. I can't hold it any longer."

Beaver could only hold back the water for a time, and then he began to sink.

Great Turtle, the oldest of the beings spoke out and said, "My shell is hard; let me make the attempt."

The rest of the Earth divers gathered the dirt from Beaver and placed it on Great Turtle's back. Great Turtle said to them, "I think I can hold it. Don't worry; in the future, if ever the Earth were to increase in size, so will my back as well."

The waterfowl then placed the woman who fell from the sky, Otsi:tsia, Mature Flowers of the Fertile Earth, upon the Earth on Great Turtle's back. They left satisfied. They had done all that they could to save her and help bring life to the Earth. The mingling of the female and male had begun.[24]

Not long after this occurred, the turtle's shell began to grow outward. As it reached a certain size, Otsi:tsia gave birth to a daughter. Her daughter grew very rapidly, and, as time passed, she became a young woman; she began to travel all over. She was known as Ohshe:wa, Budding Flowers. Her mother, Otsi:tsia, was the female aspect of the potential of plant life that came with the rain, while Ohshe:wa was the female essence of plant life. Ohshe:wa traveled walking counterclockwise with the Earth in her hands, spreading it in every direction. This was because she was born from the ancient beings of the Sky World, where everything was in reverse to that of the Earth World.[25]

One day as she was taking a walk, she noticed a male being watching her. He said to her, "Come over here; I am looking for a mate. Would you not consider marrying me?"

It appeared to him that she was looking for a companion as well. She looked him over and saw that his clothing was the color yellow.

She replied, "I can't answer you right now. I will have to ask my mother's permission first. It is up to her to decide whether you would be a good match for me or not."

She then returned home and told her mother about her experience. She said, "Mother, I have met a male being who wants to marry me."

Her mother asked her, "My daughter, what answer did you give this stranger?"

She replied, "I told him that I would speak to you first before giving him an answer."

Her mother said to her, "My daughter, you did the right thing by coming to me first."

She then asked her daughter, "What color were his clothes?"

She answered, "The clothes he was wearing were the color yellow."

Her mother told her, "I cannot consent to the marriage, and you should go back and tell him this. You must always be careful whom you meet, because you never know who it might be. He may try to lead you from your path and that would bring harm to you and others. Always make sure you come to me first before you marry anyone." Otsi:tsia had remembered her own experiences in the Sky World, and she knew she had to prepare her daughter on the Earth.

Her daughter then went back to the male being and explained to him, "I cannot marry you because my mother will not consent to it."

He replied, "I feel angry by your answer." He then got up and left.

The girl watched as he was leaving, and suddenly he transformed himself into a fox and ran off. She returned home satisfied that she had done the right thing. To be married and come together with the wrong male being could have disastrous consequences for the world as their essences would not match up.

Not long after, she went for a walk once again. She came to the end of the Turtle's back, where the shore of the water was. There, she saw a male being sitting on a rock.

He spoke to her, "My dear, are you looking for a companion, and, if you are, would you consider marrying me?"

She replied, "It is up to my mother to decide. I will go home and ask her first." She noticed that his raiment was a gray color and that his face was striped black.

Upon returning home, she asked her mother about the man.

She said, "Mother, I have met another male being who wants to marry me. He was a grayish color, and his face had black stripes on it."

Mature Flowers replied, "I cannot consent to your marrying him either."

The daughter then returned to where the male being sat and told him what her mother had said, "I have spoken to my mother about you, and she would not consent to the marriage."

Angry, the male being replied, "It really doesn't make any difference to me what you do." As he turned around to walk away, he transformed himself into a raccoon and left. She returned home satisfied that she had done the right thing once again.

One day the daughter went to fetch some wood, and as she began to place the wood into a bundle another male being arrived. This time it was the Great Turtle being. He looked at her and then said, "I am searching for a mate, and I would like to know if you would marry me." She looked back at him and saw that he was dirty and had large flaps that looked like scales surrounding his body.

She replied, "I cannot give you an answer until I have talked it over with my mother." She went home and told her mother about what had happened.

She said, "Mother, this dirty man with strange flaps over his body has told me that he wants to marry me."

Otsi:tsia asked her daughter, "What was the answer that you gave him?"

She replied, "I told him that it was up to you to give your consent to the marriage."

Otsi:tsia said to her daughter, "I am pleased with the answer that you gave him. This male being is known as being invulnerable to any malevolent energies. When you two mingle, you will be as one, and life will grow from your body. I will therefore confirm your marriage to him. Tell him to come and meet me." The Great Turtle Man being was the male potential in creation, and, when his body mingled with Ohshe:wa the process of life on Earth, would begin.

Ohshe:wa returned to the Great Turtle Man being, and she said to him, "My mother has agreed to consent to our marriage. She says that she would like to meet you first. Would you come with me to my lodge?"

The Great Turtle man answered, "I would like to come, but first I must go back to my lodge and prepare myself for this marriage. When I have finished, I will come and visit your mother; however, I will never live with you, for my place lies within the Earth."

Ohshe:wa went home and when she arrived her mother asked, "Where is the Great Turtle Man that you are supposed to bring home?"

She replied, "The Great Turtle Man told me that he would come and visit when he was ready. He also told me that he would never live here with us for his place is under the Earth."

Otsi:tsia said, "It is well known that this Great Turtle Man being is immune to any form of sorcery." They then waited for his arrival, but he did not show.

The Twins: Teharonhia:wako and Sawiskera

One evening, the two went to lie down and rest. Just as they were about to sleep, Great Turtle Man showed up and announced his arrival. He told them, "During the night I am going to leave my arrows to lie here, and in the morning I will come back and retrieve them."

The daughter noticed that he held two arrows and that one had an ice crystal flint point while the other had no point attached to it at all. Turtle Man seemed to repeatedly straighten out the arrow that had no point. He then laid the arrows on her body, side by side, and tied them together with a thong of deer leather. Within these two arrows was the male being's essence of life.[26]

He said to her, "Leave them here and do not untie them. I will return in the morning and undo them myself." He then left to go back to his place under the Earth.

In the morning he removed the arrows and returned to his place under the Earth. The daughter appeared to be pleased after this happened. She noticed that she was undergoing changes to her body.

Her mother said to her, "My daughter, good fortune is about to occur as you will soon be with child."

As her daughter began to get bigger, she could hear two male voices speaking from within her body.

One voice said, "What will you do when you and I are born?"

The other voice answered, "I will create human beings so that they may live as peoples. I will also create animal beings who will provide game for the people to live on. Next, I will create the rules that human beings and animal beings will live by on this Earth. As well, I will then create all the things that grow so that they will bear fruit that other beings can live on. All these things will make the human beings who will dwell on this Earth happy and content."

Ohshe:wa, Budding Flowers, then heard the voice who had answered ask the other voice, "What will you do after you are born?"

The other voice replied, "I will create the same things as you; if I am not able to do so, I will create my own things so that I will have something worthy to contribute to this world as well."

She then heard one of them say, "It is time for us to leave our mother's body and go out into the world. Which one of us will take the lead?"

The other one answered, "You take the lead, and I will follow where there is light from our grandmother and spring out that way."

The other voice answered, "I don't think that would be a good idea, because if you go that way our mother will be destroyed."

Suddenly, the first child sprang out in a natural manner from his mother's body. Soon after, the other child broke through her armpit, with the result being her death.

The boys' grandmother took the two male children and began to attend to them. She then lay the body of her daughter at the entrance of the lodge and told the children, "Don't worry, my grandchildren, your mother is not completely dead; she will have light enter her body again in ten days' time."

The children grew rapidly and were very intelligent from the time of their birth. Within a few days, they could already converse with their grandmother.

Their grandmother asked them, "Do you boys know where you came from and where you will go after you leave this world?"

One of the boys answered, "I know the place we have come from. It is the sky that is situated on the upper side of the Earth. That is something that I will never forget. I will always continue to grasp that place where I came from by using both my hands, so that when I leave this world I will be able to return there."

His grandmother said to him. "I will name you Teharonhia:wako, He Grasps the Sky with Both Hands, because you have not forgotten where you came from."

Then the other male child was asked by her, "What do you think about the question; I asked your brother about where you both came from?"

He answered, "I don't think about the place from where I came from or where I will go when I leave this world. In fact, I am quite happy that I live here and trust in the gift my father gave me to be forever content in this world."

His grandmother asked him, "What was the gift that your father gave you?"

He pulled out an arrow and showed her, "This is the arrow he gave me with the point attached to it. It is a flint-pointed arrow, which typifies the power of the piercing of the extreme winter. Maybe he intended my having it in order for me to defend myself, and that is the reason I do not fear anything here. I can stop anything from growing or living and bring darkness with this weapon."

His grandmother then said to him, "I will call you Sawiskera, Flint Crystal Ice. That is because you only think of yourself in this world."

From that time on, the destiny of the generations of the real human beings *onkwe:honwe* who would be born in the future would be set by the understanding of where the twins had come from. Teharonhia:wako would be known by them as the right-handed twin while his brother Sawiskera would be known as the left-handed twin. The *onkwe:honwe*, like other living things, would always be influenced by the twins. Their minds would either be turned toward the Sky World or turned toward the Earth World. Like the right-handed twin and the left-handed twin, their minds would be divided into the right and left sides. Those whose minds used only the left side would be solely turned toward the Earth and would bring disruptive influences to it by trying to take control over it. They would only think of themselves in matters pertaining to the world. Those whose minds are turned toward the right side would always know where they came from, try to protect the things on the Earth and always think of others first.[27]

A few days later she overheard Sawiskera ask his brother, "Do you know where our mother went?"

Teharonhia:wako answered, "I believe she is sleeping."

Sawiskera asked his grandmother, "Grandmother, is it true that our mother is only resting and that she will awaken in ten days' time?"

She answered him, "It is true my grandson. She will soon wake up after ten days' time."[28]

"Grandmother!" Sawiskera replied, "It is urgent that I see her as soon as possible because I miss her."

She answered him, "Don't worry, you will see her because I know the time when she will rise up again."

He pleaded with her, "Then you must tell me when that time is as it would really put my mind at ease." His grandmother then took him by the hand, thinking that nothing could go wrong if she showed him his mother.

When Sawiskera saw his mother's body, he asked her, "Mother, why do you just lie there? Why don't you get up?" His mother did not move at all. Sawiskera was becoming angry as he tried to prompt her to stand up.

He then said to himself, "What will I do with this sleeping woman who is my mother and who continues to ignore me."

His grandmother told him, "Do not worry; she will remain like this until she rises in ten days' time."

His brother, Teharonhia:wako, said to them, "It doesn't matter to me when that happens. As far as I am concerned, she can sleep until she decides it is time for her to rise up again." His grandmother took it to mean that Teharonhia:wako didn't care what happened to her, and she became angry with him.

Sawiskera meanwhile did not have any patience with his mother, who would not respond to his needs. This would be another lesson that the *onkwe:honwe* would teach their children in the future. They would have to learn to be patient with their parents, and their parents would have to listen to their children's needs.

Sawiskera said, "I will wait a short time for her to get up, and if she doesn't do so, I won't let it bother me again. Anyway, maybe it is better that she lay there forever."

Teharonhia:wako was shocked at what his brother had just said. Angrily he told him, "I am going for a walk so that I can clear my mind about what you said about our mother."

The boys' grandmother cared for Sawiskera more than she did for Teharonhia:wako. She had always believed that Teharonhia:wako was responsible for her daughter's having to be put to rest for ten days' time. The *onkwe:honwe* in the future would also learn from her behavior regarding what can occur when their loved ones favor one child more than another. All children had to be taken care of equally. The men would always be wary of the influence of their mother-in-laws over their children.

After Teharonhia:wako had left to go for his walk, the boys' grandmother said to Sawiskera, "My grandson, I have a few provisions left, and I will save what I have for you and your brother. I don't know where I will be able to obtain more when the rest of the provisions run out."

Sawiskera replied, "Don't worry, Grandmother, I will go and look for something for us to live on."

She said, "Then let us eat the rest of the food. Teharonhia:wako will have to be satisfied with the leftovers when he returns."

Sawiskera then asked his grandmother, "Could you make me something that I could use to hunt with? Pretty soon there will be many kinds of game animals running about, and we will have plenty of meat."

She answered, "I will make you a bow and arrow. However, after I finish making it, promise me that you will not lend it to your brother."

When Teharonhia:wako returned from his walk, he saw that his brother was carrying a bow with an arrow. He asked him, "My brother, where did you get a device such as this?"

Sawiskera answered, "Grandmother made it for me out of wood."

After speaking to Sawiskera, Teharonhia:wako then asked his grandmother, "Grandmother I have seen the wonderful device that you made Sawiskera, could you make me one as well?"

She answered, "Instead of having to go through the trouble of making another one, why don't you share your brother's." Teharonhia:wako was satisfied with the answer he received for the time being.

Meanwhile, Sawiskera attached a flint ice crystal to the end of an arrow he had made. He said, "It is now time. I will awaken our mother as she has been asleep for much too long."

He then approached the body of his mother and said, "Mother, if you do not wake up right now, I will thrust my arrow through your body to wake you up myself." He then shook his mother, and she did not respond. Next, he took his flint ice crystal arrow and held it over his head and thrust it down into her body. His mother did not move. He then cut at her throat until her head came off; then he laid it aside.

Teharonhia:wako soon became aware of what had happened. He said to his brother, "Sawiskera, look at what you have done. You have destroyed our mother. Her body is frozen. It was she who first established herself in this world, and it is now she who will be the first to depart from it. She will go back to where she came from, and one day she will begin to light up the Sky World once again. Her body will bring new life to this world through the things that will grow from it. From the life of her body in the Earth, I will form the human beings."

Our mother will now be named Kahiteh:sok, She Who Always Leads, and this is the way that she shall be remembered. Women shall always arrive on the Earth from above first. They will visit this place and then return to where they came from. Before leaving, their bodies will spring up new life. In this way, the cycle of life will always be renewed."

Later, the *onkwe:honwe*, remembered this event as the time of the first killing. They taught their children that the cutting of the creation by any other process but the natural one was wrong. They also taught their children that from death would begin new life in the ground and the mother would never truly die as long as Teharonhia:wako remained in control.[29]

After this occurred, Teharonhia:wako went to his grandmother and spoke to her about what he had witnessed, "Grandmother, I have seen what my brother has done to our mother. Now that I think about it, I don't think that it was a good idea that you favored him over me by making him a bow and arrow."

His grandmother then promised him, "My grandson, I will make you a bow as well so that feelings will be better between you and your brother." His grandmother made him a bow and some arrows, and, after giving it to him, told him, "Remember, this will be the first and the last thing that I will ever make for you. If you lose it, you will not have another." She then passed him the bow and arrow.

Teharonhia:wako replied, "Thank you, Grandmother. The *onkwe:honwe* who are to be born will learn to always treat their children equally."

Teharonhia:wako soon began to travel around turtle island with his bow and arrow. During this time, his grandmother would not allow the twins to eat together; she tried everything to prevent them from having a relationship with one another.

Teharonhia:wako traveled around the shore of a vast body of water, always returning from where he started. One day as he watched the sky, he saw a bird fly by. He went to get his bow and arrow in the lodge. As he got it out, he saw that it had perched nearby. Suddenly the bird flew off along the edge of the water. Teharonhia:wako followed it, cutting across the fields as he ran. He saw that the bird had stopped and had again perched itself on a ledge. As he moved closer, it eyed him with surprise. He took the bow and placed an arrow into it, then shot at the bird, missing it. He watched his arrow fly through the air and fall into the water. This made him sad because he knew he would not get another arrow. He began to wade into the water and tried to grab it. Just as the arrow disappeared into the water's depths, there was suddenly no more water in the direction he was going. Instead, he saw a lodge with smoke rising from its top, and, in front of it sitting, was a male being.

The male being said to Teharonhia:wako, "For a long time I have been watching you. I was hoping to see you. I have brought you here because I have seen that your grandmother does not respect you. It is time for you to do the work that you were destined to do. A grave thing is happening to the Earth, due to the fact that you and your brother are walking on different paths. This is the way it will always be between you both. Your grandmother has taken the side of your brother. In return I will replace the things that you have been deprived of by your grandmother in order that you may survive."

He then took some food plants and said to Teharonhia:wako, "Here are the items I promised. Now take them with you. From these items, you will prepare food by roasting them upon your return home. Then you shall eat the food. When your brother and grandmother find out that you have provisions, they will ask for some. You will answer them that, as soon as the food plants grow, you will decide how much you will give them. Remember, these things have sprouted from the depths of the Earth, and, like you, are the result of my mingling with your mother." Next, he told him, "You will need many things to do your work. Do not worry; eventually, you will have them, and you will lack nothing. During this time, many things will occur. If you ever need anything, come back and you will find me in this same place."

Teharonhia:wako replied, "Thank you! I now have to return home."

Before he left, the male being gave Teharonhia:wako some seed, and Teharonhia:wako proceeded toward his grandmother's lodge. Teharonhia:wako did not know that the male being was his father, the

Great Turtle, and when he had gone past his shell into the water his father had been there waiting for him.

Upon arriving back at the lodge, his grandmother offered Teharonhia:wako the leftovers of the meal that she had cooked for Sawiskera.

Teharonhia:wako asked his grandmother, "Why, Grandmother, have we never eaten together, and, when I do eat, my food is always cold and dry?"

She replied, "That is because we are so poor; we have nothing but stale food left to eat."

Teharonhia:wako then told her, "It is time that I begin to do the work that my destiny calls me to do. I will make sure that there are always things for us to eat."

His grandmother then said to him, "Grandson, perhaps it would be better if you found another place to do your work, so that you may be alone and away from me and your brother. This way, we will not be in your way."

Teharonhia:wako agreed with her, knowing inside that he was not wanted. He went to the other side of the island, where he put up a bark shelter and proceeded to begin to fulfill his destiny.

The Creation of the Living Beings on Earth

The first thing Teharonhia:wako did was plant the grass and then the Sunflower, which he planted beside his lodge. He said to himself, "The Sunflower will be a sign which will represent the coming of the families of real human beings, *onkwe:honwe*, who will one day establish themselves on the Earth."[30]

Then he made the red willow and said, "Here I have planted the eldest of all the medicines that will grow on the Earth."[31]

Then he formed the strawberries and said, "These will be the first of what will be called berries that will be planted close to the ground."[32]

Then he made the shrub or thimbleberry and said, "These will be the bushes that will carry the berries that will nourish the *onkwe:honwe*." Next, he made the mulberry bush as well as the huckleberry bush and said, "These will also carry a berry within them."

Then, he planted in the Earth the great fruit, the plum, followed by all the other fruits. When he had finished with these, he thought that he had done enough for the time being and that it was time for him to rest. After so much work, he decided he should eat so that he had the energy to continue his work later on. He kindled a fire and put the corn his father had given him onto a spit for roasting.

As he was roasting the corn, he said to himself, "After I create the human beings, they will always give thanks, first to the grasses and then to the berry life. After the Earth, these will be the first things of creation that they should be thankful for."

Sawiskera smelled the aroma of the cooking corn coming from Teharonhia:wako's direction. He went in his lodge to tell his grandmother about what was happening.

He said to her, "Grandmother, the wind brings an appetizing odor from the direction of Teharonhia:wako's place."

She said to him "Go, my favorite grandson, and find out what is going on over there." Sawiskera then went to Teharonhia:wako's lodge and saw him preparing the food.

Teharonhia:wako turned to his brother and said, "Come in, my brother, I am cooking food that the *onkwe:honwe* who will one day reside here will live upon. When I am finished, there will be so much food that no one will ever have to worry about going hungry again." Teharonhia:wako knew what it was like to be hungry. He would make sure that this would never happen to the beings in his creation.

Sawiskera then left the lodge. He looked around and saw all the things that were growing, including the beautiful flowers. He saw one shrub of beautiful colors and asked his brother.

"Teharonhia:wako my brother, what have you done to create such a beautiful thing as this?"

Teharonhia:wako replied, "What you see are the things that I have planted and will grow on the Earth."

Sawiskera then departed to his lodge and told his grandmother of the astonishing things that he had witnessed. "Grandmother," he said "I have seen many wonderful things growing from the Earth when I visited my brother Teharonhia:wako. I saw food that dripped oil, which when steamed became fat, smelling of an appetizing odor. I even asked Teharonhia:wako for some to taste, and he told me that they were not yet ready. There was one plant that pleased me the most and had a really pleasant odor to it."

His grandmother told Sawiskera, "Be watchful of your brother, and as soon you see him preparing food again make sure you inform me. Then I will go and find out what your brother is doing."

Teharonhia:wako decided to visit the man whom he had once met before and who had told him he could visit him any time. He still did not know that the man was in fact the Great Turtle Man, the boys' father.

When Teharonhia:wako arrived at the Great Turtle Man's lodge. The Great Turtle Man said to him, "The manner in which your grandmother is treating you is not right. Be careful because she will try to spoil all the things that you have created on Earth; therefore, I will tell you what you should do. When your brother Sawiskera visits you, ask him whether he would exchange that which is the substance of his life for your corn. Your brother will ask what is it that you actually want? You will answer him that you want the flint power that pierces the face in the cold that he received at birth. He will then answer, "You mean the thing that is attached to my arrow?" You will reply, "No"; you want the thing that is contained in his body. Your brother will answer that he will be willing to make the exchange. When that happens, your brother for a while will have control of the corn. However, you will have control of the main part of his freezing power and in this way ensure that the Earth is spared."[33]

The Great Turtle Man then told Teharonhia:wako, "As soon as you see his power coming out of his mouth, seize it and pull it until it is equal in length to the flint that is fastened onto his arrow. Then ask him to break it at that point. Your brother will answer that you should break it yourself. Do not by any means do what he asks, for he is the one who must break it, and only then will you be able to receive it from him. Then will you be successful in your life task of creating many wondrous things, and he will no longer have the power to spoil what you make. I will tell you truly, your brother will never be able to make the things that you can make. However, he will attempt to do as you do so that he can take control of the creation from you."

He continued, "Remember, he will not be able to do anything as long as you possess the thing that constitutes the very substance of his being. His power will be cut in half, and, although he may try to destroy your creation, he will only be able to disrupt it for a time with the aid of darkness and the winds from the north."

Teharonhia:wako listened to what the Great Turtle Man had to say and then departed to do his work. He said to himself as he was working, "Here, I will plant the great fruit, the plum, and that will be the first thing that my grandmother will see when she visits."

Then he began to roast some of the ears of corn to eat. Sawiskera again smelled the odor coming from Teharonhia:wako's place, but he didn't tell his grandmother as he said he would. He decided instead to visit his brother on his own.[34]

When he arrived at his brother's place, he asked him, "Teharonhia:wako, let me taste the thing that you are preparing. It smells so good."

Teharonhia:wako replied, "My brother I will let you try it in exchange for the substance of your life, the flint-ice crystal power to freeze things."

Sawiskera answered, "Do you mean the thing that is attached to my arrow?"

Teharonhia:wako replied, "No, I mean the thing that is inside your body and is the substance of your life."

Sawiskera thought about it for a minute while breathing in the succulent smell of the roasting corn and then answered, "I will make the exchange."

He opened his mouth and out came the lethal weapon, the piercing flint crystal ice. Seeing it, Teharonhia:wako grabbed it and pulled until it was as long as Sawiskera's arrow. He said to Sawiskera, "Here is the place where it should be broken off."

Sawiskera replied, "Break it off yourself."

Teharonhia:wako then explained, "You are the only one who can break it off, because you are the owner of the substance of your life, and only you can discharge it from your body."

Sawiskera then broke the flint from his body and gave it to Teharonhia:wako. He then said to him, "What you wanted, I now give to you."

"Let me in return have your corn," he said.

From that time on Sawiskera's power of freezing would be limited. He still had his arrow to freeze, but he could never destroy all of Teharonhia:wako's creation again.

Teharonhia:wako replied, "I will give you what you ask for."

He plucked two grains of roasted corn and said, "Here is one corn for you and one for our grandmother." Sawiskera received the two grains of corn and departed for his lodge. When he arrived at his lodge, Sawiskera told his grandmother that he had visited his brother without her permission.

He said to her, "Grandmother, here is the food that Teharonhia:wako was preparing." He then gave her one grain of corn. "Now both you and I may now eat," he said.

His grandmother, smelling the corn decided to eat it. After trying it, she told him, "This tastes really good."

Sawiskera then tasted his corn.

His grandmother asked, "What do you think of it, my grandson?"

Sawiskera replied, "It is really delicious."

She said to him, "The next time that your brother prepares food, tell me, and I will go visit him with you."

After Teharonhia:wako had planted the fruit, he began to form the bodies of the bluebird and robin. The flying things were the next order of creation that would later be remembered by the human beings in their prayers.

He said to them, "Now that I have finished your bodies, I have given you life for the purpose that you will breed here on Earth and produce many offspring." Then he let them go. There were two individuals, one male and one female. They flew into the air and sang as they soared in circles above. These creatures were as close as any would ever get to the Sky World.

Then he said to himself, "Among the flying creatures, I will create the passenger pigeon." So he made both a female and a male. He said, "These will multiply and become so plentiful in the sky that they will block out everything else whenever they fly by."

Sawiskera looked up, and he could hear the birds singing in their beautiful voices. He then went to his grandmother and told her what he had heard.

"Grandmother, there is something happening above where our brother lives, as I can hear beautiful sounds coming from the sky over there."

His grandmother replied, "Soon, we will go over to your brother's and see what is taking place."

Meanwhile, Teharonhia:wako was thinking to himself, "I will create the body of something that shall be called the deer and be very important in the lives of the *onkwe:honwe*, whom I will one day create from the Earth." After he finished forming the deer, he also formed the elk, the moose, and the buffalo. He created two of each, one female and one male.[35]

Upon finishing he said, "Now that I have completed your bodies, I plant you here on Earth so that you will continue to breed and multiply." He then released them, whereupon they ran in different directions on the Earth. The deer remained in place, while the moose ran north and the buffalo west.

Next, Teharonhia:wako created the porcupine, forming both a male and female. Then he formed the wild turkey. When he was finished, he said to those creatures that he had created, "I have made you for the purposes of breeding and creating families. You will help the *onkwe:honwe* by providing them with sustenance. In return, the *onkwe:honwe* will always remain thankful to you. You will be included as well in their words of thanks." Then he let them go. Some ran, while others flew away.

Teharonhia:wako said to himself, "It is time that I create those things which will inhabit the dry lands, along with those who will be able to climb. First, I will make something that will be called a bear. These will be among the smartest and most powerful of my creation." He then created a female and a male.

Then he said, "I will also make something that will be called a raccoon." He will always create mischief. He then created both a female and a male.

Next he said, "I will create that that will be called beaver. He will be extremely resourceful." He made both a female and a male as well.

When he had finished, he said, "I have created and planted things on the Earth for the purpose that they will breed and have families. I have used the essence of the primal beings who first dwelled in the Sky World to make my creatures. These primal beings will always look after the smaller creatures who represent them." He then let them go, and they ran off.

Finally he said to himself, "I have done a lot of work; I should now rest for a while." Teharonhia:wako then headed for his lodge.

Once he had returned to his lodge, he began to prepare food for himself. Sawiskera smelled the aroma as his brother was cooking. He also smelled the scent of the ripened fruits and various shrubs. He then ran back to tell his grandmother what was happening.

"Oh! Grandmother," he said. "Something wonderful has happened. I have smelled many different odors that are pleasing coming from my brother's place. It seems my brother is cooking food once again for himself."

His grandmother replied, "Perhaps it is time to go over and visit your brother. Let us go and see what is going on there."

The two of them began their journey toward Teharonhia:wako's place. Once they had arrived, his grandmother was surprised at the wondrous things that were going on and the fine aromas that were emanating from his place. She saw that by the door of the lodge a Sunflower grew that gave light to everything around. Also nearby, was a fruit that was covered with drops of syrup called raspberries. She and Sawiskera then entered the lodge, and they saw Teharonhia:wako roasting something, the fatness of which dripped down its sides.

She asked aloud, "Who has created all of the things that I see growing outside?"

Teharonhia:wako answered, "I am the one who has created them."

She then asked him, "Would you share any of this with us so that we can eat as well?"

Teharonhia:wako answered, "I will share everything except that which is growing from the tree standing over there." He then pointed to a tree where they saw beautiful fruit growing. He then plucked some corn from the roasting ears and gave each one of them a cob. His grandmother and Sawiskera began eating.

Teharonhia:wako said to them, "Let us go outside."

They then went outside, and pointing to the Sunflower he said to them, "This is the first thing that I planted."

Then he pointed to the red willow and said, "I have planted that as well."

As they walked, he pointed to the raspberry and plucked two berries from the branch and gave each of them one to taste. He told them, "I have also planted these."

Next, he showed them the huckleberry and said, "All the things that you see growing will ripen at different times of the year, so that there will always be new things springing up in the world. This will make the world diverse and beautiful."

They then returned to the side of the lodge. He pointed to a tree and said, "This bears the great fruit the apple." He then plucked two apples from the tree and gave it to them to eat.

His grandmother told him, "This is extremely pleasing to the taste." Then she asked him, "My grandson, can I take some back with me?"

Teharonhia:wako explained to her, "It is not possible as they have just been planted." He continued, "Soon, they will be abundant, and then you will be able to take as many as you like."

His grandmother then asked him, "Who has made the game animals that have such fine voices?"

Teharonhia:wako replied, "I created them out of my own labor."

She then asked, "Who will use these things that you have created."

Teharonhia:wako replied, "The *onkwe:honwe* who will one day populate the Earth will use them for their sustenance. They will have a duty to nurture them, just as I have done."

She then said to him, "It is time for me and your brother to leave for our lodge." The boys' grandmother and Sawiskera departed back to their lodge.

After arriving at their lodge, the boys' grandmother said to Sawiskera, "What wonderful things we have witnessed that are being created by Teharonhia:wako. Your brother is really living up to his statement that he would create many things that would be necessary in this world."

Sawiskera, feeling undermined by his brother's success and jealous of him, replied, "Oh Grandmother! You will see, I will create the same things as my brother has."

Just at that moment they heard a great noise coming their way.

When they went out of the lodge to see what it was, they witnessed several animals, mostly deer passing by. Soon after, other animals also began to travel near their lodge. They included raccoons, buffalo, bears, elks, and porcupines.

Next, they heard a great noise in the air and as they looked up, they saw many kinds of birds flying around.

The ancient woman, said to Sawiskera, "Isn't it wonderful what is happening now that the animals are beginning to multiply."

Sawiskera said to his grandmother, "I am going over to Teharonhia:wako's place and ask him how he created such wonderful things. Once he tells me, I will make them as well."

Sawiskera started out and, soon after, arrived at his brother's place. He entered his lodge and asked Teharonhia:wako, "My brother, tell me how you have created the things that we see living on the Earth."

Teharonhia:wako answered, "From this Earth that has the life spirit of our mother, I created the living bodies of what you see. When their bodies die, they will return to our mother and regenerate into new forms of life. I have imparted the spirit of the ancient beings in each one. When they depart from this world, they will be renewed in the Sky World above."[36]

Teharonhia:wako then asked his brother Sawiskera a question, "My brother, what type of device would have the ability to destroy your power."

Sawiskera answered back, "There are only two things that I fear can do that. They are the flint stone and the horns of a deer. Only they are able to chip away at my flint ice."[37]

The *onkwe:honwe* who would one day arrive would understand that by using their minds like the deer that they would be able to create shelters from the cold and use the flint stone for hunting food. Not even Sawiskera's power of crystal ice could prevent them from surviving. They would use the deer antlers due to their hard substance to chip the flint stone when making their arrows and both of these could chip Sawiskera's crystal ice that in of itself can cut the through air like sharpened flint. Whenever the thunders were to be heard, the *onkwe:honwe* would look up into the sky and see the flashing deer antlers from the west chip away at the flint ice crystals that belong to Sawiskera after he brings in the winter cold. They would then know that winter was almost over.

When Sawiskera returned to his lodge, he told his grandmother, "Grandmother, I have learned how my brother has made the many things that we see in the world. He used the dirt from our mother's body to give them life."

His grandmother asked him, "What do you think about what your brother has done?"

He answered, "I think it is wonderful what my brother has been able to accomplish. However, I will find an easier way to create the same things. What I will do first is use my power to conceal the bodies of all the game animals that Teharonhia:wako has made so that they will be under my rule. Then I will make my own creatures to rule the Earth."

His grandmother then asked him, "How will you do it?"

Sawiskera answered, "I will use my freezing power and force them into a cave in a mountain. When they think it is winter, they will fall asleep and not be able to get up."[38]

His grandmother answered, "Do what you have to do; I will say nothing more about this to your brother."

Sawiskera had set the stage, for time immemorial, of using his influence to try and gain control over the things that Teharonhia:wako had created. He would do this by putting the game animals to sleep during the winter.

Sawiskera then went to a mountain cliff and began to set to work carving up a cavern in its side. Using his freezing power, he began to freeze his mother's body. As the animals became cold, they began to get tired and looked for shelter. He then gathered all of them and led them inside the cave, placing a rock over the entrance. Once there, they fell asleep. The animals would always remember this event. Whenever winter would appear, animals like the bear would always find a cave where they would go to sleep.

Sawiskera said to himself, "Now then, the animals that Teha-ronhia:wako created are under my control. Both myself and my grand-mother will be able to obtain everything we need whenever we want." In his greed, Sawiskera would be a reminder to the *onkwe:honwe* yet to be born of how destructive hoarding could be to their survival."[39]

Sawiskera then went home and said to his grandmother, "Grand-mother, I have frozen the Earth and hid all the animals in a cave for our-selves. From now on, we will never be without meat."

His grandmother replied, "We should be extremely thankful that we now have abundant provisions for ourselves."

Sawiskera then proceeded to his brother's lodge. When he arrived, he saw Teharonhia:wako making arrows. He asked him, "My brother, what are you doing?"

Teharonhia:wako answered, "Soon, the game animals will be plenty enough to hunt, and I will need something to hunt them with."

Sawiskera mocking him asked, "What animals are you talking about? I don't see any animals around."

Teharonhia:wako replied, "That is because the animals who live on the Earth are moving about and are not easily seen."

Sawiskera said, "I have been everywhere on this island, and I haven't seen any game animals running about. Perhaps they are lost."

Teharonhia:wako looked bewildered and said to him, "That cannot be; the game animals should now be flourishing and moving all over the island."

Sawiskera, knowing he had fooled his brother, then proceeded to return to his grandmother's lodge. Upon arriving he said to her, "I have just visited the place where Teharonhia:wako lives. I saw him making arrows so that he could kill the game that he thinks are now abundant." They both decided to get some rest, satisfied that all of their needs would now be taken care of.

After they awoke, his grandmother asked Sawiskera, "Grandson, I am hungry. Could you fetch me some meat from the cave?"

Sawiskera replied, "Wait here; I will go and get some meat." He then started out toward the cave, and when he arrived he removed the rock from the entrance and went inside. Once there, he found a deer sleeping and he killed it. He closed off the entrance and left with the deer tied to a forestrap on his head and then proceeded back to his grandmother's lodge.

Upon arriving, he said to his grandmother, "Grandmother, I have done what you have asked me to do."

She replied, "We must be thankful that it is so easy for us to supply ourselves now."

This went on for some time, with Teharonhia:wako thinking that his creatures were moving about the Earth and that was why they were hard to find. Finally, Teharonhia:wako began to realize that the animals he had created were nowhere to be seen. He decided to, once again, visit the lodge of the Great Turtle Man, also known as He Who Holds the Earth with His Two Hands. Teharonhia:wako would ask him what he thought had happened to his game animals.

Upon arriving at his father's place, he asked him, "I don't know what has happened to the animals whose bodies I have created. They do not seem to be anywhere in sight."

The Great Turtle Man explained to him, "I know where they are. Your brother Sawiskera has outwitted you. He has shut them up in a cave in a mountain near the lodge of your grandmother and brother. He carved out the cave and sealed them off. They were made docile by the cold, so they followed him into the cave. Go there tomorrow and see for yourself, but be on the lookout for your brother. Do not let him see you when he comes to take meat for food. You will see what he does when he uncovers the mouth of the cave and comes out with an animal tied to a forestrap on his head. When he leaves, uncover the cave's entrance and enter it. You can then awaken all the game animals and drive them out so that they may run free. We will take care of warming the Earth sometime in the future."

After hearing what his father had to say, Teharonhia:wako went back to his lodge. The next day, he prepared his arrows and began traveling around the shore of the great water that surrounded Turtle Island. Finally, he arrived at the mountain from the backside and seated himself. It wasn't long before he noticed Sawiskera coming toward him.

Sawiskera stopped in front of the great rock and looked around to make sure no one had followed him. He grabbed the rock and lifted it over to the side and entered the cave. When he came out, he bore a porcupine tied to a forestrap on his head. Sawiskera said to himself as he was leaving, "There is something strange going on here. For some reason this animal was very difficult to kill and in fact it almost killed me when I tried to take it." He then drew back the rock and covered the mouth of the cave and proceeded home.

After Sawiskera had disappeared, Teharonhia:wako said to himself, "It is my turn now to regain control of the game animals."

He went to the great rock at the entrance of the cave, and, after lifting it aside, he entered it. All the game animals woke up and came forward to greet him.

Teharonhia:wako said to them, "When I completed your bodies, I made a big mistake. It was not good that I made you docile rather than wild. It was for that reason you were taken so easily and shut in the cave. I will now make it so that from now on, all of you will be wild animals for as long as you continue to exist. From now on, if someone wants to kill you, they will have to work really hard to do so. You are now free to go." He then released all the game animals.

As the game animals dispersed, Teharonhia:wako took out an arrow and shot it into the body of a deer as it ran off.

He told it, "Now then, run toward the lodge where the old woman, my grandmother, lives." The deer ran, and just as it got to the doorway of his grandmother's lodge it fell down making a great noise with its hooves at the entrance.

Teharonhia:wako's grandmother, hearing the noise outside, got up and yelled aloud. "What is happening out there?"

She looked outside her entrance and was surprised to see a deer lying with an arrow fixed in its side. She called out to Sawiskera, "Look at what has happened; a game animal has come to our lodge and is lying in front of our lodge and appears to be dead."

Sawiskera looked and saw the arrow, which he recognized as belonging to his brother. He said nothing and went back into the lodge with his grandmother following close behind.

Teharonhia:wako shot another arrow into the body of a raccoon. He then said to it, "Run to the lodge where my grandmother lives." The raccoon then ran off, and, when it arrived at his grandmother's lodge, it fell beside the entrance.

Next, Teharonhia:wako shot another arrow into the side of a buffalo. He said to it as well, "Run to my grandmother's lodge." It also fell beside the entrance of his grandmother's lodge.

Next, he did the same to the bear, and he told it, "Run to my grandmother's lodge." It also fell down after arriving at the entrance.

Next, he shot a moose and said, "Run to the lodge of my grandmother." The moose did the same thing and fell at the entrance to his grandmother's.

Next, he shot an arrow into the body of a wild duck. Teharonhia:wako said to it, "Now, fly to my grandmother's lodge." The duck flew and when it arrived, it fell from the air in front of the lodge of his grandmother.

Soon, there was a pile of animals stacked in front of the entrance of his grandmother's lodge. Teharonhia:wako finished what he was doing and said to himself, "That is enough game for my grandmother and my brother. They will now have enough provisions to last them for a long time."

In spite of what his brother and grandmother had done to him, he still showed compassion toward them. He was angry but he still cared very much for them.[40]

Teharonhia:wako then proceeded to his grandmother's lodge. After being let in, his grandmother said to him, "Look, Grandson, at what a wonderful thing that has taken place. Your brother Sawiskera has been hunting and look at all the game animals he has killed."

Teharonhia:wako pointed to an animal and revealed to her, "That is called a porcupine, and my brother could not have killed it because he is hunting in a place where there is no game that looks like this. Therefore, it could not have been he who killed it. In fact, I want to tell you that I was the one who killed it. I did it so that you could have food to eat."

He then continued to say, "All the game animals are in great abundance at the place where I have come from."

He said, "I will show you the many uses of the game animals. Watch me dress all the game animals I have killed, and I will show you that they can provide you with many useful things."

Teharonhia:wako then went outdoors and began to skin the game animals he had killed. He cut up their bodies and hung up several pieces of meat all around the lodge. Next, he brought skins into the lodge and smoothed out each one. He lit a fire and smoked them. Then, he tightly fastened them together and placed them around the bark of the inside of the lodge. He spread a skin over the place where his grandmother had her bed and then placed one for himself so he could lay down.

Teharonhia:wako then turned to her and said, "Oh! Grandmother, I have now fulfilled the promise that I had made to you when I was first born. You will be the first to have continuous pleasure from the things that are now created on this Earth. They have been put here for the purpose of making a person content. One day, the *onkwe:honwe* who will be born on this Earth will make use of the game animals that live with them. Their minds will always be at ease because of the many creatures who inhabit the Earth with them. From them they will always have food, clothing, and shelter."

When he had finished what he had to say, Teharonhia:wako departed for his lodge. Once there, he said to himself, "I don't think that it would be a good thing for my brother and I to live near each other any longer."

Now that his brother had shown him what kind of character he had, it had resulted in his feeling distressed in the work that he was trying to do.

He thought to himself, "My brother and I must be separated because I still have much work to do, and, if we remain on the same floating island, he will try to spoil all my work. I will cut this floating island that we live on into two halves, and by that way separate us. Then, I will thrust a great body of water between us, so that he cannot cross over to my side too easily." Teharonhia:wako then went to the shore and stood at its edge.

He said to himself, "Now, this Earth will be divided forever." He then yelled to the water, "Water, enter between my brother and I and separate our two worlds forever." Turtle Island then began to separate into two halves. As the water was traveling between the two islands, Teharonhia:wako arrived on the other side of the divided Earth. As the waters flowed through their course, he said to himself, "Now my brother and I are separated, and I can continue to do my work unimpeded." He then returned to his lodge.

From that time on, there would be two floating islands. Later on, Teharonhia:wako would separate them again so that there would be four floating islands. Two of which would be connected to one another with the other two also connected to the other. The *onkwe:honwe* and their cousins would inhabit two of the floating islands on Teharonhia:wako's side of the world. All the other human beings would inhabit the other two floating islands.

Not long after Teharonhia:wako had separated the two floating islands, Sawiskera arrived at his grandmother's lodge to tell her that they were running out of meat.

He said, "Grandmother, we only have a little meat left for us to eat. I will go hunting, as the meat Teharonhia:wako gave us is running out."

He then went out to hunt, and as he traveled around looking for game, he noticed that there were no animals anywhere in sight. After attempting to look for a long time, he spotted some animals in the faroff distance. As soon as they saw him approaching, the animals jumped into the water and swam away.

He then noticed the island floating on the other side of the water where the game animals went ashore. Sawiskera was astonished at what he was seeing. He said to himself, "I will go and tell my brother what has happened."

He began walking in the direction of Teharonhia:wako's lodge. He looked all over the island, and he could not find him anywhere. Finally, after looking all over the place for him, he decided to go back and tell his grandmother what had happened.

When he reached her lodge, he said to her, "Oh! Grandmother, an astonishing thing has happened in that I cannot find any game animals around. When I did see some, they dove into the water, and they swam to another floating island where they climbed onto its shore. When I went to tell my brother about it, I couldn't find him, or his lodge, anywhere."

She replied, "I don't think that there is anything that we can do about what has happened. It appears your brother has tricked us."

Sawiskera answered, "I know something that I can do. I will create the same type of things over here that my brother has created on his island. I will start right now with some small creatures like the butterfly."

Sawiskera then proceeded to take some Earth, and he formed what he thought a butterfly would look like. He blew into them, and they flew away. They were gray in color and much smaller in size.[41]

Suddenly he looked up and saw some passenger pigeons fly overhead that had been created by Teharonhia:wako. He said, "I will make those as well."

He then began to form the bodies of what he thought passenger pigeons would look like. When he had completed them, he said, "Now, I am going to travel around this island and create more wonderful creatures."

What Sawiskera didn't notice was that as his pigeons flew off, they had fur and teeth.

Next he said, "I am going to make the Sunflower that will bring light to this world." He then formed what he thought a Sunflower would look like but instead made a thistle with thorns on it.

Then he said, "Now then, I will make the great fruit, the apple, that will bring me nourishment." He then formed what he thought an apple would look like. They looked almost like Teharonhia:wako's apples but were to sour to eat.

Then he saw many small creatures fly by and he said, "I will make an abundance of these as well."

Just at that moment, he saw his brother Teharonhia:wako, approaching. Sawiskera, said to the creatures that he had created, "Hurry! Go quickly before my brother sees you." The creatures then flew away making a great buzzing noise as they left.

Teharonhia:wako arrived and asked his brother, "My brother, what was that I saw you doing as I was walking over here?"

Sawiskera answered, "I was just resting. However, I want you to see all the things I have created while you were gone."

Teharonhia:wako then asked him, "What were all of those strange creatures that I saw flying away as I approached? "

Sawiskera replied, "Didn't you hear the great buzzing noise they made while they spoke to one another. Those are the creatures I have just completed."

Teharonhia:wako said, "It is true, the different languages they are speaking creates a great buzzing noise. They will from now on be referred to as flies. In fact, they will assist me as some will live upon the carcasses of game animals. In fact, all creatures that have been created will have a purpose."

Teharonhia:wako knew the value of even the smallest and ugliest of creatures. He also did not want to hurt his brother's feelings for he had compassion for his brother.

Sawiskera laughed and said to him, "Come and see the Sunflower I created?"

Teharonhia:wako looked at it and said, "This plant bears a beautiful flower; when it ripens it shall assist me as well. Several animals will live near it, and it shall be called a thistle."

Sawiskera's mind was gratified, and he said to his brother, "Come and see the apple I have created?" When they arrived, he showed his brother the apple he had planted.

Teharonhia:wako said, "This is good as well, as this thing you have planted will assist me as the game animals will live upon it. It shall be called a crab apple."

Sawiskera then said to him, "Now, let us go and see the bird that I have created. When they arrived, he pointed to the bird he created.

Teharonhia:wako said to him, "The thing that you created is also good, and I see no reason why they cannot travel around the Earth. They will be known as the vulture, and they will get rid of any waste left over." Sawiskera was again gratified.

Sawiskera said to his brother, "There is only one thing left for you to see. However, I may have made a mistake in my creation, and when you see them you can decide what can be done with them."

When they arrived at the shore of the lake, Sawiskera pointed and said, "Look at those creatures flying about; they are my pigeons."

Teharonhia:wako looked up in the sky and said to the flying creatures, "Come to me? " The creatures then flew over to him.

Teharonhia:wako, upon seeing them close up, said, "It is not good that your creatures flying about have fur and teeth, as they will do harm to the other flying creatures who are more vulnerable. I will call them bats."

He continued, "This gives me an idea. Perhaps, it would be good, if everything were divided into two parts. From now on, I will make it so that there will be daylight only for a short time. Then darkness will appear, followed by daylight again. This cycle will repeat itself forever. Those beings that have feathers will continue to fly about while there is daylight, while at night they shall rest. It would not be good to have things flying around with teeth during the daylight. From now on they will live in the trees and they will hide in other places. They will come out only at night." He then said, "The night shall be yours, my brother, while the day mine."

Sawiskera was taken by surprise at the things his brother had just told him. He liked the idea of having his power enhanced during the cold of the night.

Teharonhia:wako turned to Sawiskera and said, "It is time for me to return to my island. The next time it will be your turn to visit me and see the work that I am doing."

The Renewal of the Sky World, and the Creation of the *Onkwe:honwe*

When he arrived at his lodge, Teharonhia:wako thought it would be nice if he created an orb that could light up the whole Earth. He went to visit the home of He Who Holds up the Earth, the Great Turtle Man, his father. After they had greeted one another, he said to him, "I want to make an orb of light that will forever give light to the Earth. How do you think it could be done?"

The Great Turtle Man, upon hearing the proposal, said to him, "It is time that I tell you something."

He then explained, "Near the place where your grandmother came from, she has a brother who watches and waits to see if she remembers him. You should go to him and assign him the duty of giving daylight to the Earth. At one time, your grandmother's brother had said that he would be remembered by shaking the Earth. Before his sister left the Sky World, he had told her that he would one day go to the place where she had fallen and search for her. You can help him find her. Therefore, I think that you should invite your great-uncle to come here. He will then watch over the things that you create and assist you with your grandmother who has been against you."

He continued to tell Teharonhia:wako, "There is a way that you can find him. You must take the red willow plant that you have planted and cut off the young shoots that have sprouted from it. This should be done two at a time. Take one of the sprouts and scrape off the bark. Then steep it for medicine by cooking it in water. Scrape the bark from the other shoot and cast it into the fire. When that is done and the smoke starts to rise, cast yourself into the smoke. This is the way that you shall meet him. He will be about halfway up. Tell him what you want from him. He will be able to give you what you need because his light on top of the celestial tree is very powerful."

After Teharonhia:wako had arrived back at his lodge, he kindled a fire. He then went out in search of the red willow bark. When he had found some, he cut off two shoots and took them back with him. He scraped the bark from one shoot and made the medicine. He then took it as an emetic by boiling and drinking it. He scraped off the bark of the other shoot and threw it into the fire. As the smoke from it rose into the air, he leaped into the fire as he was asked to do. He then began to rise with the smoke.[42]

He had not gone very far when he saw a male being approach him. The male being spoke to him saying, "We have finally met, my Great-nephew. How can I help you?"

Teharonhia:wako replied, "I need you to help me with something. I have completed all the things on Earth in their various forms, but I need something that will give more light than the Sunflower. It should give as great a light as possible, because the Earth has become very large, and there are now two floating islands that must be lit up. In fact, one day I may even add to the Earth so that there will be four main floating islands instead of two. In that way the creatures that I create will spread all over, and there will be different ones living in different places. Therefore, I will need something bright so that it could give daylight to the whole world below."

He further explained, "I have been sent by Earth Grasper to ask you if you could help me in this task."

The man being replied, "It has been a long time that I have waited for someone to remember me. During that time, I have watched all that has happened to you on the Earth. I will be willing to help take this problem off your shoulders and will do whatever you ask of me. I will attach myself on the underside of the sky, and I will begin at a certain place over the middle of the Earth each day, beginning in the east and ending in the west. Then I will rest for a while and proceed to repeat the same thing over again. This I will continue to do as long as the Earth below continues to exist. I will always take care of those things that you have created by keeping the Earth below warm."

Teharonhia:wako replied, "Now that this has been taken care of, the Sunflower will continue to grow as a reminder of your approaching daylight."

The male being answered, "I have waited a long time for my sister who happens to be your grandmother to remember me. It will be up to you to decide what to do with your brother who beheaded your mother. Her head still lies where your grandmother lives. I would like to make a request that you assign your mother's head a duty that would give her movement and life once again. In this way, she and I could aid one another. Your brother is very worrisome to me as he will continue to try in every way to make a mockery of everything you have created. You did the right thing in separating yourself from him, as this will cause him difficulties in what he is attempting to do. It is known that he will try to destroy you and take over the creation."

Teharonhia:wako answered him, "Perhaps it is time that we settle this matter once and for all. Do not attach your body to the sky until I tell you to do so. Only then will it do the Earth any good. Those below will know the time when you will use the power that is within your name."

The male being replied, "That is why they will also know me as He Who Shakes the Earth. When the time comes when the world approaches its end, the people will feel the Earth shake, and they will then call out my name. For my power above will influence what happens below."

Teharonhia:wako then said, "From now on, as you rise above this very place where we have met, the midpoint in your path, you will rest for a while and then continue on your journey." He continued to say, "During that time, the human beings who will inhabit the world will direct their thoughts at you. You will be able to answer them in a positive manner as you will have had time to reflect on their thoughts. The human beings living on the Earth will always look at you and refer to you as their Elder Brother. This will be the way it will always be as long as the Earth continues to exist. In much the same way, the human beings will refer to the first one to set herself below on this Earth as your younger sister."

"Finally, it is time for us to separate. Tomorrow you will come for the first time over the horizon and cause daylight and bring brightness and warmth to the Earth," said Teharonhia:wako.

They then separated and Teharonhia:wako floated down to the Earth below.

When Teharonhia:wako returned to his lodge, he said to himself, "Now it is time for me to make the *onkwe:honwe*, real human beings, who will inhabit this floating island."

It was not too long after this that he began to create the bodies of the real human beings. He took up some red Earth from his mother's body and said aloud, "This Earth that I have taken is alive with the spirit of my mother's body, and so I will form a human body from it. When the human body passes from this Earth, the body will return to my mother's body and regenerate new life from it."

He then molded the flesh of the *onkwe:honwe* from the Earth, saying to himself, "It would be a good thing if the *onkwe:honwe* has life, just as I have."[43]

He then took a portion of his own essence and placed it inside the *onkwe:honwe*'s body. Then, he took a portion of his mind and enclosed it in the head of the *onkwe:honwe*. Next, he took a portion of his blood and put it inside the *onkwe:honwe*'s flesh. Next, he took a portion of his sight and put it in the *onkwe:honwe*'s head. Next, he took a portion of his speech and put it into the *onkwe:honwe*'s throat. Last of all, he blew his breath into the *onkwe:honwe*; then the *onkwe:honwe* came alive and stood up for the first time on Earth.

Teharonhia:wako said to himself, "Last of all, I have now completed the *onkwe:honwe* who will now stand upon this Earth. I have finished completing everything I had set out to do. I have made myself master over all that the Earth contains, and I will continue to give comfort to those that live on it whenever it is needed. I have placed the *onkwe:honwe* on Earth to dwell so that he may beautify my creation by cultivating it."

At that moment, the Elder Brother came over the horizon and caused it to be daylight, and at the same time he warmed the Earth. It was a beautiful daylight with beautiful light rays shining on everything in the creation.

Teharonhia:wako yelled to his creation, "Look at the orb of light coming over the horizon causing it to be daylight. This will forever result in pleasure for you all, in that it will warm the days as well as the nights to come. As a result, all the things on the Earth—plants, animals, human beings—will continue to live in comfort. You will be able to travel everywhere on the Earth as long as your Elder Brother causes it to be daylight. When the daylight ends, darkness will then occur and at that time you will rest. I have completed that that shall continue into the future, as long as the Earth continues to exist."

During that time, Sawiskera and his grandmother became aware of what was happening as they saw the daylight appear over the horizon.

Sawiskera said to her, "I am going at once to where my brother lives to see why this most astounding thing has just occurred."

When he arrived at the shore of his island, he saw that the other floating island was very far off and only slightly visible. He said to himself, "I will make a canoe to cross the water."

So he began to search for something he could cross with. He knew that even though his power to freeze was limited, he still had enough to create a white stone canoe bridge. With the help of the night, he would be able to cross the water to the other side. That night he completed his white stone canoe made from ice. As the Earth became colder with the setting Sun, he walked across the ice bridge to the other side. Once there, he disembarked and in front of him appeared an *onkwe:honwe*, the first he had ever seen.

The Era of the *Onkwe:honwe*

Sawiskera asked the *onkwe:honwe*, "Who are you and where did you come from?"

The *onkwe:honwe* answered, "I came to life in this place we are standing on."

Sawiskera, then asked, "Who was it that created your body?"

The *onkwe:honwe* answered, "The one who created me lives near here. Let us go and visit him. You will then meet the one who created my body."

They then proceeded together toward the lodge of Teharonhia:wako.

After they had arrived and Sawiskera saw who it was, he asked his brother, Teharonhia:wako, "Was it you who created the body of this *onkwe:honwe* whom I just met?"

Teharonhia:wako answered him, "I am the one who molded the body of the *onkwe:honwe* from the red Earth where our mother lay."

Sawiskera replied, "There is another thing that I want to ask you? Who caused it to be daylight?" he asked.

Teharonhia:wako answered, "It is our grandmother's Elder Brother who has returned from the Sky World."

Sawiskera was astonished at what he was hearing.

Teharonhia:wako then spoke and said, "My brother, let us go for a walk. You will then see the condition of the things that are growing on our mother's body and that I have planted."

They began to walk where the many fruits were growing. Suddenly various animals ran by them.

Sawiskera said to his brother, "It is amazing how quickly the things that you have planted have multiplied themselves."

"How did you do it?" he asked.

Teharonhia:wako explained to him, "In the beginning the Earth was small, and then it continued to expand and kept growing. This is how it will be for all life, including the game animals and the human beings. As they multiply, their numbers will also increase in size."

Sawiskera replied, "I will return home to our grandmother's lodge and tell her the wondrous things that I have seen."

When Sawiskera arrived home, he said to his grandmother, "I have been across the water and have seen astonishing things over there. Teharonhia:wako told me that your older brother now gives light to the world."

His grandmother answered, "It appears that my brother has kept his promise when he said that one day he would arrive and look for me."

Sawiskera, feeling jealous of his brother's work, said to her, "Do not worry, Grandmother; I will also make a human being to inhabit this side of the world."

Sawiskera then began working to create a human being. He took some Earth and molded it into what he thought a human being should look like.

After it was completed, he said, "Human being, stand upright and walk." Suddenly the creature leaped up and ran into the water immersing itself there. In a short time, he thrust out his head and looked around.

Sawiskera said to his creature, "Come over here and let me look at you."

The creature did not answer or move.

Sawiskera then said to himself, "Perhaps I made a mistake. It seems I did not form this human being's body correctly. I will try once again."

He then molded another creature and when he was finished, he spoke to it saying, "Human being, stand upright." The creature rose up and as he walked, he saw a tree and began to climb it.

Upon seeing his creation, Sawiskera said to himself, "It appears that I made another mistake, for it seems that my human being is too small in size to be human and that he has a long tail."

He then called to the creature, "Human being, come over here."

The creature did not reply but remained in the tree. Sawiskera then said to himself, "I will make another human being who will be much larger this time." He then molded another body from the Earth.

When he was finished, he said to it, "Human being, stand upright." The creature then stood up.

Sawiskera watched him with glee, and said to himself, "Perhaps this time I have succeeded in creating a human being."

This creature looked like a human being but was much larger and more powerful. Unlike a human being he had much more hair on him.

Next, he said to himself, "I will now make a game animal."

He then molded a game animal, and when he was finished he said to it, "You will be called deer." The creature stood upright and cried out as it ran off.

He made another game animal and said to it, "You will be called bear." His creature then rose up and walked away.

At that moment Sawiskera saw his brother coming toward him along a path. Sawiskera said to Teharonhia:wako, "Now, I will show you the kind of things I have created." They both then began to walk together.

Sawiskera pointed and said to his brother, "There is the human being that I created." Teharonhia:wako looked and saw a creature seated at the edge of the water.

He then asked his brother, "What kind of creature is that sitting at the edge of the water? That's not a human being; that is a bullfrog." The bullfrog then plunged into the water out of sight.

Sawiskera pointed again and said to his brother, "Look up there, I have made another human being."

Teharonhia:wako answered, "That is not a human being, your creature has a tail and fur grows on its body."

Teharonhia:wako then asked the creature, "What type of creature are you, sitting up in a tree?"

As the creature began to weep, Teharonhia:wako said to it, "From now on you will be called a monkey."

They then went a short distance and there sat another of Sawiskera's human beings.

Teharonhia:wako asked it, "What kind of a creature are you?" The large creature stood up and also began to weep.

Teharonhia:wako said to it, "You will be called hairy human being."[44]

Sawiskera said to Teharonhia:wako, "There are two beings still remaining that I have created that I will now show you."

He took his brother to where he had created the creatures and said, "That one there I call a deer while the other is called a bear."

Teharonhia:wako looked at one of the creatures and said, "That is not a deer." The animal then cried out.

Teharonhia:wako said, "You will be called saber-tooth tiger, while the other creature because of its great size will be called mammoth instead of bear."

Teharonhia:wako said to Sawiskera, "Tomorrow, you and grandmother should return to my island together." Teharonhia:wako then crossed over to his floating island.

Sawiskera went back to his grandmother's lodge to tell her what happened. When he arrived at her place, he said to her, "My brother arrived and changed the human beings I created. He changed my deer into a tiger and my bear into a mammoth. In fact, every creature that I created and showed him, Teharonhia:wako would not acknowledge. Since the creatures that I had made are turning out different from those of my brother, I will destroy his creation with mine. Soon, I will send them over to Teharonhia:wako's island, where they will eat all his food. Once there, my creatures will eat all Teharonhia:wako's creatures. If that doesn't work, I will challenge him to a fight. Tomorrow, we will go over to visit Teharonhia:wako's lodge.

His grandmother asked him, "How will we cross to the other island?"

Sawiskera, replied, "I will make a white stone canoe bridge so that we can cross, and it will be completed by daylight. This is how all my creatures will arrive on Teharonhia:wako's island as well."

"When you have done this, I will go with you," his grandmother replied.

That evening, Sawiskera said to himself, "I will build a white stone canoe between the two Earths where we may cross."

Because Teharonhia:wako had taken half of Sawiskera's power to freeze in the exchange for corn, he could not build the canoe bridge by himself.

Sawiskera told his grandmother, "Do not worry; we will leave after your Elder Brother, the Sun, has set in the west, and it becomes dark."

Sawiskera then called out, "Oh! Black night. You have the power to help me complete the white stone canoe bridge in the space lying between the two islands during the night. Once this is done, my grandmother and I shall cross the water, just as Elder Brother rises in the east."

As the night came it became very cold, and the temperature continued to get colder until Elder Brother reappeared in the east.

That evening Teharonhia:wako said to himself as he felt the cold air arrive, "Perhaps, Sawiskera has enough power left to destroy the things that I have planted on this island. If that happens, the rest of the creation will have nothing left to eat. Sawiskera seems to have augmented his power in the darkness."

Teharonhia:wako decided that it was necessary that he assign someone to make sure that it did not become excessively cold or dark.

He said to himself, "I will await the arrival of my grandmother before I decide to do something about it."

The next day, Teharonhia:wako was surprised when he saw his grandmother and brother crossing the waters. After they had arrived, he asked them, "How is it that you were able to cross the waters?"

His grandmother replied, "Sawiskera has caused a white stone canoe to float between the two islands, and we crossed over on that."

At that time Turtle Island had once again become very cold and some of the plant life died.

Suddenly, Elder Brother the Sun began to appear. Sawiskera told his grandmother, "We will have to leave soon, because the Elder Brother will make it difficult for us to get back across to the other side."

His grandmother replied, "We should wait to see what your brother wants before we leave."

Teharonhia:wako then said to them, "Let us first eat from the food that I have planted. As soon as we are full, we will examine all the things that my island contains and that have been newly created." He then went and brought back some corn and began to roast it. As it got hot, it gave out a pleasant odor.

His grandmother asked him, "Could I pluck one cob and eat it?"

Teharonhia:wako replied, "That is not the way things should be done. Wait until it is cooked first, then together we will eat. Everyone has an equal right to the things that grow from the Earth. From now on, everyone will share with each other the things that grow upon it."[45]

His grandmother replied, "All I want is the small uncooked end for myself."

Teharonhia:wako answered, "That is not the way things are to be done."

She persisted, saying, "I just want a small quantity to take back with us."

He told her again, "That is not the way things will be done. From now on, everyone will eat together because everyone has an equal right to share in the things of the Earth. That is the way it will always be on the Earth."

The old women replied, "I am amazed at what a stingy person you are."

Teharonhia:wako could see that his grandmother had become very agitated. She then went to the fire, picked up some ashes, and threw them on the roasting corn. When this happened, the appetizing odor of the corn ceased, as well as the flowing fat that dripped from the cob. At that time, the lands of Turtle Island were filled with drought from the ashes that filled the air from when the grandmother scooped them from the fire and threw them on the corn. This made it hard for the plant life to grow.[46]

She then asked Teharonhia:wako, "Is it only human beings that will get pleasure from this? Cannot your grandmother have some pleasure from it as well?"

Angrily Teharonhia:wako replied, "What you just did was not good. You have spoiled the one thing that would have given the most comfort to the *onkwe:honwe* who dwell on the Earth." He knew that corn was not good to the taste until it had fully ripened and that it was important that everyone shared equally from it. When the rest of the corn was cooked, they then ate together.

When they were finished eating, feeling conciliatory, Teharonhia:wako said to them, "Come over here."

He pointed to a tree and told them, "You shall be the first to eat the fruit of the tree that you are standing close to." There they saw a growing shrub that bore fruit that were slightly sweet in taste and like drops of syrup.

Teharonhia:wako said to them, "The large fruit on this tree is called an apple. Each of us will pluck one from the branches of the tree, and then we will eat together." They each then plucked off an apple and ate it.

His grandmother then asked Teharonhia:wako, "Wouldn't it be all right if I plucked off some more apples to take back with us."

He replied, "You must wait for them to ripen first before you eat them. Then you can take as many as you like, and the game animals will do the same." Once again in anger, the old woman entered the lodge and took a handful of ashes from the fire.

She went out and threw the ashes over the growing fruit. When the fruit had turned black from the ashes, she said to Teharonhia:wako, "Are only the people of the Earth allowed to get pleasure from this as well."

Once again, Turtle Island became covered in ash that ruined the plant life.

She continued, "From now on, since I cannot enjoy an apple when I want, neither will the *onkwe:honwe*. From this point on, the *onkwe:honwe* will refer to it as the sour fruit, and no human being will ever want to eat it again."

Teharonhia:wako replied, "I think you have tried much too hard to injure your grandchildren. Perhaps, it would be better if you no longer see the things I have planted or the game animals I have created."

She answered him abruptly, "I will leave this place with your brother and return in ten days time. Then, we will settle this matter once and for all in a bet with the winner having control of all the food supply. If I win the bet, then I will control all the things that you completed on the Earth. If you win the bet, then I will no longer disturb you or the things that you have created."

Teharonhia:wako responded, "I will do whatever you wish."

While they were visiting, Sawiskera studied the *onkwe:honwe* who had come to life. He then asked Teharonhia:wako, "My brother, how did you make so physically perfect a being as this human?"

Teharonhia:wako answered, "The Earth is still young and continues to grow from its power of *orenta*. This is the same for the animals, the *onkwe:honwe*, and the other forms of life as well. In the beginning, everything is born this way. They begin small, and, as they grow up, they use up more of their *orenta*, until finally they pass from this Earth and return to the Sky World."

Sawiskera replied, "I have a better understanding now as to why things are the way they are. Grandmother and I will now leave for home."

Sawiskera and his grandmother both departed toward home, hoping to walk over the ice bridge. Upon arriving they discovered that the ice bridge had melted away. Sawiskera's grandmother asked him, "How will we go back to our floating island over the great water with no stone white canoe to cross on?"

Sawiskera answered, "I will use my abilities to make another white stone canoe that I will complete shortly by using the help of the north wind." He then called for the north wind to arrive, and suddenly it became very cold.

Not long after, Sawiskera began to complete the white stone canoe. When it was finished, he said to his grandmother, "Come now, Grandmother, get aboard and we will cross." They then crossed the water to their floating island that had also become frozen.

Upon arriving on the other side of the water, Sawiskera said to his grandmother, "I will create all the same things as my brother, but this time I will not show my brother the things I have created."

Sawiskera began to work by first making the body of a game animal. When it was completed, he told it to stand up. The being dragged his body along as it slithered away. Unsure as to why his creation was so unusual, Sawiskera said to his grandmother, "My brother must be using his influence to disrupt the things I am creating. I will try to make something else."

He then made another creature and said to it, "Stand up." Instead of standing, the being also slithered away on its belly. Sawiskera said to himself, "This must be what all the bodies of the creatures I have formed look like. If these creatures ever become numerous on the Earth, I will let them cross under the water to my brother's island, and I will make sure that they will continually cause trouble while they are over there."

Sawiskera continued making bodies for his creatures, and just as quickly as they were made he thrust them aside. Soon they became numerous and were formed in all shapes and sizes. Some of them became very monstrous in size and appearance, and they began to multiply. When he had finished forming all his creatures, he gathered them together and told them.

"Now that you have been created, I will assign you the duty to cross over the water and go to my brother's floating island on the other side. Once over there, you will find abundant plants, animals, as well as human beings for you to feed upon."

His creatures then began to travel around his floating island looking for a place to stop. Many of them were fierce-tempered and fought with one another. Sawiskera created another white stone canoe, and some of them began to cross over to Teharonhia:wako's island. Others swam across the water as Sawiskera had asked, landing on Teharonhia:wako's floating island. Once there, they began to attack and destroy Teharonhia:wako's creation.

It was not long before Teharonhia:wako became aware of what was happening. He said to himself, "These creatures who have invaded my island should not be mingling with my creation. I will send them back from where they came."

He then gathered all the monstrous creatures and forced them back across the water to Sawiskera's island. He then followed them, forcing them toward the cave of the mountain that the first animals had been shut in by Sawiskera. There were serpents and various other creatures that Sawiskera had created. Once he had driven them into the cave, he placed a rock in front of the entrance. After this was done, he crossed the water back from where he came.

After returning to his lodge, he thought to himself, "Something is still missing in my creation. The human being is alone and needs a companion. I will make another human being to be a companion to him so that they can reproduce."

He gathered some red Earth from his mother's body and formed the flesh of women from it. He said to himself, "This human being will also be made in my image."

He then took a portion of his own life and placed it in the body of this new *onkwe:honwe*. Then he took some of his own life, so that the being would have voice and sight. Finally, he put a portion of his breath into her, and then she came to life. He then told the human being to stand up.

After she stood up, he said to her, "I have completed your body as well as all the other things in the world."

He called the male human being over to him and told both of them, "You will have the duty to look after all the things in my creation."

He then said to the female human being, "Because you are a female like my mother, whose body is in the Earth, you will have the duty to look after the plant world. When my mother's head is placed in the sky, she will always aid you in your work."

He then turned to the male human being and said, "Your duty will be to look after the game animals on the Earth. My grandmother's brother will always give you guidance each day, as long as you ask for it when he rises each morning."

He then told them, "There is one final thing that I will ask of you and that is that you must be married. If you do this, you will be more capable in performing the tasks I have given you to do. You will travel all over the Earth and spread your offspring.

He continued, "Your tasks will not be easy, and you will have to work very hard for there to be peace between you both."

He turned to the male human being and said, "Make sure that you do nothing that will put your companion in distress."

He then turned to the female human being and said, "Your male companion will have to work even harder than you, and there will be times when you will both suffer because your bodies are made fragile from the Earth and can be easily destroyed. You will make a circuit around the fire so that the male *onkwe:honwe* who will aid you will remain at peace. This will bring both of you joy."

He then said to them, "All human beings from now on will take the form of your bodies. One day, the Earth will be covered by human beings. Each human being will have a different length of days to spend on the Earth until death takes them away. Until that time you are to be united in marriage."

He continued, "Now, I have mixed together the minds and the blood of you both. Other humans will take their form through your bodies. I state that you should have one mind at all times, so that you don't hurt one another during your days on Earth. Only that which is called death should ever separate you from one another. This will be the same for future beings who will also marry one day. This will be the way it shall be as long as the Earth continues to exist."

Then he said, "I have now completed everything I set out to do."

Sawiskera traveled the island looking for the wild beasts he had formed, but he could not find them anywhere. He then decided to cross the water to his brother's island, believing that they might have swum over there as he had requested. When he arrived at Teharonhia:wako's island, he asked him, "My brother, have you seen any of the wild beasts I have created?"

Teharonhia:wako answered, "You can look all over the island to see if you can find any of your wild beasts, but I don't know where they might be."

Sawiskera began to travel over the island and saw many game animals around, but none of the ones he had created. Suddenly, he saw the two human beings.

He asked them, "What are you two doing?"

They answered, "We have been left here to reproduce by our Creator so that there will be other human beings in the future."

Sawiskera was astonished at what he had seen and heard, and he went back to Teharonhia:wako's place. Upon arriving there, he asked his brother, "I have been everywhere on your island and have not found any of my creatures. However, I did meet two of the human beings that you formed and noticed that you made them slightly different from one another in order to reproduce. I would also like to create two human beings like the ones you created on my floating island. Would you mind if I tried?"

Teharonhia:wako answered, "That would be all right, as long as you took great care and made an exact copy of the human beings that I created. If you do this, your human beings will be able to inhabit your island as well. If that happens, I will make it so that our Elder Brother will pass right through the middle of both of our islands. It would make me happy that there will be more human beings on the Earth."

Sawiskera was really pleased with his brother's answer. He then asked him, "Help me create the human being on my island? Also, I would like you to help me find my game animals that have disappeared?"

Teharonhia:wako answered him, "I will consider it."

Sawiskera then told him, "I will now go home, and my first task will be to create a human being such as you have made here."

After arriving back on his island, Sawiskera told his grandmother about everything that he had seen. He said to her, "I have been to Teharonhia:wako's island, but could not find any of my game animals. However, I did see two human beings that Teharonhia:wako created. He told me that if I were to make a human being like his, I would have to be very careful and make sure that it was in the same form as his own."

His grandmother answered, "I think it is a good idea that you follow your brother's instructions. I wouldn't be happy if your human being turned out to be half as good as your brother's. As well, I think something must have been done to your game animals, but I don't know what. Let us hope that we can find them."

Sawiskera replied, "I am ready to begin to create a human being. I only have a short time to do it as my brother will arrive tomorrow to examine my work."

He then took some snow that had fallen from his body and said to himself, "Perhaps, if I use the white foam of the water to create my human being and mix it with the snow and Earth from my mother's body, my human being will be different from Teharonhia:wako's and I can call them my own."[47]

Sawiskera took some white foam from the water and mixed it with the snow and Earth from his mother's body. He put great care in forming the body of a human being. He then attempted to bring life to it but was unable.

He said to himself, "Very soon my brother will arrive and I will ask him to help me in bringing my human being to life. I have tried hard to bring peace between us, and he has agreed to let me make a human being. I will go to meet him tomorrow and tell him that I have failed in making a human being come to life."

He noticed his brother was approaching in the distance. When they met, Sawiskera pointed and said to his brother, "Over there, lies the human being that I made out of the snow from my body, foam from the water and the Earth. I now have a human being that I can call my own."

Teharonhia:wako replied, "Your human being looks good in form. I will help give your human being life. I will add to what you have already created by giving him the ability to move his body." He then took a portion of his life and placed it in the lifeless body of the human being. Then he took some of his mind and placed it in his head. Next, he took a portion of his blood and placed it in its flesh. He also gave the human being the power to see and talk. Finally, he gave the human being some of his breath, and the being came to life.

Teharonhia:wako said to the human being, "Now then, stand up."

The human being then raised himself up.

Teharonhia:wako said to his brother, "I have fulfilled your wishes, but with some regrets. One day your human being will try to control my creation and will become hostile to my work. That is because you did not use all my instructions in creating him."[48]

Sawiskera then asked Teharonhia:wako, "Could I have an equal control over the creation as it would be a good thing if I also had some influence on the world." Teharonhia:wako agreed with his brother's idea, knowing that the world should consist of balance between their two powers.

He then told Sawiskera, "From now on, I will allow you to use your power half the time if this will make you happy. You will use both the night and north wind to augment it. After that, with the help of our mother and her brother, my power will have pre-eminence over the creation."[49]

Sawiskera replied, "The human being that we formed together is made in both your image and mine. In this way, he will always have two minds."

Teharonhia:wako said to Sawiskera, "You are right, you will influence the left side, while I will influence the right side of his mind. As long as the human being learns to use the right side, his thoughts will be with me. If he learns to use the left side only, his thoughts will be with you, and he will want to control the creation.

Sawiskera asked, "What should we call this new human being?"

Teharonhia:wako replied, "The first human beings, which I created from the red Earth of our mother and with the red skin will be called *onkwe:honwe*, real human beings. Their thoughts will always be centered more toward me. The ones I helped you create shall be known as the One Whose Body Is White, and they will be known simply as human beings. Their thoughts will be centered more toward the way you think. One day they will destroy their part of the floating island by trying to control everything upon it. When that occurs, they will try to arrive on my floating island, and then the *onkwe:honwe*, real human beings, will have problems. That is why they should remain separated from one another.

Teharonhia:wako then said, "There are other human beings created as well. They will live on the other floating islands. However, they will have little effect on the lives of the *onkwe:honwe*. Some will be like the *onkwe:honwe* in their manners and customs and even look like *onkwe:honwe*."

Sawiskera said to his brother, "I will then make other human beings from a portion of our mother's body."

Teharonhia:wako replied, "I will not help you any longer as I have assisted you enough already."

Sawiskera then said to his brother, "There is still one matter yet to be settled, and it has to do with the disappeared animals that I created."

Teharonhia:wako pointed and asked him, "Who made the mountain and the cavern inside it that runs to the depths of the Earth?"

Sawiskera became angry as he knew he had been put on the spot. He replied, "Maybe it was the game animals that made the cavern."

Teharonhia:wako answered, "If your game animals are that powerful to create a cavern, perhaps your animals became lost in it as well."

Sawiskera then said to his brother, "Let us go together and find out if they are there."

They started off toward the mountain where the cave was. When they arrived, they saw the cave with the large rock in front of it.

Teharonhia:wako pointed and said, "This is where your game animals are." He picked up the boulder in front of the cave and threw it aside. Soon all kinds of monsters began to appear, dragging their bodies along by crawling. Some of them were small while others were large. Many of them had teeth and snarled as they slithered out.

Teharonhia:wako then said to his brother, "It would not be a good thing for your creatures to associate with the human beings. They would kill all the human beings in the world. I think it is better that your creatures remain underground forever."

Sawiskera replied, "There are even larger beings that even I have not seen and that are even farther underground. He then took the rock and placed it over the opening of the cavern. He continued to tell his brother, "The day will come when they will be let out by those who have white bodies. It is now time that we return to our grandmother's place and tell her what we have done."[50]

Upon arriving, Sawiskera said to his grandmother, "I have finished completing everything that I set out to do. What do you think we should do next?"

His grandmother answered, "I am worried about the head of my daughter as it has been hanging from my lodge for a long time."

Teharonhia:wako said, "Perhaps, we could hang it above in the sky so that the human beings will always remember what had happened here a long time ago."

His grandmother replied, "That sounds like a great idea."

Teharonhia:wako then said, "Perhaps, it would be good if we brought her head back to life again as well. We should place her head above in the sky and assign her a duty, so she could help light up the Earth when it is dark. Her duty will be restricted to a certain time when the Elder Brother, the Sun, takes a rest. This will cause it to light up and bring peace to the animals and the human beings below. She will be fullest for three days, when she will begin to re-create herself once again. This will guide the human beings and those other living things below, as their life cycles will be governed by it. She will work together with the female human beings and the plants to regenerate the Earth."

Sawiskera said, "I agree that she should be fastened high up where the human beings will be able to see her. However, a time may come when someone may try to hide her. Grandmother and I will watch over her in case someone tries to rob her head. In fact, I believe that there might be a time when this might happen, so I will guard her day and night. If anyone tries to take her, I will destroy them whether they be a human being or an animal."

Sawiskera wanted to retain control of his mother's head because he had already lost control of her body. Teharonhia:wako knew he was being deceived.

In later times, every once in a while, Sawiskera would try to hide the Elder Brother, the Sun, or the Mother, the Moon, and Teharonhia:wako would have to return for a short time to release them.

Teharonhia:wako told Sawiskera, "If you do that, then our mother's head will be of no help to anyone."

He continued, "I am still waiting to settle the matter of who will control the creation once and for all, since our grandmother has challenged me to a bet when she struck my door post. The challenge our grandmother has made to me is that whoever wins the bet will gain control over the creation in the world. I will watch and be ready for you to arrive, as the bet has been scheduled for ten days' time. Only after the bet is finished will I consider creating more things on the Earth. Until the time the bet has been won, I will stop creating things."

The boys' grandmother replied, "I am also ready for the bet, and you, Teharonhia:wako, should be on the watch, for I will be arriving on your island with Sawiskera to win control over the creation."

Teharonhia:wako went back to his floating island. As soon as he returned to his lodge, he informed his created beings that they were about to face a great crisis in a short time. He explained to them, "Tomorrow the old woman who is my grandmother and my brother Sawiskera who brings in the winter will be coming to seek control over you. If she wins the bet we have made, she will make sure that not a living thing will grow upon which the human beings and the game animals live. If I win, then I will continue to rule over all the things on the Earth, and the things that I have given you human beings to nurture will continue to flourish and grow. Only if I win will I add more to the creation. However, those things that have been planted will live only a short time, because they will continually seek to ruin them. I have allowed my brother some of his power in the hopes that it will satisfy him."

He continued, "Therefore, two things will occur, with the first taking place on the Earth. It will become warm for a certain period of time, and things will continue to grow. When the plants mature, it will turn cold and the Earth and the water will harden, just like when Sawiskera caused the ice bridge to float. This will last for a while, until once again it will begin to warm up and the Earth's crust will soften and life will again be renewed. Plants will then begin to grow and provide for the game animals and the human beings until the cycle is repeated again."

He continued, "The second thing that will occur is that there will be an orb of light at night as well as in the day, and they will aid one another.

The human beings will call the Elder Brother the orb of light in the day, the Great War Chief; they will call the light of the night, Our Grandmother. They both will be held in great respect by the people on Earth. The orb of light in the night will disappear for three nights and then will renew herself. The human beings will always revere her." Teharonhia:wako then took a seat to rest.

Not long after, his grandmother and brother came along, ready to win the bet over who would control the creation. Teharonhia:wako said to his creation as they arrived to witness the game, "Here comes my grandmother, Mature Flowers, and my brother, Sawiskera, to try and destroy you."

Teharonhia:wako then told them, "Watch what happens when we come to grips with one another and our bodies begin to sway back and forth."

He continued, "You will have a story that will be remembered by the coming generations until the end of time. There will be many other things that will happen in the future that you will one day tell your grandchildren. Sawiskera will repeatedly do things that will go against my creation, so that the coming generations will face many fearful situations in the future."

Once his grandmother and Sawiskera had arrived, Teharonhia:wako said, "Now the time has come. On this day, it will be decided whether the human beings, the plants, and the game animals will survive or whether they will be destroyed forever."

His grandmother said to him, "We will play a game and use my own bowl and plum pits to throw for control of the creation."

Teharonhia:wako replied, "To make it fair, I want to have a say in the rules of the game as well. We will use your bowl; however, when I throw, I will use my plum pits. As to yourself, you may use your own plum pits when you throw. We will each throw once, and the winner will then be decided. Hopefully, the pits will fall in my favor."[51]

His grandmother agreed and said, "Are you ready with your pits?"

Teharonhia:wako replied, "Wait a minute, I will go get them." As Teharonhia:wako went to get his pits, he called out, "I need six chickadees to come over here and assist me." Six small chickadees flew toward him.

Teharonhia:wako appealed to them and said, "Assist me in my bet with my grandmother. She wants to take control of the plant world, and if she wins all the other beings will be affected."

The chickadees, upon hearing Teharonhia:wako, cried out and began to sing. They then perched themselves along his body. Teharonhia:wako beheaded six of them and took them to his grandmother's place.

Upon arriving, he told her, "We will throw the pits once in the air from the bowl and that will be all." He then sat on the ground.

The old woman said, "I will be the first to throw the pits in the bowl." She grabbed the bowl and threw the pits into the air and when they landed back in the bowl, nothing turned up.

Teharonhia:wako said to her, "Now take your pits out of the bowl, and I will use mine." He then placed his pits in the bowl, and they strangely enough seemed to be alive. They scrambled back and forth in the bowl while he held it.

Teharonhia:wako whispered to the chickadees, "You must put all your *orenta* in the game, so that you can win and the creation can survive." He then grabbed the bowl and threw the pits up into the air. Suddenly there was a loud noise and all the living beings cried out including the things that grew on the Earth. The pits then flew out of the bowl and out of sight with a great sound seeming to follow them behind. Both the grandmother and Sawiskera put their *orenta* together to prevent them from returning.

Teharonhia:wako said, "Let there come a field." This meant that the pits would all be turned upright when they returned.

His grandmother yelled, "It isn't over yet."

After a while they heard the pits in the distance coming downward, crying out loudly.

Teharonhia:wako kept shouting, "Let there come a field."

The old woman yelled back, "Let three come together."

The pits flew into the bowl and kept rolling around until they finally stopped. Once stopped, they all rolled black.

Teharonhia:wako yelled out to the creation, "I have put down the field."

He turned to his grandmother and said, "I have met your challenge. For a long time you have tried to get control of my creation and from this point on you will never succeed."

He continued, "Now the human beings who have just come to life will look after the creation for me. When they remember you in their stories, they will refer to you as the ancient woman and will be reminded of the time the creation fell from your control. This story will be related by the *onkwe:honwe* for generations to come. " His grandmother had helped control the rain and now her power would be held in check. She could never use her power to flood the Earth but only to help replenish the plant life.

Teharonhia:wako turned to the male *onkwe:honwe* of his creation and said to him, "You are the youngest in the creation and will therefore be known as Otetonia, Sapling. Your partner will be known by the generations to come as Awenhaniyota, the Blooming Flower."

He continued to tell them, "Both of your lives will endure as long as the Earth continues to exist. All the grasses, bushes, trees and flowers are still at a young age, but in the future more new things will be springing up.

He then said, "Otetonia, you will be the first to give thanks by crying out three times. Everyone will then repeat your words and be happy, and this shall be done for all time to come."

He turned to Sawiskera and his grandmother and said, "There is still one unresolved matter that must be dealt with." He continued, "You must give back the head of my mother that is hanging in your lodge, because I now have control over everything, and she is needed by the creation."

Sawiskera answered, "I have not tried to have control of her head so I don't see why you should have control either."

"Will you try and take something from me before I even have control over it?" he asked his brother.

Teharonhia:wako replied, "I am trying to do the work that will benefit everyone, so that we may all live in this world together in peace."

His grandmother said to Sawiskera, "Maybe it would be better to leave well enough alone since we have lost control over the creation. Let us go home, for we have lost the bet."

Meanwhile the two *onkwe:honwe* began to travel around with their family. Teharonhia:wako gathered them together one day and told them,

"I have decided that we must bring back the head of my mother from my grandmother's and Sawiskera's lodge, and you must assist me. You have to prepare yourselves for this task by getting the red willow to make medicine, and you are to use it as an emetic to purify yourselves. Before the Sun rises, you will use the medicine three times, and you will do this for three days in a row. When you are cleansed inside, then we will divide our work between us. "

He then told Sapling, "Look over the whole of the island and find a horn of a deer lying on the ground and then place it high up in a tree. If you find a flint, you may do the same. Look thoroughly, and do not let any deer horns or flint remain on the ground. The work that I have asked of you will help us pass through this crisis. If we all work together, we can ward off Sawiskera. He may try to return to cause you problems. Meanwhile, I will go to Sawiskera's island and place all the deer horns, as well as the flint that I find, high above the ground. Once Sawiskera sees the deer horns and the flint placed up high, he will know that everyone is against him; he will then remain in his lodge. By the time I return, all this work I have assigned to you must be completed; otherwise, we will fail."

After Teharonhia:wako had left, Otetonia began to do the thing that was asked of him. He and Awenhaniyota began to collect the flint and deer horns, placing them high above the ground. When Teharonhia:wako arrived at Sawiskera's island, he began to travel all around, looking for deer horns and flint. Within a short time he found them and placed them above the ground. As he came around the side of Sawiskera's lodge, he found more of them lying about, and so he placed them up high above. When he had finished, he saw a tree standing nearby with his mother's head at the top of it which Sawiskera had placed there. It was not that difficult to get to the top of the tree. However, he noticed Sawiskera standing ready in ambush in case someone tried to take the head. Instead, Teharonhia:wako turned around and walked toward a mountain that was standing in the distance. There he met a male being standing in his way.

The male being, upon seeing Teharonhia:wako, asked him, "Where did you come from?"

Teharonhia:wako replied, "I came from the floating island that lies beyond the water, and I am taking care of some personal business on this floating island."

Teharonhia:wako then asked the male being, "Where did you come from?"

The male being answered, "From the direction of the setting Sun, and I too am taking care of business here on the Earth. After all, it is my creation to look after, as I have completed it myself."

Teharonhia:wako then asked the male being, "What is your name?"

The man being replied, "My name is Hato:i, Master of the Winds. Brother of the uncle who sits on top of the celestial tree and is sometimes called the Great Dew Eagle.

The man being then asked Teharonhia:wako, "What is your name?"

Teharonhia:wako replied, "My name is Teharonhia:wako, which means Holder of the Heavens."

He continued, "I am the Creator of the things that live on the Earth as well as the human beings who inhabit it."

Hato:i then held up a Great Turtle shell rattle and began to shake it making a loud sound. Many of the animals of the Earth began to become frightened when it seemed to thunder in the sky.

Seeing he was being challenged, Teharonhia:wako pointed toward the mountain and said, "If you are as powerful as you say, see if you can move that mountain closer to us."

Hato:i replied, "I am not worried. I will meet your challenge; just watch what happens. Come then. Let us turn our heads this way." They both turned in the same direction.

Hato:i then spoke to the mountain saying, "Move closer toward our backs."

He then said to Teharonhia:wako, "We should each hold our breaths while this happens." The two held their breaths for as long as they could.

Hato:i then said, "Let us turn our heads around once again." The two of them then turned their heads, and they saw that the mountain had moved a little bit but not much.

Teharonhia:wako mocked the male being, laughing and telling him, "Someone who has so little power as yourself could not have created the world."

He continued, "It is now my turn to move the mountain and, if I succeed, it will prove that I am the Creator of life on the Earth. Now, let us both turn our heads once again."

He then said to the mountain, "Mountain, come forward. Here at our backs you will rest." They both then turned their heads around.

He then said to Hato:i, "Let the two of us hold our breaths and then it will be decided who can hold it the longest. Only then will we look around."

They both began to hold their breaths. Hato:i felt something graze across his back, and, as he turned around to see what it was, his face struck the mountain edge that had moved behind him.

Teharonhia:wako said, "Let us turn and face about once again as the mountain is now at our backs."

Teharonhia:wako looked at Hato:i and saw that his face had changed. Both his nose and mouth were now twisted.

Teharonhia:wako said to Hato:i, "As you can see, I am the master of the Earth and am the one who could have created it. The proof I have is in what has happened to your face."

Hato:i answered, "It is the truth. You have great power as you showed it by moving the mountain, which slammed into my face. I now acknowledge that you are the one who created the living things on Earth as you are the one who controlled the movement of the great standing mountain. It is true that you are the ruler on Earth, and I now humble myself before you. If you will have mercy on me, I will help the *onkwe:honwe* who are now settling on the Earth. Soon the *onkwe:honwe* will begin to have dreams of me. Inside my flesh there is much *orenta* that I have implanted on the Earth. It was I who was the first to wander upon it. Whenever the *onkwe:honwe* who live on the Earth have dreams of me, they will imitate my face and the form of my body. During this time the *onkwe:honwe* will undergo a spell. They will travel to each of the lodges in order that other *onkwe:honwe* will recover from illness. Before doing this, the *onkwe:honwe* must remember to make a human form patterned after my face and my body. This will not only make them well but will also allow them to be content inside themselves."

He continued, "Sawiskera, your brother, will try everything to destroy your creation and the people will become ill in their bodies as well as their minds. This will result in the end of the days of the *onkwe:honwe*. During these times of suffering, I will continue to aid those who address me as their dear grandfather. In return I will address them as my dear grandchildren."

Teharonhia:wako replied, "I will accept your giving aid to the *onkwe:honwe* on one condition: that you don't reveal yourself to them, as it would frighten them if they ever saw you in person. You will abide in a place that will always be available to the human beings so that they may be heard by you."

Hato:i accepted this proposition and said, "This is what I will do. I will dwell in a place where there is rough ground, stone cliffs, and high banks. In this way no one will see me, and I will stay there as long as the Earth exists. It is true, that neither humans nor animals nor things that grow should ever see my face. Instead the human beings will use the basswood tree, which has a long life. From its trunk they will carve a face that resembles mine. Using this face, they will call on me, and I will come and blow on them and cure them of their illness. The *onkwe:honwe* will place my face over theirs and travel to the different lodges of the people, and this will be done by a society named after me called Hato:i. When they arrive, they will blow on the person who is ill, just as if it were me doing it. Those who call on me and do what I say will then be helped. The Hato:i society will pledge words to me while using Real Tobacco on a fire, whereupon smoke will rise that I will draw into myself. They will then take hot ashes from the fire and blow them over the ailing person. Then the sickness will go away and, the person will be cured. The society will also prepare corn mush, which I enjoy, and blow it out on the person repeatedly. This may be done if a person is ill at any time of the year in order that they may recover their health."[52]

Teharonhia:wako said, "Your task is now complete, and it will be known by those who have dreams of you what it is that you will do for them." They both then departed.

Teharonhia:wako went back to his lodge and met Otetonia who was waiting for him. He said to him, "Otetonia, we should go to the place where I originally came from."

Otetonia replied, "I have done everything that you have asked of me, and I am ready to leave with you."

Teharonhia:wako said to him, "Let us make a canoe and a paddle for our voyage. We will also have to choose someone to help us steer the canoe."

They then made the canoe and Teharonhia:wako assembled all the creatures on Earth and told them not to be frightened. Soon all the beings of the Earth began to appear at Teharonhia:wako's lodge to get their instructions.

Once assembled, Teharonhia:wako told them, "My mother's head still has a duty to perform that will benefit all of you. I want to get her head away from my brother."

Upon hearing what Teharonhia:wako wanted them to do, Fox was the first to say. "I will volunteer to steer the canoe."

Teharonhia:wako asked Fox, "What would you do once you arrive at the other floating island and we have my mother's head?"

Fox replied, "I would take the head once it fell to ground and run with it, for I am fast."

Soon, many more of the beings of the Earth began to arrive. Fisher said, "I will be willing to help as well."

Teharonhia:wako asked him, "What kind of help could you give?"

Fisher answered, "When Fox comes running with the head and gets close to the great water, I will take it from him and swim with it."

Teharonhia:wako said, "I don't think that the plan will succeed."

Beaver jumped in and said, "I will help as well."

Teharonhia:wako asked Beaver, "What do you think that you could do to help us?"

Beaver answered, "I will remain in the canoe, and if necessary I will cut down a tree and block the way. I can even carry the head if I am needed to do so."

Teharonhia:wako felt that with Beaver's help, they would be able to succeed. Both Fox and Fisher agreed to go along with the plan. They all got on board the canoe and paddled toward Sawiskera's floating island.

When they had arrived at the place where the Elder Brother began his ascent each day, both Teharonhia:wako and Otetonia stood at the bank of Sawiskera's island. Beaver alone remained in the canoe and told them that he would keep watch, but that if they needed him they were to call out his name and he would come. The others also said that they were ready, and they would come if called. Fisher ascended the bank from the water and said that he would sit on the bank and wait for the call until he was needed.

Teharonhia:wako addressed Otetonia and the rest, saying, "Now then, let us begin." They then departed for Sawiskera's island, until finally they arrived at a tree whose light shone from the head of Teharonhia:wako's mother, only to find that no one was there.

Otetonia said to the others, "I will try and climb the tree to retrieve the head." Otetonia began to climb the tree, and after a short distance he fell to the ground.

He said to Teharonhia:wako, "I don't have the strength in my legs to make it. My feet couldn't seem to grasp the tree."

Teharonhia:wako told him, "That is because you have only recently been brought to life and your body is still lacking in something."

He continued, "The problem is that when I created you, I didn't complete your feet, as I had not foreseen that you may need to use them to walk fast and climb. I will repair the error that I made by hollowing out an instep in your feet. That will make it easier for you to climb the tree."

He then said to Otetonia, "Hold up your two feet." Otetonia did as he was asked, and Teharonhia:wako took hold of his foot and pressed into the middle part. He then did the same to the other foot.

He then said to Otetonia, "I have completed what I had failed in doing when I first created you. Now try to climb the tree again before my grandmother and Sawiskera arrive."

Otetonia began to climb the tree, and, when he reached the top, he removed his mother's head. He then started down the tree, carrying the head in his arms on his side. He yelled down, "Watch out. I am coming." He then began to slide down the tree so quickly that he couldn't stop himself. With a thud he hit the ground. The bark on the tree had been scraped right off, and when he got up he showed Teharonhia:wako the head that he held in his arms.

Teharonhia:wako said, "In the future, the *onkwe:honwe* will tell the story of what happened to this particular tree that will from now on be known as the Sycamore."

Not long after this happened, Sawiskera and his grandmother appeared. They saw that the head was no longer attached to the top of the tree. His grandmother cried out, "They have taken the head of my daughter. Let us hurry and find out who it is."

Next, all the animals cried aloud, and there was a great noise in the air when they heard her coming. Sawiskera understood what had taken place.

He said, "Something is about to happen to me. I have a feeling that someone wants to kill me. It seems that everywhere I look, the things that I fear the most, the deer horns and the flint, have been put up high above the ground so that I cannot reach them. I cannot do anything about it. Grandmother, you have to follow them and get the head back."

His grandmother ran toward the Tree of Light, and she noticed the tracks of the beings that had taken the head. She saw that they had gone toward the direction from where the Elder Brother the Sun had set. She then began to pursue them.

Teharonhia:wako and his companions could hear running behind them.

They could hear her yelling, "Bring back the head."

Fox yelled to the others, "Give me the head for I am the quickest, and she won't catch me."

Otetonia said to Fox, "I don't trust you because you are always deceitful, so I won't give you the head."

Black Squirrel yelled, "Let me have the head, for I will cross the tops of the trees and prevent her from having it."

Otetonia said to him, "I will use you, only if it is necessary and as a last resort."

Otetonia became aware that the grandmother was close behind him, and he began to run faster. Both Fisher and Squirrel ran along the treetops trying to keep up with him. The grandmother meanwhile was catching up.

Teharonhia:wako said to the others, "Have courage and take strength. We can outrun her." Both he and Otetonia ran even faster.

Finally, they made it to the canoe where Beaver was waiting. They got in, and Teharonhia:wako told them they had to paddle as quickly as they possibly could. Otter and Muskrat jumped aboard, offering to assist in the paddling by pushing the canoe. They began to paddle with all their strength just as the ancient woman arrived at the shore.

She was in an angry state, and she pleaded with Otetonia, "Otetonia give me back the head; take pity on me."

Otetonia would not listen.

She then pleaded with Beaver, "Beaver give me back the head."

He also wouldn't listen to her.

Next, she yelled to Otter, "Otter give me back the head." Otter also remained silent.

Next, she pleaded with Muskrat, "Muskrat have pity on me. Give me the head."

Feeling sorry for her, Muskrat replied, "I will give the head back to you." Muskrat, then tried to get the head from Otetonia.

Teharonhia:wako looked at Muskrat and said, "Your actions and reply were a mistake. Now you have to take responsibility for what you tried to do. From now on, you will have no more power on this Earth, and you will walk humbly along the shores of the waterfront for the rest of your days." He then threw Muskrat overboard.

Otter became frightened at what had just occurred and said to Teharonhia:wako, "I don't like what has just happened to Muskrat. I want to get out of here."

Teharonhia:wako replied to Otter, "No one has forced you to take part in this. From now on, you will be wild, always hiding in the waters and traveling from place to place." Upon hearing this, Otter jumped overboard.

As they reached their destination, Teharonhia:wako said to the rest of them, "Finally, we have arrived, and my mother's head can now fulfill her duty."

He turned to Beaver and said, "Because you have assisted me, you will have control over the water, by using the Earth to dam it if you choose.[53]

Teharonhia:wako told them, "I will now restore the flesh of my mother's body, so that she will be whole again."

Over and over, with the use of the winds to help him, he restored the form of his mother's body. When he was finished, he said, "Now, my mother's flesh, body, and power are made whole once again."

He then spoke to her, "It was my brother who caused your ruin as you became the first victim on Earth, and he has tried to do the same to the other beings here as well. It seems it is his destiny to do wrong as long as the Earth continues to endure."

He then explained to his mother, "Now then, my Mother, you will have a duty and purpose for the rest of your days. You will attend to the Earth—the grasses, fruit, bushes and forests and all the things that grow for the benefit of the game animals and human beings."

He continued, "I will assign a duty for you. The time, when the orb of light passes in the daytime and the Earth begins to warm up, will begin the season known as early spring—when the things that grow will begin to renew themselves. This is also the time when some of those plants will grow flowers. It will continue like this until it becomes cold on the Earth once again. You and the Elder Brother, the daytime orb of light, will always assist one another. After it becomes dark and the Elder Brother appears in the east, he will heat your body, and then the dew will fall upon it. You will always think of your grandchildren as they travel about the Earth."

Teharonhia:wako took some red willow and scraped off the bark and said to his mother, "Now that your body has a duty to perform, your head will also have a duty. Your grandchildren, the *onkwe:honwe,* who look upon the setting Sun, will see your renewal. Each night, you will draw nearer to them and slowly increase in size, moving toward the place of the Elder Brother, the Sun. When you reach your destination, your form will be complete and you will then become smaller until you reach the place once again that you had originally departed from. Upon your arrival, your grandchildren will not see you for three nights, and then on the fourth night you will return. Your path will be fixed in this way, so that your grandchildren will always hold you in high esteem. They will watch you as you draw closer and they will follow your cycle during both winter and summer. You will be in charge during the night, and you shall have the power to light up the sky. In this way, you will continue to help the human beings who travel about the Earth. The human beings will then be able to travel to their homes with their minds filled with peace during the night."

Teharonhia:wako then said, "This matter has now been completed. Both you and the Elder Brother the Sun will now share a responsibility. Those on the Earth will address you both by saying, 'Oh Sun, our Elder Brother, the great male being.' Or when speaking to you they will say, 'Oh, our Grandmother Moon, the great female being.'"

Teharonhia:wako continued, "I will leave something here on Earth that will be used by the *onkwe:honwe*. It is the great precious smoke known as Real Tobacco. The *onkwe:honwe* will continue to use it no matter which direction they face on the Earth. Whenever they think of the world above, they will take the Real Tobacco growing near them and hold it when they speak. They will then throw it into the fire they have kindled, and this will become their words. For the rest of the coming days of the world, the Real Tobacco will be used in this way."

He then turned to his mother and said, "As to what I have asked of you to do. You will use that which first grew on the Earth, the Red Willow to help you fulfill your duty. Now, go to the place where I have assigned you your duty. Until the time that I say so, no one will be able to defeat either you or the Elder Brother in the future. You will assist each other until that time comes. Now I will prepare the Red Willow for your departure."

Once he had done this, Teharonhia:wako took the Red Willow he had prepared and threw it into the fire. He then said to his mother's head, "Cast yourself into the fire." His mother's head then jumped into the fire, and soon the smoke began to rise. From that time on the Moon, the Earth, and the female beings would always be connected as one.

Teharonhia:wako told Otetonia and his mate, "You must now watch and see what happens after three days' time."

He said to Awenhaniyota, Blooming Flower, "You will see a change come over you when you see your Grandmother Moon in the sky."

He continued, "Your grandmother will grow and for you, Blooming Flower, it will be a sign that life is being renewed inside you. It will be a sign that this is the beginning of the forming of the human beings who will one day overflow the Earth as dwellers upon it. It will be from the Earth that you will see your Grandmother the Moon appear. This is the way it will be for all time to come, as long as the Earth shall continue to exist. Things will continue to grow upon the Earth, along with human beings and game animals. Those *onkwe:honwe* who follow you in the future will remember what you both saw for all time to come. There will still be some frightening things left in the future that you and they will witness."

At that time, Otetonia and Awenhaniyota watched the sky. After three nights Awenhaniyota noticed a change come over her. She said to Otetonia, "The thing that Teharonhia:wako has told us about is now occurring in my body."

Otetonia looked toward the west and saw the Moon begin to rise.

He said to Awenhaniyota, "I will go and tell the one who created us what is happening."

When he arrived at Teharonhia:wako's, he said, "Teharonhia:wako what you promised would happen to Awenhaniyota is now being fulfilled. A change has occurred in Awenhaniyota's life, and the new Moon has risen as promised."

Teharonhia:wako replied, "What I said would happen has now occurred. The life and birth of human beings on Earth will always be tied to the cycle of the Moon. Now, I will go and travel, and you will be free to do the same. I give both of you the stewardship of the Earth in order to take care of the things that are upon it. I will come and visit you both every once in a while to explain what will happen in the future. In fact, I am certain that my brother and I will disagree with each other once again when we meet. The sign that this is about to happen will occur when unknown beasts come from the ground, slaughter, abuse, and eat the flesh of the creatures that live here. When you see this occurring, you will know that my brother and I are disagreeing once again. When Sawiskera becomes angry, he will have control of all those creatures that once lived in the water and the land that he has completed."

He continued, "When this happens, I will arrive and try to restore order to those things that are out of control. If I must, I will even remove my grandmother to another place. My brother and I will then be alone to decide the issue. The only way that there can be peace is to remove ourselves from this place for the benefit of your children, for if we stay everything will be destroyed. That is why we must leave, and you will rarely see me in the future."

Teharonhia:wako knew that both he and his brother Sawiskera had too much *orenta* to remain on the Earth. If they stayed and remained fighting, they would end up destroying the world. Instead they would both leave, and when Sawiskera's influence over the human beings became too strong on the Earth Teharonhia:wako would then return for a short time to restore order. He said he would do this only so many times, and, if it didn't work, he would then send someone to help the *onkwe:honwe* restore balance to the natural order.

Teharonhia:wako then departed back to Sawiskera's floating island. Upon arriving, he discovered many wild beasts roaming about. They were huge, ugly, and fierce in temperament. He then walked to his grandmother's lodge and found out that Sawiskera was not there. He approached his grandmother and asked her, "Grandmother, it is you that I have come looking for. I think that it is time that you left this place to go live somewhere else."

She answered him, "Your brother is not here, and, when he comes back, I don't think he would be pleased to find out I was gone."

Teharonhia:wako then told her, "Go to where my lodge is and wait for me there. I will wait for Sawiskera here and when he arrives I will tell him that I asked both of you to leave."

His grandmother replied, "Sawiskera will not know where I am, and I should be here when he comes. Right now his mind is troubled because someone has carried away the head of your mother."

Teharonhia:wako told her to look up into the sky. He then said, "The one you are talking about is looking at us right now from above." Just as his grandmother looked up, the Moon rose in the air with its rays bursting through the forest.

She said to him, "You are right; that is my daughter. My mind is comforted in seeing her alive once again. I now feel at ease, and it no longer matters if I leave this place, even if it means departing from this world. I am sorry, my Grandson, for taking sides against you when your mother was killed."

The *onkwe:honwe* would learn that all things pass away for only a short time. Whenever they lose someone that they care for, they would know that they would meet again in the world above. Therefore, they should not grieve too long. In the end, to kill someone only hurts the one who kills.

Teharonhia:wako said to his grandmother, "Leave now, and I will promise that it will not be long before you will again be a part of the Sky World from where you first came. When that happens you will also have a duty to perform, in that you will assist your daughter. After all, there is still someone that I will need to attend to the things on the Earth. I am not here to spoil any of the things my brother Sawiskera has created. It does not bother me that I did not create them. They have a purpose here as well, as long as they don't harm the rest of the creation. They are here to keep the world in balance and are therefore needed to remind the human beings that the balance can shift against them if they do not continue to perform their duties."

She replied, "It would please me greatly if you and your brother would agree with one another, rather than fight with one another all the time."

Teharonhia:wako replied, "That is also my wish, and if that occurs, then things will also change for the better on this floating island."

His grandmother, satisfied with his answer, then left toward Teharonhia:wako's floating island.

Once she was there, she sought out Otetonia and Awenhaniyota but could not find them anywhere, so she returned to Teharonhia:wako's lodge. At the lodge she found that it was empty; so she took a seat and waited. Not long after her arrival, the two for whom she was looking for arrived.

She said to them, "I have just arrived here and I am not sure what will happen at the other floating island. Sawiskera is not at my lodge and Teharonhia:wako is waiting for him there. I am afraid of what might happen when he does arrive, as Sawiskera is still angry at having his mother's head stolen from our lodge."

Otetonia told her, "Do not worry. Continue having good thoughts as everything will be all right. All things, including the one you are most concerned about, have an important duty to perform."

At that moment, the ancient woman looked up and saw her daughter above. She said to them, "It is true. It is my daughter who brings peace at night to the creation." Her mind was then put at ease. The three of them then waited for Teharonhia:wako to return.

A few days later Teharonhia:wako began to wonder what had happened to his brother, as Sawiskera had not yet returned to the lodge. He then decided to go looking for him. He traveled over the whole of the floating island but could not find him anywhere. He was surprised to see two human beings, lighter in color than the *onkwe:honwe* walking about. He stopped them and asked, "Have you seen my brother Sawiskera ?"

The two human beings replied, "He was just here a few moments ago. We are sure that he is not far away."

They asked Teharonhia:wako, "Who created the orb of light that now shines during the night, and what is the reason for it being placed up above in the sky?"

Teharonhia:wako answered, "It is I who created it so that it may guide the human beings who will arrive in the future. They will govern themselves and count the number of days by looking at it. In fact, you both will govern yourselves by its cycle. You will always cohabit together depending on the condition of Awenhaniyota on this floating island. During that time you will not see the orb of light for a period of three days, and when that occurs the female will then renew herself. At the time when you notice a change come over her, she will be alone. Once the renewal has occurred within her, it will be the beginning of the new human beings on Earth. You will then count the numbers of them when you begin your clan family. There should be no more than three children to a family. In this way the Earth will always be able to replenish itself. Your children who are formed from your bodies will be descended through the female line. One day all the Earth will be covered with human beings who will be born in this way."[54]

He continued, "If ever you see my brother and I disagree, do not let it interfere with your purpose in life. This is because we will always quarrel. My brother will always want to control the creation, and I will not let it happen. I have given all the human beings the duty to be caretakers of the Earth. You will travel and add to this island more human beings in the future, that is, as long as I get through the ordeals that my brother has in store for me. Now I'll go look for him." Teharonhia:wako then left to look for Sawiskera.

Teharonhia:wako went back to his grandmother's lodge. As he approached it, he saw a pile of flint stones and picked them up and carried them with him. He looked around and saw that Sawiskera hadn't yet arrived. Teharonhia:wako placed the stones in the place where Sawiskera usually sat down in the lodge and then went outside to wait for him. Sawiskera was waiting for him to come out.

Teharonhia:wako said to his brother, "I have been waiting for you inside the lodge. When I entered no one was home, and I didn't see anyone around."

Sawiskera asked him, "Is not our grandmother in her lodge? She was there when I left."

Teharonhia:wako answered, "Let us go inside and you will see that no one is there."

They both entered the lodge. Sawiskera, began looking for his grandmother but couldn't find her. He then went to sit down in his place and was surprised to find several pieces of flint lying nearby.

He then went to the entrance of the lodge and said to his brother, "Our grandmother has turned against me. She has forsaken me. I no longer care if I live or am taken a prisoner. Even the human beings I created seem to have turned against me. I will defend myself, even if it means I have to become a slave. No matter what, I will attempt once again to gain control of the creation."

Teharonhia:wako pleaded with Sawiskera, "Why do you think everyone has turned against you? I don't want to fight with you any longer. I would like to help you as I want peace to be here on the Earth, as well as in the world above."

Sawiskera replied, "What have I done here on Earth that warrants you wanting my destruction? Look at the place where I usually sit. Someone has laid out several items that could kill me. In fact, no matter where I walk, I find the things that could destroy me placed up high above so that I cannot reach them. That must be the reason why someone took our mother's head, as well as why our grandmother has disappeared from her lodge. I will defend myself to the end as there is nothing further left for me here to lose. As long as I continue to live, I will never assist or show pity to anyone. It would give me pleasure if there came a day sometime in the future that I could control all the things on the Earth. To achieve my task, I will use my power both in the day and the night. It doesn't matter to me what time or what place."

Teharonhia:wako answered, "What are you talking about? There is nothing wrong in what has happened. No one wants to harm you."

Sawiskera answered, "I am not pleased that all the human beings look to you in all matters concerning the Earth. I will only be happy when I have control of the creation. When that happens, all the human beings will turn away from you. I will make it so that the human beings' minds of this island will be turned from you so that they will also want to control the creation, and they will help me in my task. I will give them dominance over the rest of the creation. One day, they will have dominance over all the creatures and plants on your floating island. They will even have control of the minds of the onkwe:honwe who live on your floating island. When that is done, I will have control over the Earth."[55]

Teharonhia:wako said, "Let this matter end in harmony, and let there be peace between us as no one wants to harm you."

Sawiskera answered, "At this moment I will do nothing more as I admit that I have lost everything, including my grandmother and mother. However, I promise you, I will be back with a vengeance."

Teharonhia:wako pleaded again with his brother, "Why is your mind so troubled about the death of our mother? She has come back to life again and will live in the future for all time. In spite of this, your mind is still troubled. I believe that it is because of the fact that you killed her, and this means that you may never be close to her again. This is the way it shall be for the human beings on Earth as well. Anyone who kills another human being will also suffer when their time on Earth is ended. Each human being is given a certain length of time to live, and it is wrong to cut the creation of another before it is their time to depart. That is because in the beginning I gave them a part of my life, and they are all related to each other through me. When they kill each other, they also destroy a part of themselves and their connection to me."[56]

Sawiskera was extremely angry. He said to Teharonhia:wako, "Let us go outside and settle the matter once and for all."

They then both went outside the lodge. Sawiskera then spoke to his creatures, "Let all those creatures, whose bodies I have formed and are alive, eat those things that have been created separately from mine. This includes the *onkwe:honwe* as well. In fact they will be the food of my creatures. Both daylight and darkness as well as the springs of the water will one day be overcome by my magical power. At that time, the sky will become unclear and the waters murky. Disease will wander about inhabiting all kinds of things that will affect the minds of the *onkwe:honwe*. There will even be a water of fire that will destroy the minds of the *onkwe:honwe*."

Teharonhia:wako answered, "You will have done wrong if it is your desire to end the days of the *onkwe:honwe*. If that is your wish, you should begin with the one who created them."

Sawiskera replied, "I have promised myself that, whatever occurs in the future, if you ever become displeased with my actions again you and I will fight over it."

Teharonhia:wako said, "You have threatened me and told me what you are going to do. How do you want to settle this matter and what would you like to use to settle it with?"

Sawiskera answered, "We will settle it by your using your power of *orenta* that you have boasted about and my using my power of *otkon*."

Teharonhia:wako replied, "Then I will use my power of daylight and make sure that it will be bright when we meet each other in battle."

Sawiskera answered, "I will use the night to bolster my power, and it will be in a place of darkness that we shall meet and settle the matter."

Sawiskera then pulled out his flint-tipped arrow, and, holding it in his hand, he said to his brother, "I have already killed one person with this, and there is about to be another killed shortly."

He threw the arrow at his brother, and the air became very cold. Teharonhia:wako caught the arrow in the air. They then both began wrestling over it, pulling and struggling to get control.

Suddenly, a loud sound was heard on the Earth, and it began to get cloudy. The wind also began to pick up in strength. Teharonhia:wako let go of the arrow and picked up a nearby mountain and hurled it toward Sawiskera, with it falling on top of him. Sawiskera feeling overwhelmed began to flee with Teharonhia:wako in pursuit. They circled around the floating island repeatedly. Teharonhia:wako kept picking up mountains and knocking down Sawiskera with them. Sawiskera kept getting up and provoking Teharonhia:wako. As this occurred, the mountains kept getting closer together, and they soon began to be joined with one another. Sawiskera picked up rocks and threw them at his brother. Teharonhia:wako caught them and threw them back, where they piled on top of one another forming a ridge that linked them together. Meanwhile, the wildlife began to be frightened, so they hid themselves from the battle that was taking place. Sawiskera tried to do the same thing but could not conceal himself from his brother.[57]

Teharonhia:wako called out, "He Who Shakes the Earth, it is time for you to help me make sure the Earth remains filled with light."

At that moment, the Earth began to shake and rumble, the trembling increasing in force, and the world began to quake. Teharonhia:wako then took a deer antler and flashed it through the sky at Sawiskera. Each time he swung the antler it turned bright. Again and again he did the same thing. At the same time he did it, a great noise rumbled through the air as the thunders arrived.

Sawiskera yelled out, "You have too much power. I submit and give myself up to you. From now on my body will remain still and only my mind will survive."

Teharonhia:wako said, "You are right. Like myself, you will always continue to live. However, you should not continue to inhabit this place. Perhaps you should go to another place where you will do less harm to the world."

Sawiskera then asked his brother, "Would it be all right if I did not have to be too far away from you and the creation?"

Teharonhia:wako answered, "You may remain close by as long as you no longer do any more harm. If something like this ever occurs again, I will make sure that you are confined away from this place forever."

Sawiskera replied, "I give myself up to you and won't create anymore disturbances as long as what you say is true, that is, unless you attempt to shut me away like you said you would. I ask only that you give your consent to one simple request. I would like to be able to visit the Earth as long as it is possible to do so." Once again, Sawiskera was using deceit on his brother so that he could remain and gain control of the creation.

Teharonhia:wako replied, "Perhaps I will allow it once I finish the work that I have begun. Until that time, I still have some unfinished business to take care of during the night. I am still not satisfied with what occurs during a certain period of time at night."

He continued, "Usually, when the head of our mother the Moon goes missing for three nights, it becomes too dark for the rest of the creation to see. I will form something that will help her during this time. These will be called stars, and they will cause light when our mother is unable to do so. I will give one of them a duty to appear during the day as well as the night, and it will be called The Day Bringer, *Tewenhawetah*, or morning star. When one sees this star that will stand alone in its brightness, then the night will change, and a new light of day will appear once again on the Earth."

He then said to Sawiskera, "When you see this large star appear, then you will leave and go to the place where my lodge is. There, I will be expecting you." Teharonhia:wako then went back to his lodge to wait for Sawiskera.

When he arrived at his lodge, his grandmother was waiting for him. She asked him, "What has happened. It seemed like two people were fighting all night. As soon as the light of my daughter's head rose in the air, the Earth began to shake, and I thought you boys may have destroyed one another."

Teharonhia:wako answered, "Grandmother, we have settled the matter once and for all, and I will tell you what happened. It is true that one of us was almost killed, but that is now over and we are both alive. You have accomplished your duty here on Earth, and it is time for you to leave and go back home to the Sky World. You will go to the place where you came from, and, after you arrive, you will be restored to the body of flesh that you originally had when you first left through the hole in the sky. You will be going back to the place where you first acquired thought and reason. At the end of ten days, you will watch for us, for my brother and I will return as long as we no longer disagree. Prepare yourself as I am now ready to send you back home."

Teharonhia:wako went to collect some red willows. He then scraped the bark off them and threw it into the fire. He then said "Grandmother, cast your body into the fire and make your return journey back home. When I arrive, you will be waiting for me. However, before I leave I will make something that will help the things on the Earth continue to live. Both you and I will aid one another, and, from this point on, fresh water will fall from above, which will be known as rain. In this way the Earth will always be renewed." His grandmother then cast herself into the smoke that emanated from the Red Willow in the fire, and she flew upward toward the sky. Through the falling rain, she would always aid in keeping the Earth fertile.

Teharonhia:wako then turned to the male and female *onkwe:honwe* and said to them, "You, who are the first humans beings to live, have witnessed, She of the Ancient Body return back to her home by way of the Red Willow. From this point on, only words and thoughts will be able to travel upward in this manner. You will use the Real Tobacco and cast it onto the fire, and, as the smoke rises, you shall speak your thoughts. The spoken word will be just as good as traveling on the smoke, and this is the way it will be done from this time on. No one will ever be able to travel by smoke again."

Teharonhia:wako continued, "I will now place the stars to be fixed in different places in the sky. When human beings fulfill their duty on Earth, and, if they have lived an honest and good life when their days are over, it will be possible for those who remain to see them when they look up. When it is their time to depart the Earth, they will be able to mingle with their ancestors once again, and they will become stars. As long as the Earth continues to exist, the stars will increase in number. There will come a time in the future when there will be so many stars in the sky that no one will be able to count them."

He went on, "As long as the animals fulfill their duty here on Earth, they will also be visible as stars fixed in the sky. Whenever the *onkwe:honwe* looks up at the stars, they will be reminded by their ancestors of their life duties."

He told them, "Look up and watch for your ancestors when they go hunting in the sky. You will see them chase the Great Bear with a knife, a bow, and an axe. At that time the leaves on the trees will turn red from the blood of the Bear and that will mean that the hunting season has begun. You will know that soon the Earth will become cold." He continued, "During the midwinter point you will see a cluster of seven brothers in the sky, and you will know that provisions are scarce and it is getting near the time of planting."

Then he told them, "Whenever a great leader passes from the Earth World to the Sky World, you will look up and see a particular star near the Grandmother Moon."

He said, "If you ever become lost, look up and you will see a star that remains stationary. You will use this to lead you home."

"When it is time to take the three sisters from the ground, the seven dancers will appear in the sky," he said.[58]

Finally, he told them, "As long as you acknowledge the stars by watching them, they will always guide you. I will now go and make the first star that the human beings will see in the sky."

Teharonhia:wako then departed to where the Great Turtle Man, his father He Holds the Earth by Two Hands, had his lodge.

Upon arriving there, he told his father, "I have come because there is still one thing I have left to create here on Earth. I am troubled about the way I should go about this task. I was thinking that perhaps I should make a new star that would be called Tewenhawetah, He Brings in the Day. I would like you to be the one that they will refer to as that being."

He continued, "The reason for this is that no one has ever seen you before, and I would like you to show your face to the beings who dwell below during the early daylight. After all, it was from you that I got the idea to create all the things here on Earth."

Tehaohwetsia:wako, He Who Holds the Earth, replied, "Everything that you have done until this time has been done correctly. I will volunteer to make your resolution come true. You have achieved your purpose and have accomplished everything you set out to do. I will tell you one other thing, and, that is this: when your brother arrives, make sure you watch him closely. When you leave here, do not let your brother convince you to allow him to stay, as he will try to attempt to do so. If you let him, he will try to get revenge against you by destroying everything that you have completed. Remember, when you leave, make sure your brother goes with you. In that way, whenever you both set your feet in the world above and your brother tries to harm you in any way, you will still be in control of the creation."

He continued, "There will be a pathway to be seen in the sky, Teyothahokeh. The path will be divided just as you and your brother's minds are. The two paths will be visible in the night sky when the human beings look up, and they will last until the end of time. The *onkwe:honwe* will know from this that when Sawiskera sends his human beings to try and control them, they will be reminded that they must not deviate from your path. They will always remember these two paths in the future. When they depart from this world, they will follow your path toward your lodge. In order for them to get on this path, they must remember to follow the instructions you have given. If they do that they will follow the path toward the Sky World where they will be greeted by you and their ancestors. As long as they stay on this path, they will be safe. If they try to cross to the other path, they will become lost. Sawiskera will try to get them to follow the other path and many will take it. There will come a time when Sawiskera's human beings will try and convince them to take his path. They must not do so or they will become lost and the consequences will become grave in both the Earth World and the Sky World."[59]

Teharonhia:wako replied, "Now, it has been decided what will happen, and I will now complete the final thing that I had set out to do. In fact, this will be the last thing that I will do before I leave the Earth."

He turned to his father and said, "I will now turn you over to the dawn where you will show yourself for a short time only. The human beings who dwell on the Earth will finally be able to see you. After that, they will see the orb of light, the Sun, on which you and the others depend.

It will be him who will attend to my creation, so long as he causes it to be light. Both he and the orb of light known as the Moon who overlooks all of the things of my creation when it gets dark will be overseers of my work for the rest of time."

Then Teharonhia:wako finished by saying, "It is time for me to leave for the Sky World, and, as soon as my brother sees the large star appear, he is to depart for my lodge and then leave with me. When that happens, I will know what his intentions will be. I have thought that maybe it would be better for me to be rid of all the beings that my brother has created before they try and smash my own creations. They will then not be able to cause any more problems to the human beings who travel and inhabit the floating islands. Some of the beings he created are so potent that just the sight of them could overpower someone by way of their *otkon*. Those beings will forever remain among the mountains under the Earth and will continue to live like this as long as the Earth remains as it is. They will stay like this until my work begins to fail and only then will they leave the Earth. It will be the human beings from Sawiskera's island who will release them. They will be poisonous and create a fire that will be so hot that it could melt anything in my creation. Then Sawiskera will bring in his freezing power to destroy the rest of the creation. I will guard the entrance to the cave that Sawiskera made with a White Buffalo. Whenever the White Buffalo escapes, I will assign little helpers to return him to the cave. When the White Buffalo finally falls because of the human beings wanting to control the creation, Sawiskera's terrible creatures will be released upon them."[60]

He continued, "I will give someone a duty so that at all times, both day or night the Earth will be cleansed so that things may grow upon it and the streams replenished for the contentment of the people. It will be they who will keep the beasts confined so that they cannot leave the Earth. They will be known as the Thunders. They will work with my mother and the deer antlers to keep the Earth fresh. They will come from the setting Sun and they will move through the clouds using their power to keep the hot beasts below the Earth. This will last as long as the Earth continues to exist."

Tehaohwetsia:wako spoke and said, "All your ideas are good ones. In this way the human beings will not be afraid when they hear the voices of the Thunders, as they will know that their purpose is good. They will also be cautious about trying to control the creation lest they let out the beasts."

Teharonhia:wako replied, "I have completed all the things that I had set out to do on the Earth, and I will now return to my lodge."

After arriving at his lodge, Teharonhia:wako said to the two *onkwe:honwe.*

"My children, there will be a morning star that will appear that will foresee the daylight to come. You are to call it, Tewenhawetah, or Day Bringer. When you see it in the sky, you will know that my brother and I are leaving, and everything is settled between us." After hearing Teharonhia:wako, the *onkwe:honwe* couple then retired for the night.

That evening, Otetonia said to Awenhaniyota, "I will stay up and watch for the Day Bringer to come."

That night Otetonia stayed up, waiting for it to arrive. As the morning approached, Otetonia watched as the great star began to rise beyond the horizon. He yelled to Awenhaniyota, "Look! This is the first time that we can see the great star arriving, and it is true that the day is following its appearance."

As the star rose up in the sky, Teharonhia:wako said to himself, "We may be once again coming to a time of crisis. As soon as my brother arrives, I will have to inform him of my decision."

It was not long after he said this that Sawiskera arrived saying, "I promised that as soon as I had seen the large star appear in the sky that I would come over at once, and so I have arrived."

Teharonhia:wako answered him, "Now that you have arrived, it is time that you and I end our fighting. I will ask you something in front of both Otetonia and Awenhaniyota so that they will hear your answer for themselves. I will tell you what my wish is and see if you will consent to it. There are many creatures that roam the land and the waters that you have created that are dangerous to the human beings, and I would like those that are left on the Earth to be confined some place."

Sawiskera answered, "I will agree to what you have asked, only if you allow me to stay and administer the Earth."

Teharonhia:wako replied, "That will never happen." He continued, "The reason that I want to confine your creatures is because neither one of us will be here to control them when we are gone, and they will do great damage to the human beings."

Sawiskera asked him, "Does this mean that the human beings will be able to be independent of us?"

Teharonhia:wako answered, "That is the way that it will be from now on. Not only will the human beings be independent but the game animals as well. This is because the game animals do not live to destroy others but only provide for themselves what they need."

Teharonhia:wako then said, "We must depart from here and go where our grandmother now lives in the sky above."

Sawiskera replied, "I would like to make a last request before we go and that is that we travel around the islands for one last time. In the beginning there was nothing here; during the time that we traveled on our islands we created many things and I would like to see them one last time before we leave. In the future, the human beings will tell stories about what we did, and we shall be remembered by them for all time to come."

Teharonhia:wako answered, "I will agree to your request." They then traveled one last time around the Earth.

After they had returned, Teharonhia:wako spoke to Otetonia and Awenhaniyota. He told them, "When I depart from this Earth, you two should still think of me. I will leave you Real Tobacco, the Great Precious Smoke, to help you. The both of you should never forget to say words to me whenever you turn your heads toward the sky. I will see and hear whatever you are doing. You should do the same whenever you look into the sky and see the Sun, Moon, or stars. You should then direct your thoughts toward them and give them thanks. As long as you do this, they will fulfill their designated duties and be watchful of the things on Earth. I promise that sometime in the future when you have settled with your families, I will return. You must watch closely, as my brother and I will leave footprints behind us when we go to the other world. There will be a clear path in view where he and I have gone. When it becomes dark, the path will become visible and that will be the path that the human beings will follow to the other world when their days are completed here on Earth. When you arrive at the end of your journey, I will be waiting for you, and once again we will be together."

He continued, "One thing that you will continue to listen for, once you arrive on my path, will occur toward the direction in the west. You will hear singing, and this you are to follow when you depart from the Earth. Another thing that will happen is when you see the human beings from the east arrive on your island, you will know that the time of the end of the Earth is near and that many will take that path shortly after. Finally, I will leave this entire matter with you both. Never allow the generations that will come in the future to forget what I have told you. Now my brother and I are leaving toward the upper world. Remember, you will only have the pathway for a sign to remember where we have gone. Whenever you see it divided, it will remind you that there are two types of minds that have come into the world above and to the Earth below. The same will occur among the human beings as well. There will be those who will live among the rest of the creation, and there will be those who will try and control it."

Otetonia and Awenhaniyota watched as the two brothers then departed homeward toward the Sky World where all things first evolved.

It was not too long after that the brothers had left the Earth when Otetonia and Awenhaniyota heard a loud sound, beginning in the west and traveling toward the east.

Otetonia said, "The reason for the noise in the sky means they have arrived at their destination. What we just heard are our grandparents or Thunders who have uttered their voices everywhere to announce their arrival. Let us greet them and give them thanks for telling us what has happened."

Otetonia then cast the sacred tobacco over the fire as he had been told to do by Teharonhia:wako. When it had become dark, the pathway in the sky became visible to them.

Otetonia said to Awenhaniyota, "You and I have seen all the things that our Creator has done for our behalf. We still have our own responsibilities to take care of in this world, as we have been designated its caretakers. This is something that we and our grandchildren will do for as long as the Earth continues to exist."

The *Onkwe:honwe* on Turtle Island

As time passed by, Otetonia and Awenhaniyota began to have children. Soon their families became numerous so that there was a large body of people living on their part of the floating island. They all knew from the stories they had heard from their parents that Teharonhia:wako would return some day as he had promised.

As the years passed by, there came a time when the *onkwe:honwe* seemed to be traveling around the Earth with no purpose in life. There were no ceremonies to perform or business to attend to. They seemed to walk about the Earth with their families aimlessly, and, pretty soon, everything began to be neglected. It was as if they were just going through the motions of living.

After many years of existing in this manner, the *onkwe:honwe* heard a great noise coming from the west and Teharonhia:wako's name being called out. They soon realized that Teharonhia:wako had returned but they did not know where he was. Many of the *onkwe:honwe* began to look for him until one day he appeared before them.

Teharonhia:wako told the *onkwe:honwe* when they had assembled, "I promised you that I would return when there would be many of you roaming the different parts of the floating island. I have now come back to fulfill my promise to you. I have seen what has occurred since I have left. It seems that everyone is going about neglecting everything, including their families. The *onkwe:honwe* are standing around with no purpose in life, and that is the reason I have returned."

He continued, "Listen all of you and pay attention to what I have to say. I will leave some customs upon the Earth that I regard as extremely important to me, which will be shared equally by all of you. They will be done into the future and will be known as the four ceremonies or rituals. You will continue to keep these customs and observe them always. The way you will do this is by assembling yourselves at certain times. The first time that you will come together will be during the beginning of the growing season. As soon as you see the new fruits appear, you will then assemble. You will take the first fruits and put them together in one place. Once assembled, you will rejoice and congratulate one another that so many of you have come to celebrate the new crops that you will live upon."

"At these assemblies," he continued, "you will give thanks to me in the order of the four sacred ceremonies that I am about to teach you. These have been patterned after the ceremonies performed by those who reside in the Sky World and are considered extremely important to the beings residing there. I want you, who live below on the Earth, to appreciate the ceremonies and perform them the same way as those in the Sky World do."

He continued, "The first of the ceremonies that will be carried on will be the Great Feather Dance. The second will be the skin-covered Drum Dance. Third, will be the Personal Chant. Finally, the last will be the Strike Bowls or Plum Bowl Game. These four ceremonies will be carried on at certain appointed times during the seasonal year."

He continued, "The first time they are to be performed will be when the season changes, and the crops that sustain you are ready for harvest. There will then be a great festival and feast. When all the crops are harvested and collected, it will be referred to as the sharing of the great foods. Every family will then contribute a small portion of their cooked crops as well as game meat, and, once that happens, the Great Feather Dance will begin. It will be at that time that the *onkwe:honwe* will rejoice and be thankful that they are still alive and in good health. In the future, they will be grateful that the ceremony given by me is still taking place, and they will remember the time when I first returned. The *onkwe:honwe* will then call out one at a time using these words, 'I thank you always Creator, you who have formed my body and who lives in the Sky World. I give you thanks that it is still possible for me to perform this ceremony.'"[61]

Teharonhia:wako continued to tell them, "Customarily, you will perform all these ceremonies, and when you do you will make a circuit around the fire in one direction, from the east to the west. Do not let anyone make a circle in the opposite direction and never let the left side of the body be on the outside of the circle. This is how it is done in the Sky World where things are opposite from the Earth World. You will make the circuit around where the two singers are sitting, and at that time you will wear your ceremonial hat that will identify which family you are from.

Once you have completed the four ceremonies, everyone should then be content and happy."

Teharonhia:wako continued to explain to them, "Another time when you will perform the four ceremonies is when everything begins to become cold and the days become shortened and what is left of Sawiskera's power is at its fullest. The *onkwe:honwe* will then say it is wintertime. When that happens, the game animals will be one of the principal things sacrificed for the festivities. That is because when it warms up in the spring, the game animals are at their weakest, and their meat is not tender. The reason for that is, by the end of the summer with the cold arriving, the meat of the game animals is at its best, and the animals have had a chance to renew their species. It is during this time when the animals are renewed that they are to be felled and that their meat becomes the main substance of the ceremony. The people will know the time when this begins because when they look up they will see three of their ancestors hunting the Great Bear in the night sky. They will hunt only until the time when the seven brothers begin to rise in the air at midwinter time. They will know then for a period of time resources will be few. Once the people have assembled themselves, they will refer to this as the midwinter festival. At their lodges, the *onkwe:honwe* of the extended families living on each side of the fire of their lodges will put their hands over their fires and stir the ashes. Then they will each speak in turn and give thanks for being alive and being healthy."

He continued, "These are the words they will use: 'Teharonhia:wako listen to me. I am thankful to you that it is possible that we are once again assembled at this place where you gave us this ceremony.'"

He continued, "After they have said those words, the *onkwe:honwe* will lament and sing and then dip their paddles into the ashes, stir them, pick them up and then let them fall back down into the fire once again. Their voices will accompany this action, and all will rejoice. When everyone has completed the entire ceremony, all their minds will be one in unity. Then it will be time to use the creatures, the white dogs, which we refer to as being trussed, for they are my messengers that I have sent to you. I will prize this ceremony as one of the most important done by the *onkwe:honwe* of the Earth who are clansmen of my father, the Great Turtle Man of the second order of things created."[62]

He continued, "The Great Turtle being is the grandfather of the human beings on Earth. The performance of this ceremony will be greatly appreciated by me and bring me great satisfaction. The white dog used in the ceremony must be pure and unblemished. It will be dressed as if it were myself soon to depart, and it will symbolize me. A person will be chosen to cast its body into the fire with the Real Tobacco. He will then direct words to it saying, 'Today, you who live in the Sky World, continue to listen to us. Look at how many have come to the place where our father's clansman first kindled a fire to you. Now continue to listen to us, as we who are alive on the Earth will now speak.'"

He continued, "'As you can see, we now speak with one voice unanimously. Our words are placed with the thing that you prize the most and known as the trussed or white dogs, both female and male. The white dogs will tell our Creator whether we have done things correctly. We, the onkwe:honwe, have said our words to you our Creator and have sent them with the white dogs during your highly prized ceremony during the midwinter. We who are the offspring of our father's clansman have done this ceremony in the way in which you told us that we must always observe.'"[63]

He continued, "'Now, all of us who have attended this assembly have spoken with one voice together and have performed our duty to you. We thank you repeatedly for allowing us to once again attend this sacrifice of these white dogs and the Tobacco Burning Ceremony. We ask of you, that all who are here be spared, to see the change in the season when it will become warm on Earth once again. We also ask that you send us the game animals, both small and large, as well as the things that grow upon the Earth, that we may mature and provide for our children to live. We also ask that those many things that bear fruit, that you planted for your fathers' clansman, will also grow and that we will see them come to maturity. Another thing, that we ask, is that you continue to send us children, so that they may be born on the Earth and your wishes will be fulfilled so that the generations to come will continue to prosper. We, the people of the Earth World and our children, beseech you so that you know once again that we have attended this assembly and have marked this ceremony with our words and thoughts with the sacred Tobacco that you have given us.'"

Teharonhia:wako continued with the instructions and words with which the *onkwe:honwe* were to address him, as well as the other great beings. He said, "The *onkwe:honwe* will turn their faces and speak in one voice and ask all those appointed by their Creator to fulfill their duties on behalf of the creation in the hope that those appointed will continue to listen and bring them prosperity."

He continued to tell them, "They will then begin by saying to the Earth mother these words. 'Mother, upon whose body we stand, we give thanks to you and encourage you to continue your duty by bringing life to the Earth, so that we may continue to be at ease within ourselves and with our children, every day and night. Elder Brother, the Sun, who travels on the visible sky continue to hear us. All of us *onkwe:honwe* who remain alive have offered something to show our thanks to you. We encourage you to continue your duty, as designated by the one who gave us form, in keeping the Earth bright and warm for us—Grandmother Moon, our nocturnal light, and our brothers and sisters, who make up the stars, give us direction in our life duties. All of us people who are alive on Earth have offered something in order to thank you. We ask that you continue to fulfill your duty in keeping the night safe and bright for us, as long as the Creator of our bodies wishes it so.'"

He continued, "'We next ask our Grandfathers who come from the west, whose voices are heard all around and who are appointed to protect us, to continue in your duties. Everyone has gathered and offered you something and thanked you in order to encourage you to continue to do your good work in overseeing us, as appointed by the Creator of our bodies.'"

"Finally," Teharonhia:wako said, "'We wrap together all the things in a single bundle who have an overseeing duty on the Earth: the grasses that grow; the growing shrubs; the growing trees; the different bodies of water; the winds and the air; the day and the night; the orbs of light; the stars; the thunders from the west; and you our Creator who completed our bodies. We thank you repeatedly.'"

Teharonhia:wako then told them, "Next, you *onkwe:honwe* will say to me, 'Teharonhia:wako continue to listen to us, as we want you to know that the ceremonies, most notably the four ceremonies you gave us, will be performed by us here on Earth for the rest of time. You will see that when the ceremonies begin, you will be the principal being whom we will thank repeatedly.'"

Teharonhia:wako then told them, "Early in the morning of tomorrow, the Great Feather Dance will begin, and the songs will be repeated three times. The day after the skin-covered drums will begin, and then someone will be chosen who will give repeated thanks. He will begin by thanking all the things that give pleasure to the minds of the *onkwe:honwe* on the Earth, as well as to those things that you have given the duty to oversee the Earth; and, I will be there among them."

He continued, "Next, the chanting ceremony, which will be your own individual song that will tell of all the things you have accomplished, will begin, and during the singing of it you will give thanks to me once again. Finally, when the great offering Plum Stone Game starts, you are to take the thing that you cherish the most, that is your most useful item, and you will use it to wager. That will keep up the strength of the noise and excitement when the ceremony is in progress, and I will be entertained in this way by my father's clansman, the human beings. It will also remind you that there is nothing on Earth that is more important than giving thanks to me."

Teharonhia:wako continued, "After you have given thanks to all the things on the Earth, as well as the bodies I have formed in the sky, including myself, then, at your bark lodges by the fires where your families live, the eldest woman in your families will have a duty to perform each day. She will continue to give thanks as soon as she sees it is daylight. These are the words she will use at that time. 'We greet one another as we rejoice in this new day. We unite our thoughts together to give thanks to all those things that are important to our lives. We thank our Mother the Earth and the things that grow on her that sustain us. We thank the animals who live among us. We thank the Sun, our Elder Brother. We thank the Moon, our Grandmother. We thank the Thunders who come from the west. Now, all our families give thanks that our numbers are full and that we are living in peace and good health and that we will again see a new day present. Finally, to you, who has made us and appointed our duties for us, we give repeated thanks so that we may travel from place to place in peace and that we will continue to think in peaceful thoughts so long as the daylight continues. We beseech you that we may get through the days in peace and that when it becomes dark all our families that are at rest in their lodges may feel safe. And that peace should be foremost in their thoughts.'"

He then told them, "When it becomes dark, you will say, 'I am thankful that we have passed through the day in peace. We now have made offerings of thanks because we have gotten through another day with our numbers undiminished. You upon whom we live, the animals and the foods of the Earth, we thank for sustaining us and allowing us to pass through another day in peace. You, our Elder Brother the orb of light, who gives us warmth, we thank that we passed another day in peace. You, our Grandmother the Moon that gives us light in the night, we thank for helping us get through another day in peace now that night has fallen upon us. You the grandfathers whom we call the Thunders, we thank you for allowing us to get through another day in peace. Finally, you, who have formed our lives along with the bodies we have been given and who is overseeing the duty of protecting us, we thank repeatedly. We ask that you allow us to remain at peace throughout the night in our lodges so that when we awaken we will not be diminished in number when it becomes daylight.'"

Teharonhia:wako then told them, "It should be this way as long as the kinship groups and the Earth continues to exist." He continued, "There is one other important thing that I have to say. It shall be the duty of all human beings on the Earth to possess the ability to be happy, to give thanks for all the creation, as you will all have an equal right to its use."

Another thing he told them, "Whenever you go traveling and fires are kindled or whenever you may meet other male human beings traveling and you come upon their firesides, if it is at the dawn of the day, you will say to them, 'I am thankful that you and I are alive in peace as a new day has dawned upon us both.' Then you will move forward and give that person a hug. This will be the same if it is a female that you meet. You will say to her, 'I greet you with all of my heart. I am thankful that we have met and that you and I can greet each other both alive and living in peace. Now, we will both give thanks to the one who formed our bodies.'

Then the other person will say, 'I am thankful that both you and I are so fortunate as to see each other alive and living in peace.'"

"Another thing," Teharonhia:wako told them, "if the day is half over and you come upon another person, you will observe the same procedure as I have just mentioned. You will hug each other and say, 'I am thankful that you and I have come together alive and are living in peace.' Then you and they will greet myself who has formed your bodies with a Thanksgiving offering. Then the other person will say, 'I am thankful that you and I have again met in peace.' If you both should separate and meet each other again when it is dark, you will greet one another and then hug one another as well. One of you will then say, 'I am thankful that you and I have passed through the day in peace as now the night has befallen us. We will now make an offering of Thanksgiving to the Creator that he should have pity on us and that there should be peace and health during the night so that we may awaken to another day.'"

Teharonhia:wako then said, "All of you have an equal right to the things that I have just mentioned. You will continue to comfort one another and greet one another with Thanksgiving when you visit each other's lodges. Whenever you travel along the different paths and you meet one another, happiness should be the most important thing, and you should give thanks to all things as well as myself. In this way, it will affect everyone, so that all will be of peace of mind each day and each night. Remember these things that I say to you for all time, because, if you don't, a grave thing will happen to you if you ever forget about peace. You will cease to continue to live if you forget about peace, and that is the reason I have set things down this way."[64]

Teharonhia:wako then said to the *onkwe:honwe*, "Now you will talk these things over with one another and be clear in your minds about what I have told you. The time is getting closer when my brother and I will disagree once again. I believe he will let loose on the Earth something that will kill you *onkwe:honwe* off once and for all, and that is the reason I have left these instructions for you to follow. In the days to come, there will be divisions among you and the other lineal families. There will be nothing but contentions among you, and you will continue to dispute with one another. In time, you will forget about happiness and peace. You will also forget about me, and when that happens you will destroy one another. Your blood ties will die out, and you will see the Milky Way divide, and then there will be two kinds of minds of human beings on Earth."

Teharonhia:wako finally ended by saying, "I am finished with what I have to say to you, and now I will depart for my home in the sky. I will be listening whenever someone wishes to speak to me. It shall come to pass that I will once again visit in the future. If you ever stop living in peace with one another, I hope I will see you get through the ordeal. I also hope that I will be fortunate and be able to retain control of the creation from my brother who will attempt once again to try to control my handiwork." Teharonhia:wako then departed for the Sky World.

Otetonia then began to travel around the floating island, telling all who would listen about the instructions he had been given by Teharonhia:wako. Everyone took what had been revealed to him to heart. Pretty soon they were able to travel wherever they wanted in peace. The things that they lived on grew from the Earth, and the *onkwe:honwe* flourished. One day, they began to assemble for a ceremony they had been taught. This included everyone from the youngest to the oldest.

Otetonia then stood up and spoke to the crowd, "We will now commence with the ceremony that Teharonhia:wako gave us. Now that we are together, we are of one mind. We will first greet one another by giving thanks. First of all, we will direct our words to the first of creation our Mother the Earth upon whom we travel and live. We thank her for providing all the things that we need to live on. We thank her for fulfilling her duty in the way that the Creator had ordained."

He continued, "Next, we are thankful to the grasses and everything that grows from the surface upward, even though the species may differ in appearance from one another."

He continued, "We also give thanks to the different bushes that grow, especially to those that give us fruit for nourishment."

He continued, "We give thanks to the trees, especially those who give us fruits to live upon."

He continued, "Other things that we are thankful for are the springs and the streams of water. We greet them with thanks, as well as the other things that we have already mentioned, so that they will continue to live life to the fullest. That is because we have all been placed here together, and we must take care of one another."

He continued, "Once again, we thank the wildlife who travel upon the Earth. They also differ among themselves. Some of them are small and live close to us. Others have outstretched wings and fly above us. Still others are large and live in the forest away from us. We greet them with thanks because he who made us left us both to live together in this place. We wish that they also live peaceful lives."

He continued, "Now again this day, we greet the light of our Elder Brother; we hold him in esteem. It is he who causes the floating islands to be lighted and to be warm. Through him there is peace and health, for the plants, the animals, and the human beings also on the Earth. Day after day he continues to attend to us. Now we must prepare to greet our Elder Brother the Sun by giving him thanks repeatedly."

He continued, "Now, we will turn our attention to the stars, as well as our grandmother's head, the nocturnal orb of light, the Moon. Our Creator intended that it would turn dark for half the time and so he appointed her to cause the night to light up. It is because of her that the dew falls on the plants to help them grow. We hold her in esteem because our lives are governed by her. We therefore greet her, as well as the stars in the sky, repeatedly with thanks. We do this so that our minds will remain content."

He continued, "Now another thing, we greet our grandfathers the Thunders, who come from the west and protect us each day and night, that they will continue to care for the Earth and everything that it contains, including us human beings. It is they who cause the mist to fall and the waters to remain fresh. Now we will prepare to greet them with all our thanks repeatedly."

He continued, "Now again, another thing, we give thanks most of all to the one who created everything else and gave each thing a duty to perform. It is for that reason we think thoughts of peace. Now we will prepare to greet him who dwells in the sky with thanks."

Finally, he said, "We end our words, now that we have fulfilled the ceremony he gave us concerning thanks. Now, the ceremony for which we have assembled will begin. We will greet one another with thanks, and the songs of the Great Feather Dance will commence."

The ceremony began, and all the *onkwe:honwe* were happy, from the eldest to the youngest. They shook hands and danced happily during the morning. When the Sun shone at midday, everyone stopped.

Otetonia stood up and said to the human beings who were assembled, "Now that we have completed the ceremony of Thanksgiving to our Creator, the plants, the animals, the water, the orb of light of the day and the nocturnal orb of light, and our grandfathers the Thunders who come from the west, we must now bring them all together and place them in one vessel and thank them repeatedly once again. All of us who have attended this ceremony are left with thoughts of peace. Once again we greet him who created all our bodies. Those of us who participated in the ceremony until its completion, we greet one another in repeated thanks."

Then Otetonia said, "We have started from the very beginning of the ceremonies that he gave us, that is, the giving of thanks from below to above. In the same way that we performed them this time, they will continue to be performed into the future. We began the ceremony of thanks starting with the Earth that we stand upon and finished in the sky above where our Creator lives. The *onkwe:honwe* will continue to use the same kind of words and perform the same ceremony in the future."

Otetonia then told those assembled, "Everyone has a right to perform the ceremonies that the Creator gave us. It is our duty to prize them and make sure that they are always performed. In fact, all the ceremonies he has given us will be done during the different seasons at the time the Creator has designated for us."

From that time on, the *onkwe:honwe* held their ceremonies in esteem and made sure they were always done at the proper time. For a while, everyone was of one mind. One night, the *onkwe:honwe* looked up and saw that the path was divided in the sky. Soon after, they began to argue with one another and began taking sides against one another. It seemed that they argued about everything, even including how and when to perform the ceremonies. It wasn't long before they stopped doing the four ceremonies all together.

Otetonia assembled the *onkwe:honwe* and said to them, "Teharonhia:wako told us not to forget to care for one another. He said that we would have pleasure in life, as long as we lived in peace and performed the four ceremonies. He also told us that if we ever forgot them, we would cease to exist. He said we would know that would happen by looking into the night sky and seeing that the path was divided. It would mean that our minds would become divided as well. It means that there will be two types of human beings living on Earth with two different minds. One will live with the creation and give thanks while the other will try to control the creation. One will live in peace while the other will live for killing. When that happens, we will no longer be able to reason with each other and we will stop doing the ceremonies that he has given us. That is why it is important that you urge one another to observe the ceremonies and that you have courage to continue doing them."

Even though Otetonia tried to speak to the people, they still would not listen or work with one another. Each day and night the extended families bickered with one another. This continued for some time. Soon after, strange things began to happen to the *onkwe:honwe*. Frequently, one of them would vanish and it would turn out that person had been killed. One day the orb of light that shone in the day underwent an unnatural change as it disappeared. Some of the children became lost, and no one knew where they went. The time had become so critical that the women of the extended families began to weep in fear.

Not long after, the *onkwe:honwe* heard a loud noise come from the west. The thunders were heard and the winds began to blow. For three days it continuously rained. The *onkwe:honwe* began to become fearful as to what it meant. They believed that something terrible was about to happen to them. After three days, the rain finally stopped. As they looked up toward the sky, they saw beautiful colors in the form of a ray of light. The ray seemed to begin on the Earth and to travel upward toward the sky and then to return back toward the Earth on the other side. There were colors in it that the *onkwe:honwe* had never seen before. In fact, they had never seen anything like it before.

One of the Elders said, "Let us go and ask Otetonia about it. He should be able to tell us what has caused the arch in the sky. No one has ever mentioned that this would happen."

Many of the *onkwe:honwe* gathered together to ask Otetonia about the strange occurrence that was taking place, and so they departed toward his lodge. When they arrived, an Elder asked him, "What is the reason for the colorful arch that travels from one side of the Earth toward the sky and then to the other side of the Earth."

Otetonia answered, "The reason that this has happened is that it is a sign to us that we have not fulfilled our duty to Teharonhia:wako and the rest of the creation. I believe that Teharonhia:wako has returned to set things straight, as he has promised that he would one day if we became lost in our ways."

The Elder said, "Let us hope that it is true so that we may see him again."

It was not long after that Teharonhia:wako arrived among the *onkwe:honwe* once again. The people did not recognize him at first as he seemed to be changed in appearance.

He said to them, "I have returned to put a stop to the harm that you are doing to one another. It seems that there are now two streams of thought running in the minds of the human beings. It seems that even among the *onkwe:honwe*, your minds are becoming divided, just as the path in the sky is. It appears that my brother's power can still influence you. From this point on, there will be divisions taking place on the Earth. There will be those who will continue to do the ceremonies that give thanks for the creation, just as there will be those who will try to subdue the Earth. The path in the sky will become broader and fork out. I shall leave a sign to remind you of my presence, as well as of your duties that I have given you. With the help of my Grandmother, I will manifest my power in the rainbow that you see. As long as it appears, the Earth will continue to exist. All persons will guide their lives by it. As long as it exists so will the things that grow and the animals who travel on the Earth, as well as everything that I have given a duty to perform. If you ever see it beginning in the Sunrise and traveling in an arch toward the west in the middle of the sky, that will be the time when the Earth will come to an end. I have given the duty to the Thunders who will come from the west to help guide you as well. You will know when they come that the rainbow is near. It is their duty to help my Grandmother cleanse the Earth so that it may be renewed. At that time you will see my handiwork receive new life and the great bow appear in the sky. This will continue as long as everything that I ask is accomplished."

Teharonhia:wako then said, "There was a time when I was here on the Earth and I received my power from the great bow. It was made from the things that come from the Earth. The first of these was the Sunflower, which was the color yellow. Next, was the Red Willow, which was the color red. Then, it was the Great Blue Heron, who was the first of the creatures that were made. In these three things came the three colors from which I began making the creation. As long as you look up and see these three colors in the great bow, the Earth will continue to exist. Whenever you hear the Thunders coming from the west and see the rain, you will know that the great bow is near and will shine above. With this sign, you will always remember me, your extended families will continue to exist, and the orb of light in the sky will continue to shine bright."

Teharonhia:wako continued, "Now, I will renew the four ceremonies and add something to them as well. This will ensure that you will continue to do them once again. When the season changes and the spring season begins, you will know that it is time for the wild strawberries to begin to grow. At that time you will gather the berries and assemble the entire community from the youngest to the eldest. You will then make a juice from the berries that everyone will drink. You will choose two persons, a boy and a girl, to distribute the juice. They will be of the age, just past puberty, when the boy's voice begins to change and the girl has her first Moon cycle. They will divide the juice among the assembly, and those who drink shall do so from the same vessel. Before they take a drink, one will be chosen to say these words."[65]

He told them to say, "I greet you repeatedly with thanks. I also greet all the things that have been given a duty to perform with repeated thanks. I greet you who lives in the sky with thanks for bringing up once again the fruits of the Earth. I also greet you with thanks once again, for allowing me to drink from this vessel."

Teharonhia:wako continued, "When that is done, you may take a drink and then speak when you are finished. If you cannot speak then, it would be sufficient to say, 'I am thankful that I am able to drink this juice. I greet with repeated thanks the one who created our bodies.'"

He continued, "If a person is not able to speak at all, then let them think to themselves these thoughts, 'I am thankful to be alive and living in peace. I am thankful to you who has created my body and lives in the sky.' I will know their thoughts."

Teharonhia:wako continued, "Once, everyone has had a drink of the juice and has spoken their words, the Great Feather Dance will begin. Everyone will then stand up and dance around the fire. Everyone should be happy in their thoughts, thinking, 'I am thankful that I am alive and living in peace. I now understand the time and the place for the ceremony and am grateful for being able to participate in it. Once again, I repeatedly give thanks to the one who dwells in the sky and has given us our life.'"

Teharonhia:wako continued, "You will then say, 'I will do the ceremony once again when the raspberries begin to ripen.' At that time, you will do the same as you did with the strawberry. You will assemble the community and prepare the juice of the raspberry. You will then do the same ceremony that you did with the strawberry."

Teharonhia:wako then said, "You will take some of the ripened fruit such as the mulberry and keep it for the ceremony of the highly prized food, the Harvest Ceremony. At that time when the great dance of the four ceremonies takes place, you will prepare the mulberry juice. That will be the first thing that will go around the fire and everyone shall have a drink of it and say thanks once again several times. At the time that the ceremony will begin and the juice will have been prepared, it will be put in the middle of the assembly, and anyone will have a right to drink it if they think they are thirsty. As soon as that happens, they will greet everyone with repeated thanks once again. Then they will greet the one who gave them life and say, 'I will do this ceremony again into the future.'"[66]

Now then, Teharonhia:wako told them, "Both the men and the women will work together to bring forth the fruit of a certain tree. I will assign this tree the duty to exude a sweet sap. When the juice is made, the sap will be used to sweeten it. The tree from where the sap will come, will be called the maple. At the time that the days on the Earth begin to become warm once again, it will be then that the sap will be gathered and become sweet. You will then once again utter thanksgiving when it arrives and drink from it while it is still fresh. That will be called the gathering of the maple sap. At that time you will perform the same ceremony as you did during the gathering of the fruit."[67]

Teharonhia:wako then said, "I have only one other thing to say to you. I will leave, but will return one day to the Earth. I have placed in your minds the idea that you must take care of one another's interests so that you can continue to live in peace. Now, I will leave once again for the Sky World."

Teharonhia:wako then disappeared, and no one knew exactly where he went. The *onkwe:honwe* made use of the things he had told them before he left. From that point on the people performed the ceremonies in the order he had given them and they remained content, enjoying what they were doing.

For many years, the *onkwe:honwe* carried on the ceremonies, performing them correctly. Then one day they began to argue with one another over how they should be conducted. They began to use any means available to win their argument. Some would say they must be done one way while others would say that they had to be done another way. Each tried to take control of the ceremonies, telling the others that they were in the right. This happened repeatedly, day after day, night after night.

Once again Sawiskera's presence could be felt. Even the forests became more dangerous for the *onkwe:honwe*. As they went hunting, strange animals would appear that were larger than the ones they had known before. Sometimes they would hunt them down while at other times they would be the ones who were hunted and killed. The Great *Kwis Kwis*, Mammoth, the Great Bear, and the Great Mosquito appeared and killed many. When the people looked up into the sky, they saw that the paths had become even further divided. It came a time when there were only a few *onkwe:honwe* left who remembered the original ceremonies that Teharonhia:wako had taught them.

Soon after, even stranger events began to occur. Some of the *onkwe:honwe* began to die in their villages for no apparent reason. This seemed to occur more and more often. The *onkwe:honwe* had never had such a thing happen before, and the people began to grieve as more of them expired. Soon the grief began to become unbearable. It seemed that no one performed the ceremonies any longer. They felt that the ceremonies were not helping to provide for their needs. Just when things seemed to becoming unbearable and when everything seemed to be lost, a great noise was heard coming from the west. It was Teharonhia:wako returning to find out what had gone wrong.

When he had assembled the *onkwe:honwe*, he said to them, "I have come for a short time only, and this will be the last time that I will set foot on the Earth. After this time, the people will only have my name to remember me by. If anyone does want to see me in the future, they will have to work very hard to do so. Therefore, I will tell you something that will help you to continue to live on the Earth while I am gone. This will be the last thing that I will do while I am here. After that, it will be up to you, the *onkwe:honwe*, to decide what you want to do."

He continued, "The time is coming when my brother will do his best to control the creation and the minds of the *onkwe:honwe*. He will try to spoil all the things that I have given you. The only way that you can protect yourselves from him is to continue to perform the four ceremonies and try to care for one another. You must always remember caring and peace. If you remember me every day and every night, you will be taken care of. I have now said the last thing that I wanted to tell you, so I will now return home."

Teharonhia:wako then left the Earth World. He promised that he would always watch over the creation from the Sky World. However, he had given the *onkwe:honwe* the free will to make choices for themselves. He knew that, over time, many would falter. Sawiskera's power was strong but not as strong as those who remained faithful in the things that he had given them.

As time went on, there were many *onkwe:honwe* who remembered the history of what had taken place during those years when the Earth was still young. Those who used the sweatlodge to foretell what would happen became afraid of what they saw in the future. In time, many of the oldest and the youngest *onkwe:honwe* in the communities began to die off. Others went insane because of their grief. There were those who began to gossip and lie against one other. The people of the extended families were no longer happy and content with their lives. They even began to kill one another; this was the worst thing that they could do. Soon there was little respect between the families who sat across the fire from each other.

The *onkwe:honwe* began to fear walking upon the trails, lest they were attacked by someone who was mad. Once again the four ceremonies ceased to be performed. There was only sadness and despair among the families. Pretty soon all that could be heard was the weeping of women and children. Even the fruit no longer grew as it had before. Each season there seemed to be less and less to provide their families with. The *onkwe:honwe* began to starve, as there never seemed to be enough provisions. So great was the grief among the *onkwe:honwe* and the expectation that a miracle would happen, that there were rumors that Teharonhia:wako had returned and was living among the people. They began to search for him but to no avail. They had forgotten how to ask for him the way Teharonhia:wako had taught them to.

Teharonhia:wako looked down from the Sky World and was saddened to see what was occurring. He felt compassion for the *onkwe:honwe* and thought about what he would do. Suddenly, out of nowhere and to everyone's surprise, Teharonhia:wako appeared. In spite of this, the *onkwe:honwe* continued with their self-destructive behaviors.

Teharonhia:wako called for an assembly to be held, and, when the *onkwe:honwe* had come together, he told them. "It is time for me to tell you why I have come back. Once again you have failed in doing what I had asked of you. I told you that my brother's power is strong and that you would have to be vigilant in the ceremonies. Now, you will truly be on your own. You will have to watch over your children and teach them what they have to do in life. You saw what can happen when you do not follow the instructions that I gave you. There are all kinds of things that can bring you sorrow if you are not ready for them."

He continued, "You *onkwe:honwe* do not seem to care for each other in the way that you should. You do not seem to be aware of the reason that you act the way that you do. You should know by now that my brother is influencing you to do wrong. He will continually do this to get at me. He will work through you to spoil my creation. He is trying to control the creation by controlling your minds. In the end, his objective will be to destroy the creation, and he will use you to do it. He will use every devious means to do so."

Teharonhia:wako continued, "The first thing that I have to say is that you must cease hurting one another. You will again care for one another and live in peace with one another. Remember, there are two paths that one can take. The first is for those *onkwe:honwe* who follow the ceremonies and live their lives as good people and in peace with others. When their allotted days have expired on the Earth, they will take the path that will lead them to the Sky World, where I will be waiting to greet them. Upon arriving in that place, they will find happiness. There, they will find the four ceremonies continually being performed, for they help keep the universe in motion."

Then he said, "The other path is for those who continually do wrong. When their days on Earth are allotted, they will travel on the other path until it forks off to the left. There they will come to my brother's lodge. When they arrive in that place, they will see every manner of thing that is ruinous to see. They will witness disease and destruction like they have never seen before. This will be tenfold to what can occur on the Earth. That is why you *onkwe:honwe* have to continue in the duties that I have given you. Only through hard work will you get through. I wish it could be easier, but because of my brother it never will. If you fail in the duties I have given you, you will certainly perish on the Earth, as well as in the sky. In fact, you will experience death twice. You must keep your mind in constant awareness, for it can deceive you."[68]

Continuing, he said, "Each of you have a part of myself as well as my brother within you. Those who live on my brother's island have an even greater task as they were the ones formed by my brother. Because I gave them life, they also have a chance to live well in this world and in the next. However Sawiskera's influence will even be stronger on them to control the creation. This is the way that it will be, as long as the Earth continues to exist. There is nothing that you can do to change it, except what I have told you to do."

He continued, "Now, I will give you something called medicine that will help you to continue to live. The reason that I will do this is because there will be something called disease that will travel around the whole Earth causing a great deal of death and suffering. It is malevolent by nature and faceless. However, it has the power to end the days of the *onkwe:honwe* and the other human beings on Earth. It doesn't matter what age you are, it can strike suddenly and destroy my handiwork. It is my brother who has caused this to happen. If ever the Earth becomes spoiled and you forget your instructions, there will be more disease to come. That is the reason that I have come to deliver medicine from the plants to you. You must always take care of the plants, for they will help you prevent the effects of disease with these you can continue to live your days in peace."

Teharonhia:wako continued "You will now go out and gather the various kinds of grasses, shrubs, and trees and bring them together here." The *onkwe:honwe* did as they were asked. They collected the medicines and placed them in a pile in front of Teharonhia:wako.

Teharonhia:wako stood up and spoke. "Now then, you must pay attention to me. All of you know the various kinds of plants as well as their names. I will take one and hold it up high in my hand and will then ask you questions about it. If you know what it is, you will say so and explain to us what you think it is."

Teharonhia:wako then took one of the plants and held it high above his head and asked, "Does anyone know what type of plant this is?"

There were only few that could pick it out and say what it was.

Teharonhia:wako then said, "This will be used to make medicine. It will help you counteract several diseases. Because there are only a few of you who took the time to know this plant when I asked, there will therefore be only a few of you who will be taught to use these medicines in the future."

Teharonhia:wako continued, picking up different plants and asking the people if they knew what they were. There were only a few who could respond in the affirmative. They were the ones whom he taught the different uses of the medicines. When he had finished showing them the medicines, he told the crowd of people gathered, "You will have to go to these select few, if you want a cure for disease."

He explained, "You will use the medicine plants, as well as the Real Tobacco to aid you in the future. Whenever you need help with a medicine, you are to take Real Tobacco as a thank you offering to the one who will make the medicine. When you approach the person, you will say, 'I have come to you for help. Something serious is happening to me and it is sickness. I have chosen you to help me with this.'"

Teharonhia:wako then said, "Next, the medicine person will look for the medicine and pledge these words upon it. Once he arrives at the place that the medicine grows, he will say, 'You have been selected because there is someone who is dependent on you for help. That person is sick and is unable to help himself. I am offering these words of thanks for your help in curing the person.'"

Teharonhia:wako continued to tell the medicine people, "You will then offer tobacco to the medicine plant as a gift for its services. Only then may you take the medicine plant and carry it back to the one who is sick. When you arrive, you will say to the sick person. Now I have brought you the medicine; I have asked that the medicine aid you."

He continued, "You will then say, 'You, who lives in the sky and has completed all things on Earth and above, continue to listen to us. Both the person who is sick and myself pray that the medicine will aid him so that he may travel once again upon the Earth in peace. We leave this to you to decide what to do, for it is you who gave us our lives.'"

Teharonhia:wako continued to tell the medicine people, "That is the way it should be done, and that is the way you will continue to do it into the future."[69]

"Now again, another thing," Teharonhia:wako continued, "I will deliver the things that you need so that you may continue to live. At that time, you will have to set yourself up for some hard work. You will put your hands on them and care for them until the time comes when the ground becomes warm again. At that time, you will then place what I give you into the ground. Once you have them, you will never go hungry again, for they will care for you as long as you care for them in return."

He then said, "There will be three things that I will give you. The first shall be called the corn; the second shall be called the bean; and the third shall be called the squash.[70] When the time comes for them to be planted, you will place them into the ground. When that is done, you will assemble the people and give thanks to them repeatedly. You will then participate in the first of the ceremonies that I have given you, the Great Feather Dance. At that time, you will continue to greet each other with thanksgiving. When the seeds have sprouted from the ground, you will begin to care for them. Be careful that you do not spoil them when they are being attended to."

He continued, "The next thing you must do is assemble all the people to participate in all the ceremonies. You will first gather up the beans, cook them, and set them aside. There should be enough to support all the people. After that you will choose a person to speak. He will begin with the preliminary ceremony of giving thanks, starting with the things that come from the Earth. Then he will continue upward until he reaches those things in the sky who assist and protect you. Then, you will continue to greet me by giving thanks for having been allowed to participate in the ceremony once again. At that time the Great Feather Dance will commence. Everyone will give greetings of thanks repeatedly. They will also greet me by giving thanks once again. Everyone should continue to be happy and participate in the ceremony by dancing around the fire. You will then divide up the beans so that everyone gets an equal portion and that everyone will share in it. The same will be done when the corn and the squash comes up. When that is done, you will combine the three, who are sisters to each other and are your mothers, so that they can work together. At the ceremonial place you will gather the great food and rejoice with the four ceremonies."

Continuing, he said, "Now then, I have completed what I have to say on the matter of the things that you will be accustomed to do on Earth. Whoever continues to hold the ceremonies in high esteem and continues to care for others will live in peace. When their allotted days are numbered on Earth, they will take the path that will bring them to my lodge on the upper side of the sky. There, they will find the four ceremonies being continually performed, and there will be rejoicing forever. In that place, they will find that death does not exist. Nor is there any illness. They will find that they will not have to struggle in order to live, for there will be no sorrow. There are only things that give pleasure to the mind, which are never without end. There, they will find all kinds of fruits, flowers, and animals, including those who dwell in the sky whom you have never met on Earth. When people arrive in that place, they will be possessed by all kinds of joyous things; these will continue to give pleasure to the mind forever."

Then he said to them, "Now, another thing that I will tell you *onkwe:honwe*. I have said before that there are two kinds of minds. One type follows what I said and uses the ceremonies that I have left to you. Those of this mind set will continue to use the things I have given. Those of the other mind set will fall into my brother's traps. Those who continue to use that which is not right and who show that they don't care for others or of peace upon their departure from this place will take the path to my brother's lodge. There, they will see great suffering and famine. They will also suffer by sharing the same fate as my brother. Like him, they will not live in liberty, and like him they will be confined to that place. There, I have made him a fire ten times hotter than any you have on Earth so that his anger can be controlled. The fire I made is eternal and is there to cool his cold heart and his power. My brother will never stop trying to gain control of the Earth or the minds of the human beings who dwell on it. Now, I have told you the way things exist. Whichever path you choose to take will be your decision, and you will live with the consequences of it."

Finally, he told them, "Now then, I will tell you one more time, I will not return here. I have finished my three visits and have completed what I had set out to do. I have given you the way that you are to conduct yourselves here on Earth for the rest of the days and nights to come. If there ever comes a time in the future that you forget to live in peace with one another and are without caring for one another, I will send someone to help straighten you *onkwe:honwe* out. He will assist me in bringing you back to having a good mind. In fact, I will send someone in the future three times to assist you. When the third person appears, you will know that something is going to happen to the Earth shortly after he arrives."

Continuing, he said, "The first thing that you will notice is that all the things that help sustain you today will begin to disappear. The things that grow in abundance will no longer do so. The same will be for the animals and the birds. The passenger pigeon, that are so plentiful that when they pass over they cover the sky, will cease to exist. The large animals on which you live will also disappear. When that happens, you will see strange things happen on Earth, and you will be awestruck by them. This will occur more and more each day and night. At that time, the Earth will quake and release the things that have been hidden in the ground whose *orenta* can outmatch those of the human beings. All of these things that I am mentioning will take place. Even though my brother has been put away, he is still powerful, and he will try to seduce the minds of all the human beings. When that happens, everything will be spoiled and become destitute on the Earth. He will even spoil the way that human beings live with the rest of the creation. He will turn your minds from me, by deceiving you with sudden wealth, so that your minds are corrupted. Soon, I will leave to go back to my lodge in the sky once again, but remember these words."

Just before leaving he told them, "Everything that I told you about shall continue to exist after I leave. They have been put there for your pleasure. I will make a path here on Earth, and, if you follow it to its end, you will find the corn, beans, and squash growing. Once you have found them and they mature you must care for them. Never waste them, for they will sustain you into the future. You will divide them up so that everyone has a suitable share for each of the existing extended families. You will always continue to live on these three sisters: the corn, the beans, and the squash."

Continuing, he said, "You will call to them before you pick them, 'Oh! Our mothers.' The reason that you will do this is because they will always care for you until your dying days. They will provide strength and bring sound minds among you. Your children will develop a healthy breath from them so that they can travel far distances when they get older. They will grow up strong and healthy and be of sound mind because of them. They will be like your first mother, Awenhaniyota, who first gave you life. They will help your children continue to grow in height."

Continuing, he said, "I shall make a path that the *onkwe:honwe* can follow to reach them. When I have departed, you will choose two young persons at the point of maturity to follow it. One of them will be male and the other female. The boy will be of the age where his voice is about to change and the girl will be at the age where her body is going through a change and she is denied certain things. They are at the age that I will refer to as being hidden under the husk. Like the corn, you will find they are protected by the husk until they are fully matured."

He continued, "You will ask them to follow my path to its end. There, they will find a mound of Earth where they will see a corn plant, a bean plant, and a squash plant growing. The young woman will stand to the west of them and the young man to the east of them. The young man will then speak and say these words. 'Oh, our Mothers, we have arrived. We both have been sent here by your children. We have come to take you with us, to live with our people. Now then, we whose bodies were made from this Earth by our Creator will come together, and yours will help fulfill ours.'"

He continued, "At that time, the young woman will take the first standing corn and then the first bean that she sees. The young man will then take up the first squash. When they have done this, they will then understand the meaning of the open grave. Whenever the *onkwe:honwe* departs from the Earth at the distance where the corn, beans, and squash grow from the village, your path will have ended where the ground is opened up. The *onkwe:honwe* shall always keep the ground in good order. By keeping the opening at that distance, you have the responsibility of preserving the Earth with your bodies. It will continue to be this way forever."

He continued, "In the future, you will continue to depart from one another on this Earth. When that happens, the one who takes the lead in departing and who has exhausted their days on the Earth, will always be the first to rest in this place. That is because each person is given a certain amount of allotted days to live on the Earth. That is, each person departs from the Earth at a different pace. You must therefore walk a straight line to the place where the path ends to where you will find the corn, beans, and squash. When members of the extended family come to the end of their life in a place that is far from their village, that is where they were intended to depart from and that is the place where their bodies are to be left. At that time, you will bring some corn to them in a bowl. You will then guide their spirit back to the village where it will make its final departure. If that happens, I will leave it up to those who remain to take care of this matter. You have a duty to make sure that the generations who are coming ahead will live in happiness."

Teharonhia:wako then told them, "Now I must leave it up to you to care for each other. I have completed my work. I have established the things that are to be included in the creation of this world in order for it to exist. This includes the plants, the animals, the human beings, the waters, the four ceremonies, caring for one another, the Elder Brother the Sun, the Grandmother Moon, the sky, those that come from the west, the Thunders, the winds, and the medicines. These are things that you have a responsibility toward. As long as you fulfill your responsibility to them, they will continue to aid you. By way of these things, your bodies will continue to have life, so will the Earth below and the sky above. One thing that I will do is hide from you the number of days that you have on Earth. I will also not tell you where I have gone. Only when your days are ended will you be able to find me. I will never let anything come between us. I will always be looking down at you and watching how you are doing. I will be looking at the manner of how you think and will know when I am included in your thoughts. I will know if someone is asking for something of me or if they are offering thanks to me. Now then, you should have your eyes fixed on the direction that I will depart."

Teharonhia:wako then departed from the Earth for a final time. The *onkwe:honwe* watched to see in which direction he traveled and saw that he went west. They soon lost sight of him. All the *onkwe:honwe* marveled at what they had seen and heard from Teharonhia:wako. They regarded everything that he said to them with the highest of esteem.

The male Elders of the village said, "It would be good if we attended to the things that were given to us and to hold them in reverence always. Now, we understand the way Teharonhia:wako put things in order for us. He has left it up to us to continue to observe them and to live in peace with one another. The first thing we must do is choose two young people to follow Teharonhia:wako's path. They will find the corn, beans, and squash that Teharonhia:wako promised us that will help us live. The *orenta* of the young are at their peak. They both should be virgins and have been born with a birth veil, a caul, over their faces. They will have the strength to follow the path that Teharonhia:wako has given us. When they find the three things that Teharonhia:wako has promised us, they are to be brought back to us, so that we may continue to live."

The *onkwe:honwe* Elders decided that they would look for a young male whose voice was about to change and had been born with a face veil. This was a difficult task but there were two children who had been born this way some twelve years before and lived in the village. One of them was a male and the other a female.

When they had found the boy they asked him, "Young man, do you think that you will be able to follow the path that Teharonhia:wako took when he left us."

The young man answered, "I cannot promise you this. However, I will volunteer to try to find the three things that Teharonhia:wako had promised us."

Next, the Elders sought out the young woman to travel with the young man. When they had found her, they told her. "You have been chosen to go with the young man who is following Teharonhia:wako's path. When you arrive it will be your duty to pick up the corn and the beans. It will then be the young man's duty to pick up the squash."

The young woman answered, "If that is what has been asked of me on behalf of Teharonhia:wako, I will do as requested."

One of the Elders said, "We are fortunate to have found the two young persons who are most capable to do as Teharonhia:wako has asked. Now then, you both must pay attention to what I have to say. Each one of us has prepared to greet you with continuous thanks for what you are doing. We know that you are open-minded and ready for this mission; therefore, you have been chosen to carry out this important task. The two of you will follow his tracks on the path he has made, and, when they end, you will look carefully around. When you find something growing from the ground, which neither of you have ever seen before, that will be when the male will stand on the east side while the female will stand on the west side of it. The one standing on the east side will be the first to speak. He will say to the three, 'We, who have been sent by your children, have arrived. We have come to invite you home with us, to live among your children just as Teharonhia:wako has asked.'"

The Elder continued to tell them, "At that moment the young woman will then pluck up the corn and the beans. When she is finished, the young man will take up the squash. You both will think deeply about the place where you will be bringing them to and why it is so important. When you are finished speaking to them, you will bring them back to us. We will be expecting you, so we will assemble everyone, from the youngest to the eldest when you arrive."

The two young people began their journey. They saw the tracks that Teharonhia:wako had left, and they followed them. They traveled toward the west for some time. Finally, the tracks came to an end. They could see the three plants growing.

The young man said to his female companion, "We have arrived at the place that we were told about. There are the three plants growing that we have never seen before this time. You must go stand to the west of them, and I will stand to the east of them." The young woman then stood at the west side of where the plants were growing. The young man stood to the east of the plants.

He then spoke to the plants saying, "Now that we have arrived at this place, we have been sent by your children and have come to take you back with us. We will return home together so that you may dwell among us."

He then turned to the young woman and said, "Now it is time for you to take up the plants." The young woman approached the corn and bean plants and pulled them from the Earth. After she was finished, the young man pulled up the squash just as he was told to do.

He then said to the young woman, "Now, that we have accomplished the deed that we were sent to do, take a look at the place from where the plants grew that we picked up."

They both looked, and it seemed to resemble where a person who had departed from the world had been placed down. It was about the same length as a person, and there was a mound of Earth on top that extended from the east to the west. It had the same shape as a person, with the head appearing to be pointed to the west and the feet pointing toward the east. Teharonhia:wako had given up his body in order for the corn, beans, and squash to grow. This would be how the *onkwe:honwe* would be placed, when they departed from the Earth. Their bodies would be returned to Mother Earth only to help bring new life back to it in the future.

The young man said to the young woman, "We understand now why it is done this way, and we will remember in the future how it was done.

It is at this place, where Teharonhia:wako's tracks have ended. It is time for us to head back to our village." They then began their journey back to the village.

When they had arrived in the village, they saw a large body of people assembled waiting for them. Upon seeing them coming, the Elders made a fire and burned tobacco. They then with greetings said, "My children, you have returned. We give you thanks repeatedly for what you have done."

One Elder stood up and said, "I have been chosen to speak for the people assembled here. You two who were chosen to follow Teharonhia:wako's path have returned. You were asked to follow the path to its end where you would find something growing there. You were also asked to examine the features of the place once you arrived. Teharonhia:wako promised that you would find three things growing there. We have assembled here so that we can find out what happened and see what you have brought back with you. We want to know if you have brought back the things that will help us continue to live. Tell us what happened while you were gone so that we can end the anticipation that we have for what you have brought back."

The young man and woman said, "We will tell you what happened to us while we were gone."

The young man continued, "When we began to journey to the west, just as far as the eye can see from here, we found his tracks." The young man pointed west, and everyone looked.

He continued, "We hadn't walked for very long before we saw his tracks come to an end. Once there, we saw three types of things growing from the ground. The young woman, that I was with, stood to the west side of them while I stood to the east side of them. Then I said these words to them, 'We have arrived to bring you three back to your children with us.' The young woman then took up the corn and the beans. I then took up the squash. We looked at the place that they had grown from. The ground was in a heap, just as if there were a human being lying there, with his head to the west and feet to the east. It appeared that Teharonhia:wako's tracks ended right where the dirt was heaped up. We then took the three plants from the ground and brought them back here with us. She has two of them, and I have one of them. As soon as we deliver them to you, you will see them. Now then, that is all we could accomplish of the things that you asked us to do."

The young man and young woman then delivered the three plants to the Elders. She presented the first two plants and told the Elders, "Here is the first sister who will help give us life."

The Elder answered, "That is what is called corn."

Then she said, "Here is the second sister that I brought back."

The Elder answered, "That is called a bean."

The young man then took out what he had brought back with him and said, "Here is the third sister that we brought back."

The Elder looked at it and said, "That is called real squash."

The young man then said to the assembly, "We have accomplished everything that you set us out to do, and we have told you everything that had happened."

When the Elders received the gifts, one of them replied, "We have now seen the three sisters that you brought back with you and have heard you speak of the good fortune that you had on your journey. These are things that Teharonhia:wako had promised us. He intended that we should live by them. You both had to face difficulty in trying to attain them at the place where they first sprouted from the Earth. It is important that you both know that we are going to burn some tobacco and thank you repeatedly for what you have done for us."

He continued, "You both have brought our mothers back to live among us, and we are grateful so that we, adults and children, can continue our lives. Now, with one voice we give thanks to the ones who have provided for us. From now on, we will follow the path that they have given us. We have burned tobacco and have greeted you repeatedly. We are the first to see the new provisions that were given to us. We will devote special care for our mothers—the corn, the bean, and the squash—upon whom we will live. We will continue to give thanks because, for as long as the extended families exist, we will live side by side with our mothers."

He continued, "Now, we will direct our words of thanks to our Mother, the Earth; next, to the grasses that grow; and to the bushes and the trees. We also give thanks to the spring waters. Next, we give thanks to the animals. Now, we will turn our words to those living above. In the first place, we give thanks to our Elder Brother the Sun. Also, we give thanks to our Grandmother the Moon. Next, we give thanks to the stars in the sky. We also give thanks to the Thunders who come from the west. Next, we thank the winds that come from the four directions. We give a special thanks to the assistants of the one who has created our bodies. We ask them to care for us each day and night. Now, we are all of one mind in these things."

He continued, "We will now burn tobacco to greet the one who created all things. We thank him repeatedly, he who has gone back to the Sky World and has told us that he would hear our words when we speak of him. He has said that he would see everything that takes place below on Earth. That is why we continue to thank him for the three sisters that he has given us and that help to keep us alive and well. They now live among us, and we call them our mothers. Now, in reference to the three sisters, these are the words of Thanksgiving."

He continued, "We will confirm what has taken place by participating in the Great Feather Dance. This is on behalf of the three sisters who have been brought here to give us life."

Everyone stood up, both old and young and began to dance the Great Feather Dance, as they were joyous as to what was taking place. As they danced, they repeated aloud, "I am thankful that Teharonhia:wako has once again provided for us."

When the ceremony had ended, one of the Elders said, "Now that we have received this wonderful gift, it is important that we decide which is the best way to distribute them."

Another spoke out, "I thought this out and believe that everyone has an equal right to a share of them."

Another said, "In that case, we should all assist one another in the planting of them in the ground, as well as in the harvesting of them. The men can clear the field, and the women will then do the planting."

The Elders thought about what had been said and agreed that everyone should take part in working to make sure the three sisters would continue to provide for them.

That year, the spring arrived earlier than usual, and the people assembled to discuss what they should do.

One of the Elders said, "The very first thing that was done to help us live was the great gamble bowl game. We will play a game on behalf of the corn, beans and native squash. We will use the pit of the plum fruit to play with, and we will bet on behalf of the three sisters. When this is done, we will place our three mothers in the ground."

Another person said, "That is an excellent idea as it will remind us of the time when Teharonhia:wako bet with his mother on who would control the things that grow from the Earth. Therefore, we men will play the game against the women as a remembrance of it."

The Elders agreed with the idea and prepared the game. The men and the women sat on either side of the bowl and began to bet on who would have control of the three sisters. The men won the first game.

When the game was over, one of the Elders said, "It has been decided, every spring, the first thing that we will do is play the great gamble game with our mothers, the three sisters, to be bet upon."

The *onkwe:honwe* then began to plant the three sisters. When they had finished the planting, they assembled and began to dance the Great Feather Dance. As they danced, they offered up their thanks for having finished planting their fields.

When the three sisters began to sprout up from the Earth, everyone came together and began to stir the soil. After this was done, they once again assembled.

One of the Elders said, "Now then, we can see that our mothers are appearing from the Earth. Those of us who have seen this take place greet one another with repeated Thanksgiving. We also greet with Thanksgiving all those things that were given duties to perform by their Creator. They will help us attend to our mothers so that they will grow to full maturity. Now then, we shall also greet with Thanksgiving the one who created our bodies.

2

The Clan System and the Migration of the *Rotinonshonni* to Their Traditional Territory

The Great Young Man Brings the Clan System

No sooner had the *onkwe:honwe* finished the ceremony of thanksgiving for the three sisters when one of them suddenly passed from the earth. The rest of the *onkwe:honwe* dug a hole in the ground outside the village and placed the body in the earth, just as the young man and woman who brought the corn, beans, and squash had told them to do.

Soon others, both young and old, began to also pass from the earth. This was occurring in spite of the fact that there was no sickness. Some *onkwe:honwe* also began to leave the villages and not return; this caused even more grief. Many of the people were no longer content, and all you could hear through the village, day and night, was weeping and sorrow. As the people began to leave, the four ceremonies were once again forgotten.

The elders got together to discuss the matter, and one of them said, "We must assemble all the people so that we can decide what to do. It is not good that we stand here and do nothing about this situation. Everywhere we go our people are crying and lamenting about their loved ones who have departed."

It wasn't long after that the *onkwe:honwe* assembled. The elders chose a person to speak for them and guide them in what they were to do.

A speaker then rose up and said, "The one who formed our bodies has given us the days that we are to live and the light that shines within each of us. He intended that the *onkwe:honwe* should always have esteem for the things that live in the world with him. We are assembled here to decide what to do about what is happening to us and what we are to do about the losses of lives that are taking place. We, who are born from the same earth, are now becoming separated from one another. We watch our people crying and pitying each other's losses. This is occurring in all the families in the village. It is evident what the cause of this suffering is. It is the result of families losing the ones they care about. We, who have assembled here, wish that someone might devise a course of action that will restore the happiness we had before. We would also like them to come up with a plan to stop the cause of the people's suffering."

The elders made the usual offerings of tobacco, then placed the problem before the assembled people and told them, "We all have a responsibility in this situation, and it doesn't matter who devises the plan. Let the women, or even the youths, be the ones to do it if they can, so that our children and our grandchildren may continue to live and have a future."

Teharonhia:wako knew that the people would be in distress, so he had imparted wisdom in a young man before he had left. He knew the day would come when the *onkwe:honwe* would expand, and as they did they would suffer from losses. At first it seemed like the *onkwe:honwe* lived for a long time and that few ever departed from the earth. As the *onkwe:honwe* grew larger in size, Teharonhia:wako knew that the earth would become too full, so he gave each one a limited life span. He also knew that there would come a time when the *onkwe:honwe* would begin to split up; they would need to find a way to stay together and come to agreement with one another if they were to remain happy in their families.

The *onkwe:honwe* contemplated the situation that had befallen them for a long time. They held several sessions; at these, they could not come to a consensus as to what to do.

A young man—who was viewed as being the quiet type and was thought would never amount to much—stood up and said to the assembled people, "I want to make a suggestion as to what we should do. The works that the Creator formed are truly great. His power and his mercy are great as well. Everything that he has done is good in its nature. These are my thoughts on the matter. The earth has life within her. She is the mother who has given birth to all the things that grow. Everything, from the many different grasses to the different trees, is charged with its own duty to perform, to live as different species. This is the same for the different birds that fly, as well as for the animals that run about. This includes the things that we live on and call our mothers. Even they have different shapes and sizes and are alive. The same goes for the pools of Water that flow, for the Elder Brother, the Sun, who warms the Earth, for our Grandmother, the Moon, as well as for our ancestors, the Stars, that keep the night bright. These are all alive. Our Grandfather Thunders who come from the west, as well as the Winds, are also alive. All of these things differ in size, types, and nature. It is these very differences that make them useful to us, as they are all charged their own duties to perform."

He continued, "Teharonhia:wako has placed them here so that we may continue to live. If we look at each of them, we would see that they all have their own duties and belong to different clans. They even have different names. Some of these Teharonhia:wako made for medicine, and when mixed together they may help the human beings when they become ill. If people use them, they will become content in their minds and live in peace. We human beings are made in the same way as these different things, and we should imitate the way Teharonhia:wako formed them. Among the flying creatures, there are robins and bluebirds. The same can be said for the bears and the other creatures that roam the earth. They may be similar to each other, but they have their own unique differences."

He continued, "The time has come when we should form clans to live in. We have to do this because we have become too numerous as a people to be one type. We should therefore portion up the people into several different clans whose members would call themselves brothers and cousins to one another. This is the way it should be as long as our extended families continue to exist. This should be the method that we use, as we are now becoming more widely spread out and beginning to separate from each other. Whenever we lose a member of one of the families who have departed from this earth, it affects the whole sisterhood. When this happens, the opposite sisterhood of the people who are still well should get together and go to the place where the person who was lost had come from. They will then say words of comfort and cheer up the minds of the bereaved and encourage them so that their minds do not get carried away in their grief. It is not good when one's mind is clouded in darkness. In fact, all young people should have a special friend to help them whenever they are in grief. You elders should consider as to whether the *onkwe:honwe* will be like other things living in the world and have differences. It is evident that there are clans of grasses, as well as shrubs, trees, and game animals."

The young man finished by saying, "I have told you all the things which I have meditated upon. I have finished what I have to say, and I leave the matter resting with you as to whether my plan should work."

The elders and people marveled at what had been suggested by the youth. They considered the matter for a while. After some time they came to an agreement that they would accept his proposition. The entire body of people would now be divided, and each would have a clan. Whenever someone was lost in one of the sisterhoods, the other sisterhood would be responsible to attend to the care of the bereaved sisterhood. It would be their duty to speak to them and encourage those who remain alive in the family, until their grief is ended and they can think clearly again.

A representative of the people then asked, "How do we go about making it possible for there to be clans."

The elders then got together to discuss the situation. They could not come to an agreement on how the clan system could work.

The elders then called another meeting and said to the people, "We have failed in the work that was given to us, which was to find a solution on how to best make the young man's proposal work. Perhaps it would be better if we asked the young man himself if he could find a solution for us. He could then complete the thing that we have been unable to do—form a clan system. It seems that in the midst of all of us, he seems to have the best abilities to come up with a solution. It will probably result in something good, if we deliver the matter for him to resolve. It is his idea, so he should be the one to complete the task."

The elders then invited the young man to come before the people. They told him, "We have decided to invite you here. The reason being is because we have failed to come up with a solution to formulate a plan based on the ideas that you came up with. We want to hand this problem over to you so that you can solve it for us. We will leave it for you to arrange how the clan system can evolve into existence. We give up our executive power and hand it over to you so that you can complete your work."

The young man answered them, "You are right, this situation has to be resolved. It is true, there is a void that is taking place within us, as we continually separate from each other here on earth. That is the reason that we must find a solution to our problem. Tomorrow at noon, all the people will assemble themselves together. At that time, I will try to arrange something so that the clan system will work. Those who are female will be the principal persons involved in this process. That is because they are the ones who give birth to the new *onkwe:honwe* on earth. The woman who is the oldest of each of the families will be the head of the entire clan that I will develop."

He continued, "Once the people are assembled we will walk toward the great long river that cuts through our floating island from the south to the north. When we arrive at the river, we will separate the people. This will occur in the morning of the next day before the sun rises. At that time, we will accomplish what we have set out to do."

The elders then replied, "This is exactly what we needed to hear in order to help us is finally about to happen."

The elders notified the people, and they were excited as to what was about to occur. They began to prepare themselves for it, and the next day everyone was ready. All the people assembled in one place.

The young man spoke to the crowd and said, "We are all assembled here, and the time has arrived for me to do what you had requested of me. I will now take my place in the front, and we shall depart; you will follow me to the river."

The *onkwe:honwe* then left with the young man, Okweta:seh, in the lead. They were all grouped in their families, and when it became evening they arrived at the bank of the river where they all stood and waited.

The river was deep and fast flowing, and they did not know how they would be able to cross to the other side. There was no log around to help cross the river. The *onkwe:honwe* all had their eyes fixed on the young man as he descended the bank. They watched him as he approached a very large tree at the water's edge.

The young man then grabbed hold of a vine hanging from the tree and said to the *onkwe:honwe*. "The time has now arrived when Teharonhia:wako has chosen to divide the people."

He then pulled on the vine and threw it to the other side of the river where it became entangled in the bushes.

He told the *onkwe:honwe*, "Soon we will cross the stream to the other side. The time has nearly arrived in which the people will be divided. However, tonight we will camp by the river. When the Elder Brother once again takes his journey in the sky, you will all watch to see what will happen. At that time, the eldest woman in the family shall go to fetch water to be used for the preparation of the food that morning. When she dips up the water, she will look to see what kind of animal will appear by the river and will remember it. I will come in the morning to see what happened." He continued, "Now you will all follow me across the river."

The young man then took hold of the vine and began to cross the river. Many of the *onkwe:honwe* followed the young man and began to cross the river one by one, as quickly as possible holding onto the vine. At that time, the sun began to go down. There were still many who were waiting for their turn to cross. In the excitement to get across before it got dark, the people started to bunch up. They were trying to cross two at a time, when suddenly the vine broke. Some of them were still crossing when this occurred, and they floated down the river to the other side. Those left on the bank could do nothing to get across to the other side. Some of them became distressed thinking that they had failed. The *onkwe:honwe* on both sides of the river set up their camps that night and kindled their fires. The camps went for quite a distance on each side of the river. They were still in a state of shock by what had happened that day.

That night the elders assembled the people and told them, "Do not worry. We will wait and see what this young man does tomorrow. It appears that something remarkable has occurred today. The young man has kept his word that he would divide the people. He has succeeded in that there are now camps on both sides of the river."

After the assembly was over, the people went to sleep. The elders meanwhile stayed awake, watching to see what the young man would do. The next morning, everyone rose up and prepared themselves for what would happen. The eldest of each of the families watched as the Elder Brother Sun began to rise up. As it became daylight, all the people were anxious to go by the river. They watched as the young man Okweta:seh started out with the elders following him behind.

He approached the lodge of the eldest matron of one of the families and entered. Once inside, he spoke to her, "I am thankful for what has occurred. I will ask you what you saw when you went to fetch the water?"

The old matron replied, "When I went to dip my ladle into the water of the river, I saw a deer standing nearby. I then departed for my lodge where I prepared some food to feed my children and grandchildren."

The young man said to her, "You have seen a game animal that was made by the same one who created our bodies. From now on this will be your family's clan. Those in your family will say, as sure as the sun moves in the same direction in the sky and the waters flow in one direction that the Deer is our clan. The Deer is the first to be chosen and is the first messenger to our Creator."

The young man then left the woman and her Deer Clan family. He arrived at another lodge, where lived another family and then approached the eldest woman. He said to her, "I am thankful that this day has arrived and we are living in peace."

The woman replied, "I am also thankful for this day."

He then asked her, "What did you see when you went to get some water at the river."

She replied, "I went to dip water from the river, and, as I bent down, I was surprised because sitting close to me was a bear. I then left, so that I could prepare food for my children and grandchildren so that they could eat."

The young man said to her, "You saw a game animal whose body was formed by the same one who gave life to us both. Your clan from now on will be the Bear, and that is what the people will call your family. Your grandchildren will say that the Bear is our clan. You will be brothers and sisters to the first family I came to, those of the Deer Clan."

The young man then got up and left. He made his way to the lodge of the eldest woman of another family. He approached her and said, "I am glad that another peaceful day has arrived."

She replied, "I am also very thankful for this day."

He then asked her, "What did you see when you went to get water?"

She answered, "I went to dip some water at the river and as I was leaning down, I saw running along the sand, a sandpiper."

He told her, "You have seen a small type of game animal that flies. From now on, you and your family will refer to yourselves as members of the Sandpiper Clan. You will be brothers and sisters of the other two clan families, the Deer and the Bear."

The youth then left and went to another lodge where the eldest woman of one of the families lived. Upon entering her lodge, he told the woman, "I am thankful that we are having another peaceful day."

She replied, "I am thankful for this day as well."

He asked her, "Did you see anything this morning?"

She told him, "I went to get some water from the river and as I dipped down, I saw an eel swimming in the current."

He said to her, "You and your family will be members of the Eel Clan. That is what your children and grandchildren will refer to themselves as from now on. You will be brothers and sisters to the other families I have already met: the Deer, the Bear, and the Sandpiper. The four of you will be a brotherhood and sisterhood. There is still some business that I have to take care of over on the other side of the river before the sun rises to its full height. I will have to cross the river because there are families who have kindled their fires that need to be taken care of on that side as well."

He then departed, and the eldest women of the four clans followed him to the river. When he arrived at the shore of the river he pulled up the grapevine and threw it over to the other side. He then crossed the river with the eldest women following him behind.

They arrived at the place where the other families had set up their camps. They then approached the lodge of the eldest woman of all the families and he entered. He said to the eldest woman, "I am glad that another dawn has come to us and we are at peace."

She replied, "I am also very thankful for this peaceful dawn that we have."

He then asked her, "What did you see after you awoke?"

She replied, "I went to dip water from the river. When I turned around, I saw a wolf running along in the back of me."

He said to her, "From now on, you and your family will be members of the Wolf Clan. Both your children and grandchildren will say we are of the Wolf Clan."

He then left her and went to the next family. When he arrived at the lodge of the eldest woman, he said to her, "I am glad that we have another day where we are living in peace."

She replied, "Indeed it is true what you say, and I am also thankful."

He then asked her, "Did you see anything this morning when you went to get water?"

She replied, "When I went to the river to dip some water, I saw a beaver swim by as I bent down."

He told her, "You and your family will from now on be members of the Beaver Clan. As long as your family and your children and grandchildren continue to exist, they will call themselves the Beaver Clan. You will also be a sister clan to the Wolf."

The young man then went to another family. When he arrived, he said to the eldest woman of the family, "What did you see when you woke up and went to the river?"

She replied, "I went to the stream to dip up some water, when to my surprise I saw a great snapping turtle swim by."

He told her, "From now on, you will be members of the Great Turtle Clan. In the future, both your children and grandchildren will say we are of the Great Turtle Clan. You will be a sister clan to the Wolf and the Beaver Clans."

The young man then moved onto another family. He went to the lodge of the eldest woman and said to her, "I am thankful that another day has arrived in peace."

She replied, "You are right, I am also thankful for this day."

He asked her, "What happened to you since the sun came up?"

She told him, "I went to the river to dip up some water and, to my surprise, walking in the mud was a bear cub."

Just then the young man said, "Something has gone wrong. That is because it is now daylight and the business I set out to do is not yet finished. Now there are two elder women, who have seen the same animal. There is already a Bear Clan family on the other side of the river. On this side there is also a Bear Clan, except that the only difference is that this is a bear cub. We will leave it like this for a while and then change it later. I think that maybe then we will put both Bear Clans together, which means one Bear Clan family will have to cross over the river to the opposite side. In spite of this, your family will be referred to as the Bear Cub Clan as long as it continues to exist. Your grandchildren will continue to say we are of the Bear Cub Clan."

The young man continued, "You and the families I have already visited on this side of the river are to be brothers and sisters. The first family is composed of the Wolf Clan, and the family beside them, the Beaver and next to them the Turtle Clan. You three clans, who have your fires next to each other, should know that this is the Bear Cub Clan."

The young man then pointed to the Bear Cub Clan and said, "Those will be the clans on this side of the fire who will consider each other as brothers and sisters. That will be the size of your sisterhood. You who are on this side of the river and those who are on the other side of the river will have a council fire between you in the same way the river is between you."

He continued, "You will sit opposite to one another and greet each other with the kinship term, cousin. When either side of the fire speaks they will refer to those across the fire as their cousins. That will be the custom from now on, and both of you will respect it. You will be equally responsible for the observances of the council, and that will be the way it will be into the future."

He then said, "You ancient ones, the eldest women of the clans, are to be in charge of this matter. Now, call all your people into an assembly so that we can meet in a council. You, who have the river between you, are now cousins and shall have a council fire between you in the same way that the river separated you. I still have a few things left that I have to say, and all the members of the council fire should hear what they are."

Then the eldest women selected a place where they could assemble. Those persons on the other side crossed the river. Once all the people were assembled at the chosen place, the ancient ones placed everyone according to where their clan was supposed to be seated. Those of the common sisterhood were placed on one side of the fire and those of the other common sisterhood were placed on the other side of the fire. The eldest women then said, "We have now completed what we were asked to do. Now tell us what you have left to say?"

The young man stood up and spoke, "First of all, we should decide once and for all what we should do, as there are now two kinds of Bear Clans on each side of the council fire. You must decide which of the Bear Clans must cross the council fire to go to the other side."

The *onkwe:honwe* then considered in council what they were going to do. This was the first decision that they had to agree upon.

After coming to agreement, the eldest matrons of the clans said, "The Bear family is something that exists in nature. Customarily the oldest mother bear travels all over the place while her cubs remain home. We have decided that it should be the ancient one, the mother bear, who should cross over the fire. There the two Bear Clans will sit together as one."

The young man told them, "I believe that you are doing the right thing. I will now ask you to ask the mother Bear Clan to cross over the fire to be with her children."

The eldest woman of the clans said, "The matter has now been attended to."

They then asked the young man, "What are you going to do about the family living on the other side of the river who still does not have a clan?"

He said to them, "Tell the eldest woman of the family to come here." Runners were then sent to get the eldest woman, and when she arrived she took a seat beside the young man.

He said to her, "Is it you whom I forgot, when I was visiting the different families on the other side of the river?"

She answered, "That is right! We thought you had forgotten us. We were expecting you to arrive and when you didn't show we became anxious about it."

He then asked her, "What did you do that morning when I told you to get water."

She answered, "When it became light outside, I went to dip some water and then I returned home. As I was walking by the place where we have our fire kindled, I noticed sitting on top of a log was a sharp-shinned hawk.

He told her, "From now on your family will be the Hawk Clan. That is what people will continue to call you and your family into the future, as long as the world continues to exist. Now I have completed the business of setting up the clan families."

He continued, "It is important that you pay attention to all the things that I am about to tell you. You ancient ones, the eldest women, have the responsibility to teach the children these things. I will start with the Deer Clan. Never forget that your Deer Clan will follow the women's lineage, and they will be the leaders of it. The reason for this is that it is within the body of the woman from where all human beings who come to live on this earth are born. You women must also give names to all the members of your children; these will be passed on when they depart from the world, so that the names will always continue with the clans."

The young man then said, "Now, you of the Sandpiper Clan. You also must be vigilant in your duty. The women will rule the family, and they will give the names to each member of the Sandpiper Clan. That is because the women are the head of the family and only they can pass these names onto their children. There can be only so many names and therefore only so many members of a family."

He continued, "The same will go for the Eel Clan. Each member should have no more than three children. In this way, there will always be plenty available for everyone. It will also ensure that the families will remain close to one another. There is medicine that can be taken to make sure that the families don't become too large."

He continued, "You of the Sharp-shinned Hawk Clan. The women will be the head and give the names to your children as well."

He then told them, "You four clans shall be sisters to one another, and that will be the size of your sisterhood that will sit on your side of the council fire."

Next, he called upon those from the other side of the river. He told them, "You, who are the Wolf Clan, will also make the women the rulers of your family, and they will ensure that the children have names."

He continued, "You, who are of the Beaver Clan, the same goes for you, in that the women will be the rulers and give the children their names."

He continued, "You, who are of the Great Turtle Clan, must also make the women the chief persons in your clan, and they will be responsible for naming the children."

He continued, "Finally, you of the Bear Clan and Bear Cub Clan who now sit together will likewise make the women the leaders of your clan, and they will make sure that all the children have names."

He then said to them, "You five clans are a sisterhood on your side of the council fire. Now you know how many clans there are who will sit on each side of the council fire. You, who sit on opposite sides of the fire, shall greet one another by the term, our cousins. This will be the way in which your families will continue to exist. Any issues that must be resolved will occur between the council fire of you both."

He then said, "The primary thing that must be remembered is the four ceremonies given to us by Teharonhia:wako. Next are the festivals that occur during the year. Finally, ensure that our days on earth end doing the above and giving thanks; this will ensure yourselves of taking the narrow road to the Creator."

Finally, the young man said, "I am finished, and this is all I am able to do. The thing that we have all participated in creating will be so durable that it will last as long as the families continue to exist. It will last as long as the grasses, shrubs, and trees continue to grow; as long as the animals endure; as long as the streams of the water continue to flow; as long as the sun and the moon take their journey; and as long as and the stars bring brightness to the earth. It will last as long as the thunders come from the west and the winds move the air on the earth."

He then finished by saying, "Now I leave it all up to you two sister-hoods who are cousins to one another to make sure that you continue to do what we have arranged. I have now finished arranging your affairs."

The ancient ones, the eldest women, considered everything that the young man had told them, from the time he had first made his proposal as to what should be done to the manner in which he achieved what he had set out to do, first by dividing the people and then making them whole again.

The ancient ones said, "It will be a long time before we see the likes of someone like him who was able to do so much for us. We will now be able to live in peace in both body and mind. Our families will be governed into the future in this way, as long as the families continue to exist. He has given us back the full power which we gave to him. Now listen, cousins who sit on each side of the council fire, and hear what we have to say. He has told us that he will leave everything up to us. He has said that this is as much as he is able to do. Now, cousins, you will hear what we of the sisterhood have to say. With one voice we thank the young man for the important work that he has done for us."

After they were finished speaking, those who were on the other side of the council fire considered what had been said. They replied, "We on our side of the council fire, with the united voice of our sisterhood of clans, think that it is a really good thing that has been accomplished. We thank the young man as well. We still have one thing that we want to contribute. Whenever we speak of this young man we shall forever remember him as Ronikohewaneh, He Who Has a Great Mind. We of the Wolf Clan and also our sister clans will from now on call this young man Ronikohewaneh. This is because he was able to do what no one else could do for us, and our grandchildren and we will remember him always with reverence. We will confirm this resolution with the *Atonwa* Ceremony. After we are finished, we will shout aloud three times, in thanks to him, for completing the work that will enable us to think and live in peace with one another into an unknown future."

At that time, they confirmed the proposition that they had come up with, and then the elders asked the young man to stand in their midst.

The eldest man, Akatuni:heno of the Wolf Clan, stood up and said, "This young man has completed the entire system of rules that will govern the assembly of people here. Whenever anyone speaks of him they will call him He Who Has a Great Mind, Ronikohewaneh. It is not certain how long he will be with us on this earth, and it may be that in the future that we will still need him for something. If anyone needs advice they should go to Ronikohewaneh, and we should always remember him when we are in need.

At that time an *onkwe:honwe*, known as the Wolf, said, "I will now confirm by a chant what Ronikohewaneh has done for us."

He then began to sing, and the entire body of people soon after accompanied him, *hiu, hiu*. When he had finished the song, the oldest of the Deer Clan rose up and spoke.

"Now that my cousin has confirmed the matter, I will confirm it on my side of the fire as well. I greet Ronikohewaneh with repeated thanks for what he has done for us. I also want to greet with thanks Teharonhia:wako, as it must have been him who gave his mind the ability to achieve this. Now we are living in good health and peace. I will confirm the proposition by chanting the *Atonwa*." He then began to sing, and the entire body of people sang with him, *hiu, hiu*, hiu and at the same time the women clapped their hands.

He finished his song and then said, "Now let us all stand up and hold each other's hands. The reason we will do this is because our Creator resides in the Sky World, and we will therefore shout three times in thanks to him."

Then, all the assembly of people including the ancient ones as well as the children stood up and held each other's hands with their arms turned upward. The entire assembly of people then shouted three times and then sat down again.

He said, "Now the whole matter is completed."

At that time, the people then dispersed with some crossing the river to their side and others staying behind.

Ronikohewaneh then said, "This is the way it will continue to be in the future; there will always be families of people living on both sides of the river and deciding issues on both sides of the fire."

The Migration

The *onkwe:honwe* soon began to multiply, and they began to contemplate moving as their resources were becoming depleted. At that time, they lived along the banks of the long river that divided the turtle's back into two. There they lived near a nation whom they called the Wolves, who referred to themselves as the Paunee. At that time their languages were more familiar to one another.

Another people that became known as the Atsha'kahnha, Algonquins, traveled through their territory at that time. They had come from the northwest and were heading east, where they would settle and people a great nation that would live along the coast of the great water. There were brief skirmishes between the Atsha'kahnha and the *onkwe:honwe* for a time until the Atsha'kahna headed east where they would be called the Lenni Lenape grandfathers of the Atsha'kahnha of the eastern light.[1]

For a time, the *onkwe:honwe* prospered, until first drought and then a famine struck. This resulted in some of the people hoarding food and even turning to cannibalism. For a people who had always shared with one another, this was a hard time. Those who hoarded were renounced as witches and were put to death if they didn't share their goods.

The *onkwe:honwe* soon began to become fearful for the future, for the land was becoming desolate. A council was called, consisting of all the leading families of the *onkwe:honwe* and their cousins. At the council it was decided that they should move east toward the rising sun. One of the ancient mothers of the Great Turtle Clan stood up and said, "It is time that we find a new land for our crops. It will mean that we must leave these barren lands. I have had a dream that Teharonhia:wako will protect us along the way."

The ancient one was called Kaihonariosk, and she led the *onkwe:honwe* along the beautiful River Ohio that led to two bodies of water. While traveling along the river, the people came to a place where a fork made up of three rivers met. As the *onkwe:honwe* were crossing the river, the vine that they were holding broke, dividing the *onkwe:honwe*, just as many seasons before when the great young man formed the clan system.[2]

Kaihonariosk spoke up, "Now then, it appears Teharonhia:wako wants us to be divided again. Those of us who remain on the west bank of the river will travel north while those on the east side of the river will continue traveling east. When we arrive at our destinations, we will set up a trail so that we will always be connected to one another." The *onkwe:honwe* on the eastern side then continued their journey.

Some of those who went east came to another river, which they called the Susquehanna. These *onkwe:honwe* would one day become known as the Kanastoka. Still others moved along rivers that led to the southeast, right to the shore of the Great Turtle's back, where they came upon a great water that had resulted when Teharonhia:wako had split up the floating islands. These people became known as Skaroo'ren and would later be known as the Tuscarora, Hemp People, from their use of the plant. The Lenni Lenape would refer to some of these people who would split off as Nottaway, Adder Snakes. Farther south, another group became known as Tslagee and later as the Cherokee. They would later call themselves Ani-Kitawagi, People of the Great Mound City. Many years later, under the influence of a people known as the mound builders, some of these people would forget that they had once been brothers and sisters of the *onkwe:honwe* in the north, and they would battle against them along the beautiful river Ohio.

Those *onkwe:honwe* who followed Kaihonariosk traveled up the beautiful river to the north and made their way east along another river settled in a valley that ended near a great falls they called Cohoes. They would become known as the Kenienké:haka, later known as the Mohawk. They were named for the type of rock that they found that looked like crystal ice. There, their land was divided by another people who were the nephews of the Lenni Lenape and also referred to themselves as the Mahican, Wolves. To distinguish themselves from the Kenienké:haka, they referred to them as Makua, Bears. Kaihonariosk decided to take some of the Kenienké:haka and other *onkwe:honwe* farther north to a place by an even greater river they called Kahnawake for its rapids. They settled on a large island that was centered by a mountain shaped like a beaver.

A smaller group of *onkwe:honwe* moved next to the southern Kenienké:haka, settling near a lake, and they became known as the Oneota:haka, People of the Standing Stone, later known as the Oneida. They were named this because wherever they settled they would find the same boulder near them. Still west of them, settled another group of *onkwe:honwe*, whose main village was just north of a lake surrounded by many hills. They became known as the Onontaka:haka, People of the Hills, later known as the Onondaga. To the west of them settled another group, and they became known as Kaokwa:haka, later known as the Cayuga. They settled at the head and the mouth of one of the large body of waters carved out by Teharonhia:wako's fingers when he was creating the things on his island. They were known as the Mucky Lake People for the murky water due to the marshes on the north shore of the lake they would paddle their canoes through. Another name given to them later was the Big Pipe People, for they had learned the tradition of the big pipe from the Tutalo.

Another group of onkwe:honwe moved west of them and became known as the Sonontowa:haka, People of the Great Mountain, for it was there that they sprang up as a great nation and would become the most numerous of the onkwe:honwe. They were later known as the Seneca.

To the west of them settled the peaceful Kakwako, Feeding People, who would always be neutral by feeding the warriors who passed through. They lived near the Great Falls, Onakara, in between the first and second great body of water. They were the eastern relatives of the Tsakonsaséronon, who would be known as the Lynx nation for the furs that they wore.

Others went farther north, bounded between the first great body of water and a third great body of water in the north and became known for their trade in tobacco; therefore they were named Teyonontatah. Their closest relatives went even farther north settling in a fertile area becoming known as the Wendat or Islanders. Some of them had branched off from those who would become the Kenienké:haka and had moved with some of them to the island with the mountain by Kahnawake, on Kaniatarowanenneh, the large river.

As the onkwe:honwe became settled on their lands, life became fulfilling for them. One day, some of the young men wanted to retrace the footprints of their ancestors back along the long river. They decided that they would canoe down the long river that divided the turtle's back to see if any of their relatives remained there.

After canoeing for many days, they reached the long river and made their way down it. By this time there were many different nations of people living along the river whom they had never known before. Finally, they came to a village the size of which they had never seen.

The people of this village had a war leader who lived on a mountain that had been made by men. The *onkwe:honwe* had never seen such a thing before. They were flabbergasted by what was before them.

When they arrived, they were greeted by the leader and his people, fed and taken care of. It seemed that this leader ruled over an area of land that was as vast as the eye could see. From the top of the man-made mountain, the spiritual leaders of the society gave thanks to the Elder Brother the Sun. The *onkwe:honwe* saw that these people sometimes sacrificed their prisoners to the Elder Brother the Sun, by removing their hearts. They were told that by eating the hearts that it pleased the Elder Brother and empowered their warriors. They said they had learned this from an even greater people who lived on the tail of the Great Turtle. These people had been very distant cousins of the *onkwe:honwe*.

After many days of visiting, the *onkwe:honwe* decided it was time to go back to tell their people what they had seen. Before they left, the war leader of the great village told the *onkwe:honwe* men that he would like to visit their lands one day. He then shook hands with the *onkwe:honwe* men, and they left on friendly terms.

When they arrived back at their villages, they told their people about the great nation of people who now lived along the long river and made mountains. It was not long after that the *onkwe:honwe* heard that a great army paddling up the beautiful Ohio toward the territory of the *onkwe:honwe*. They were told that as this army moved forward they would build forts and mounds just like the *onkwe:honwe* men had seen when they followed the long river south. These mound builders had now moved up the beautiful river Ohio as far as the second great lake, where the Tsakonsaséronon lived, the lynx people. They did not appear to be coming in peace but rather for war and conquest.

The *onkwe:honwe* held a council with one another. They invited a delegation of people from the east, the Atsha'kahnha whom they had always had an uneasy relation with since the time they had moved through their lands when they lived by the long river. They were the Lenni Lenape easterners and their grandchildren the Mahican, Wolf, and Anishnaabe, Human Beings, from the east whom the *onkwe:honwe* referred to as

Atirontok, Bark Eaters, or Tehakanus, Speakers of a Different Language. The Atirontoks referred to the *onkwe:honwe* as Menk:we, later Mingo. They were also afraid of this threat from the south. At the council, it was decided that they would work together to defend themselves. They gathered as many of their people as they could, and they attacked the Mound Builders, at their fort on the beautiful Ohio, taking them by surprise by attacking them from behind.

This happened during the winter cold, and the Mound Builders having no experience with Sawiskera's power to freeze the earth were ill-prepared to survive in the harsh climatic conditions of the freezing winter. They became bogged down and while under siege began to starve. As they had been almost solely an agricultural people, they were running out of food supplies. The war lasted for many seasons until it finally broke; the *onkwe:honwe* and their allies forced the Mound Builders back to the lands from where they had come.[3]

3

The *Kayeneren:kowa* (Great Way of Peace)

The Birth of the Peacemaker

During the disputes with the Mound Builders, the *onkwe:honwe* had become experienced in warfare. This way of life went against everything that Teharonhia:wako had taught them about living in peace. Sawiskera seemed once again to be regaining control of the minds of the *onkwe:honwe*. At that time, the *onkwe:honwe* lived in small villages. Soon the strongest males and best warriors began to take over the leadership of the people. They stopped listening to the wise men and women elders. They even stopped doing their ceremonies. Disputes arose among the different peoples, and the *onkwe:honwe* were once again fighting with each other. It became no longer safe to walk the trails at night or in the day. There was even a war trail that extended right across the country that the *onkwe:honwe* traveled upon. This war trail went from the east to the west, through the great falls Onakara into the north through the *onkwe:honwe* villages, then south down the Susquehanna. There were times when alliances were made with each other and then broken.

The women began to become worried. They were no longer able to tend to their lands, as it was no longer safe to plant the corn, beans, and squash. The men even had to put up palisades around their villages in case of attack.

During a moment of peace, it was decided that only the women had the good sense to stop the warfare. The *onkwe:honwe* held a great council that included all the different Nations. They decided that they would find a virgin girl that had been hidden under the husk, who was pure of heart and had access to a lot of *orenta*, and place her on the war trail.

If any members of a Nation were attacked and they could make it to her lodge, she would mediate in the dispute. The person would be considered safe until she made her resolution to decide their fate. A bearskin would be hung in the middle of the lodge as a divider. The persons on the run would be given sanctuary by her and placed on one side of the divider. The attacking party would be allowed to enter the lodge but could only go as far as the divider where the refugees had found sanctuary. It would be up to the woman to intercede at this time and decide the fate of the persons being chased.[1]

It was decided by the great council that the woman would be placed in the country of the Kakwako, who were considered the most neutral people in the wars between the Nations. The neutral country ran in between the two great lakes where the Great Falls stood. They would refer to her village as Kienukah, and her name would be called Tsakonsasé, Round Face Like a Cat.

So important was her duty that it was decided that, when she departed to the Sky World, another would be chosen to follow and take her place and name. As was the custom among the *onkwe:honwe*, she would also feed the warring parties as they passed through her village. It was not long after that warriors were continually passing through Tsakonsasé's lodge and being fed by her. Soon after, there were so many parties trying to resolve their disputes that she couldn't keep up.

The different *onkwe:honwe* nations still were not abiding by the teachings of Teharonhia:wako. They stopped doing the four sacred ceremonies and began to fight among each other. The young men stopped listening to the elders and women, and they began to take to the warpath. Once again it was not safe to travel the paths at night. Women became fearful for the generations to come.

From the Wendat (Huron) country in the north to the Kenienké (Mohawk) country in the east, from the Oneota:haka (Oneida) next to them to the Onontake:haka (Onontaka) and, next to them from the Kaokwa:haka (Cayuga) to the Sonontowa:haka (Seneca) country in the west, the *onkwe:honwe* warred with one another and other Nations on Turtle Island.

The *onkwe:honwe* knew that there were two spirits that inhabited a person. One of the spirits was to go to the spirit world, while the other was to remain on the earth to help replenish it. They began to believe that by eating a portion of a warrior enemy, most notably the heart where the life-giving spirit lay, that they could acquire his life spirit energy, *orenta*, and then become more powerful warriors. Elders who knew the ceremonies of thanks and peace were replaced by powerful war chiefs who began to run the affairs of the people. Some of these war chiefs had acquired a lot of *orenta* by becoming cannibals, and they became feared by the people.

They began to use their *otkon*—the unnatural force that went against the laws of the one who created the bodies of the *onkwe:honwe*—*for evil purposes*. During this time, there was much sadness in the villages throughout Turtle Island.

Teharonhia:wako looked on his creation and became troubled by what the *onkwe:honwe* were doing to each other. The taking of a life went against the natural laws of creation. Ever since Sawiskera first killed his mother when the Earth World was new, the *onkwe:honwe* had been foretold of what would happen if a life was taken before its time. It seemed that Sawiskera had been able to turn the minds of the *onkwe:honwe* against the ways of Teharonhia:wako once again. Teharonhia:wako had said the last time that, if the people strayed from the path of peace, he would not return. However due to his great compassion for the *onkwe:honwe*, he had said that he would send someone to restore the minds and hearts of the *onkwe:honwe* if they ever turned away from him again. In fact, he had promised that he would do this three times, and, if the *onkwe:honwe* would not listen, Sawiskera would cause them to suffer from many things. The first person that he had sent was the young man who had helped when the *onkwe:honwe* had begun to live in extended families and began to die or move away from each other. He had brought them the clans to unify the families. The clans were based on the natural ways of creation.

Teharonhia:wako said that the worst thing that the *onkwe:honwe* could do was to fight among each other. Now, even the clan families had become too large, and the people no longer recognized each other. They were now living as separate nations among each other. He would send someone who could bring the different warring nations together to live in peace with each other. This would require someone with even greater abilities than the first, as his mission would be even more difficult. At the same time Sawiskera promised that he would find a way to disrupt the Great Peace.

On the north side of the war trail, on the north shore of a river divided by a mountain, was a Huron village named Kahoniyen, A Place Divided Between Two Rivers. In the village lived a woman named Kaheto:ktha, End of the Field, with her daughter Kahetihsuk, She Walks Ahead. Kaheto:ktha was very fearful for her daughter. There was so much warfare going on that she asked herself what kind of life her daughter would have if she remained where they were. One day she decided to leave the village with her daughter to find a place that was safe from the warriors and cannibals.

She traveled with her daughter down the war trail to the east, hiding in the bush whenever she heard any warriors coming. They traveled along the north shore of a lake until they came to a bay situated at the end of the eastern most great lake, Kanontar:io, known for its beauty.

Here, her daughter grew into womanhood. When she reached the age when her life-giving cycle began, her mother put her away to be hidden under the husk. It was during this time that a young girl would become most powerful. Her grandmother, the Moon in the Sky World would guide her for the rest of her living days. The *onkwe:honwe* had remembered the teachings of the Sky World, when the first woman had fallen through the hole in the sky and brought life to the earth.

It had been the custom at the time for the *onkwe:honwe* to put their children away for a period of instruction. For most girls, this would later be reduced from the time her cycle began until the time of her second cycle. Later on it would be from the beginning of the first cycle until it ended. During that time, she was not to be seen by men, touch the same food with her hands, pick medicines or touch the hunting tools of men. This was a time of purification and renewal for a young woman. Boys on the other hand would be secluded after being brought into a sweat lodge. For three days, they would drink the red willow bark, fast and be purified. It was at that time that they would obtain their guardian spirit and have their dreams interpreted for the first time by an elder.

During the time of seclusion, children were taught how to conduct themselves in society. Children learned how to walk and talk in a respectful manner. It was believed that if children hollered at night they could lose their voice. Boys would learn how to speak loud and firmly so that they would be heard in council. They would be bathed daily in the cold streams to make sure that their skin remained taut. The girls would be shown the roles they had to perform as women.

Marriages were also arranged at this time. Once they had reached adulthood, the boys would be taken to the longhouse of a girl of an appropriate age. The girl would have a basket of cornbread prepared for the boy. The boy would also have a basket of venison prepared for the girl. This was to show that the girl and the boy could provide for each other as well as their future family. The boy was not allowed to look at the girl until the time of marriage when they exchanged baskets consummating the marriage. Some special children were put away for a longer time, as it was believed that at that age they could obtain powerful *orenta*, the force that is in all life things.

After Kahetihsuk was hidden under the husk, it was not long before her mother noticed that she looked as if she were expecting a child. Kaheto:ktha began to become concerned and as the days passed her concern soon turned to anger.

One day, she confronted her daughter, "My daughter I have noticed changes taking place within your body. Who have you been seeing without my knowledge?"

Her daughter replied, "I have seen no one. I can't explain what is happening to me."

Kaheto:ktha became really angry as she didn't believe Kahetihsuk. She feared that perhaps an evil medicine man had afflicted her by using love medicine. It was not long after that Kahetihsuk gave birth to a boy child.

Kaheto:ktha would not accept him as she had become so enraged with what she believed to be her daughter's promiscuity. She began to believe that the child would bring bad luck to them, and so she decided to kill him. One day in the winter she took the boy for a walk. She cut a hole in the river and threw the child into it; he was swept away.

She then returned to the camp where she thought to herself, "I will tell my daughter that I took my grandson for a walk and he slipped by accident into the river where it had not frozen over."

When she arrived at the camp, she heard a young child crying. She looked and saw that the boy child was in the arms of her daughter. She was shocked and now believed the child must have been conceived by an evil spirit. The next morning she took the child again while her daughter was sleeping and dug a hole in the snow. She then buried the child and covered him up.

She said to herself, "I will tell my daughter that my grandson was taken by wolves."

When she arrived back at camp, she looked upon her daughter who was sleeping; sitting beside her was the boy child. Now she was truly convinced that the child was *otkon*, bad-spirited. On the third morning, she thought of the most horrible death that was used against those who used bad medicine. She made a fire and took the child and throwing him into it, she watched him burn.

When she arrived back at the camp, she heard the child crying; she became very distraught. That night as she was sleeping in her lodge, she heard a knock at the doorway of the lodge and heard a man's voice speaking. She could not see who it was in the shadows.

The voice said to her, "I have come from the west to relay a message to you. What you are doing is wrong. You must stop trying to take the life of your grandchild as he had been sent by the Creator to bring an important message of peace. Even you, who left your village to find a refuge where you could live in peace with your daughter, have been affected by Sawiskera. He will always try to find a way to deceive you so that he can gain control of creation and do it harm."

The spirit continued, "The child has been sent because there is so much bloodshed on the earth and creation is being destroyed. Sawiskera's influence is once again spreading among the *onkwe:honwe*, and they are becoming more and more divided. The boy should be named Tekana:wita, Two Currents Coming Down; that name will never be used by anyone else again. He will travel among the different warring nations and bring them back to live in peace."

Finally, the voice ended by saying, "Your daughter has done nothing wrong and you should reconcile with her." Kaheto:ktha watched the shadowy figure walk away, disappearing into the darkness.

The next day, Kaheto:ktha looked out her lodge to see where the man had gone. She wondered if it had all been a dream. She noticed that the tracks on the ground were not those of a human being. They looked like they were the tracks of a Great Hare.

The next day, the grandmother took her daughter into her arms and said to her, "My daughter, I feel sorry about the way I have treated you and my grandchild. My mind was deceived by Sawiskera. I came here with you to this place with good intentions and, instead, became as destructive as the warriors. From now on, I will take care of you and my grandchild."

She continued to tell her daughter, "Last night I was visited by a messenger from the Sky World who told me that my grandson will bring a message of peace to the warring villages. We are to name him Tekana:wita, for like two streams flowing together he is born of both the Sky World and the Earth World, and they always work together for what is right. I will do everything to ensure that my grandson grows up to fulfill his destiny."

Kaheto:ktha, in not treating him well, had done the same thing to the Peacemaker that Teharonhia:wako's grandmother had done to him. It would be a further reminder to the *onkwe:honwe* that they should treat all their children properly no matter who they were. It would not be the grandmother's duty any longer to discipline a child as this could have grave consequences for his future. This would be left to the boy's uncle on his mother's side. That would ensure that the grandmother no longer took sides. It was not long after that the boy child began to grow and mature at a quicker pace than normal.

One day, Kaheto:ktha told her daughter and grandson, "I believe that it is time to go back to our village Kahoneyen."

Tekana:wita was really excited as he wanted to meet his relations whom he had never seen before. Before they left, he said to his mother and grandmother, "I am glad that we are going back to the village where you came from. I have a message to tell them so that they will care for one another again."

They then set off for the village that they had left many years before. After they had lit a fire to warn the village that they were coming, two warriors came out to greet them. They then brought them to the *rarontaron,* war chief, who was the head of the village. Kaheto:ktha asked him, "Do you remember my daughter and I who left this village many years ago?"

The war chief answered, "We thought you were killed or taken captive by warriors. It is a surprise to see you alive. Since you left there have been many who have been killed, including many of your relations. I will notify the people that you have returned."

The war chief called a meeting of the people to see for themselves that Kaheto:ktha was alive and had returned. Once everyone was assembled, the war chief stood up and said to Kaheto:ktha, "I have made a special place for you to sit; now I want to know why you have returned to us."

Kaheto:ktha answered, "I have returned because my grandson has a message to relay to the people about living in peace once again. Since I have left, there are many of you who are no longer here. Our minds have been deceived by Sawiskera into believing that it is all right to kill one another. Even I, who left with peaceful intentions, became that way toward my grandson. Now I know the truth and have come back to tell you so."

The crowd listened and became excited when they heard her story. They noticed that the boy had a way about him that was more like an elder than a child. While this was going on, Tekana:wita had noticed the other young boys, and he began to play with them. They were playing *Tewaarathon, lacrosse,* the little brother of war also known as the Creator's game. The boys began to play rough, hitting each other around the chest, as if they were being prepared for war when they got older. Soon, they began to fight among themselves, and the smaller ones were getting hurt.

Tekana:wita yelled to them, "Stop what you are doing! Why do you continue to play games of war? Did not anyone in the village tell you that using the Creator's game to prepare for warfare was against the will of Teharonhia:wako?"

Some of the elders were watching and listening, they were surprised at what he was saying. Warfare had become a way of life for the *onkwe:honwe,* and they had not heard anyone speak against it for many years. The other boys went to their lodges and told their parents about the strange ways of the new boy and what he had told them. The elders, upon hearing what had happened, wanted to hear for themselves what Tekana:wita had to say. They asked the *rarontaron,* war chief, to call an assembly where all could hear him speak. The war chief agreed and called for an assembly; when it opened Tekana:wita was told to relay his message.

Tekana:wita said to the people, "I have come to stop the bloodshed because what you are doing is wrong. I want to bring a message that consists of three things. They are peace, power, and righteousness. There is to be no more warfare from now on, and you are to put away your weapons. The rivers are the veins of Mother Earth, and everything flows in a certain orderly direction. Today, instead of the natural waters, the rivers are flowing with the blood of the dead who have been killed in battle. By continuing to war among yourselves, you are cutting off the natural creation. We are only visitors to this world, and only the Creator has the right to decide when the creation may be cut off. Inside of us, we carry both a spirit and a soul, and, when we die, the spirit remains near the body, while the soul travels the path of souls to the Sky World. It is up to us to be respectful of the natural processes as set down by the Creator. To kill each other destroys the harmony of that process. In peace we can become much more powerful than when at war with each other. This can only be done through righteous living. Righteous living only comes from having a good mind."

The people listened attentively to what Tekana:wita had to say. The elders asked the war chief if they could meet in council and decide what course of action they were to going to take. The war chief agreed with the elders and the next day they counseled with each other. They then called another assembly.

The war chief said to the people, "The war chiefs and elders have decided that the people will put down their weapons and stop living in fear. We will try to begin a new way of living in peace with each other." The war chief, then asked Tekana:wita, "Without weapons, how will we defend ourselves from the warriors of other nations?"

Tekana:wita answered, "Give it time, I still have a lot of work to do."

When the war chief had finished, the people said to him, "Let us have a feast to commemorate this occasion." They then began to hug and congratulate Tekana:wita, his mother, and grandmother; for the first time the anxiety of fear of being killed was no longer within them. Tekana:wita would be remembered as the one who brought peace to the Wendat, and from this time on he was to be referred to as Skennenrahawi, The Peacemaker.

After living in the village for a time, the Peacemaker informed his mother and grandmother, "One day, we will have to go back to the place where I was born, for I have to prepare for the great work that I will embark upon."

Every morning the Peacemaker would leave and not return until it became dark. The other parents noticed that the other male children would follow him. They began to wonder what he was up to.

One of the mothers of the boys asked the Peacemaker, "Why do you and the other children leave every morning? Where are you going and what are you up to?"

He answered her, "I am doing the work that I was sent to do."

She decided that she was going to follow the children and see what they were doing. She noticed a path that went up a hill. There she saw the boys assembled sitting in a circle.

She called out and asked, "What are you boys doing there?"

One of the boys replied, "The Peacemaker is teaching us three of the ceremonies. They are the great sacred Feather Dance, the Drum Dance and the Personal Song."

During the time of warfare the people had forgotten how to give thanks to the Creator. They had forgotten once again the ceremonies that Teharonhia:wako had given them.

The woman then said, "I had heard stories about them but have never seen them done." The boys then showed her what they had been taught, and pretty soon the village began to perform the ceremonies once again.

When the boys were older, the Peacemaker said to them, "Today is the last day that I will teach you, as I have to leave. It will be up to you to continue to teach the ceremonies to the generations of unborn."

He told them, "When you become old, you are to gather together at this same place, and I will return to show you the last ceremony." The

Peacemaker then walked around a tree, and he disappeared from sight. He was later seen in the village talking to his grandmother as they were preparing to leave the village.

Many years later, when the boys had turned into old men, they decided to visit their old learning place, wondering what had happened to the boy who had taught them so much about giving thanks. One of them looked up and saw a man appear from behind the tree. It was the Peacemaker, who was now old like they were.

He said to the boys, "I crossed the great water to where our Creator's brother had his island. He said when you see this sign, beware, for there will be a great changes coming to you as Sawiskera's influence will be hard to resist." He then raised his hands and showed where they had become bloodied.

He explained, "I have come back for one last reason, that is, to remind you how to once again do the fourth ceremony that decided the fate of the world when it was first young. This is the Plum Stone Game, which will later be the Peach Stone Game."

He continued, "Remember, to always do this ceremony as it will remind you that the world can once again be in precarious state as a result of Sawiskera's influence if you are not vigilant."

He explained, "When you offer this to the Creator, it will make him happy, for he will know that you have remembered him. As long as you perform the ceremonies and give thanks, you will be able to live in peace among yourself." Then he disappeared once again around the tree.

The Peacemaker and his family left the village to return to the place where he was born, at the hill where the eagles flew. He began to prepare himself for the journey he was about to undertake.

One day, he took his grandmother up to the top of Eagle Hill. He said to her, "*Duta*,[2] I must leave, but watch first." He then pointed to a maple tree nearby and took out his knife. Approaching the tree he slashed it, and the sap began to drip from it.

"*Duta*," he said, "After I leave this place, every once in a while take a knife and cut the tree. If ever you see the tree sap run the color red, you will know that something has happened to me."

Next, the Peacemaker began to build a canoe from white stone that would carry him on his journey. He then told his mother and grand-mother, "I am ready to leave, and I will not be returning."

His grandmother prepared him something to eat so that he wouldn't be hungry along the way. She pulverized some corn and said to him, "If you ever go hungry my grandson, eat some of this and then drink some water. It will cause your belly to swell and you will be full."

The Peacemaker Brings the Message of Peace to the Kenienké:haka

The Peacemaker then set out on his journey and crossed on the north side of the beautiful lake, Kanontar:io. On the south side of the lake there stood a man who was watching. He could see a glimmering light approaching from the other side. He had left his Kenienké:haka village because of the violence that was taking place there. He had dreamed that one day some-one would come and bring back the ways of peace among his people.

This man was named Torewater:io, which means I Do Everything Right. He had been named this because he was a man of great integrity. As he looked at the lake while the sun reflected overhead, he could see the glittering object approaching over the horizon. It was moving swiftly and seemed to be swerving from side to side as it approached. It was not long before Torewater:io could see that it was a man approaching in a white canoe. Torewater:io was curious, and, although afraid, he decided to stay and watch. As the canoe approached, he decided to hide in the nearby bushes, and, if the person appeared friendly, he would greet him. After the Peacemaker arrived on the shore, Torewater:io could see that the man had no weapons.

He then stepped from the bushes and asked the Peacemaker, "Where have you come from?"

The Peacemaker replied, "I have come from the north, where the peo-ple are now settling into lives of peace."

He then asked Torewater:io, "Where do you come from?"

Torewater:io answered, "I have come from a Kenienké:haka village with my family to flee from the warfare that is going on there."

The Peacemaker remembered that his family had also fled their village years ago for the same reason. The Peacemaker then said to Torewater:io, "I have come to stop the killing that is going on between the Creator's children here on Turtle Island."

He continued, "I want the warring peoples to have respect for one another, be generous, and live in peace."

Next, he said, "Do not be afraid. You should go home to the land of the Kenienké:haka and tell the people that I will arrive one day at their village with a message for them."

Torewater:io looked at the Peacemaker with curiosity. "Who is this strange man?" he asked himself.

He then warned the Peacemaker, "There are many other people living in the area that are killing each other. There are cannibals who eat the hearts of other warriors, as well as those who practice witchcraft, who would kill you on the spot if you tried to approach them."

The Peacemaker answered him, "That is why I am here. Those are the people that I want to meet." Torewater:io and the Peacemaker then parted ways.

When Torewater:io went back to his wife and children, whom he had hid in the bushes, he told them, "I have met a strange man that came across the great lake that divides our people in the north from those living in the south. His canoe seemed to be made from stone. I believe that this man is going to stop the warfare. We should return to our village to tell the Kenienké people of this great event that is going to take place." They then packed up and left for home.

After many days of walking, trying to avoid the paths of war, they arrived at their village near the great waterfalls and rapids. Torewater:io approached the war chief and told him about the man he met and the message he was spreading.

The war chief listened and then laughed at Torewater:io. He said to him, "We the Kenienké:haka are powerful. Tell me one other people who may enter our territory without facing the wrath of the Kenienké warriors. Why should I be concerned about a foolish man's message who has probably been killed by now?" All of the warriors except one, agreed, and

Torewater:io was looked upon from then on by the villagers as being a fool.

Torewater:io thought to himself, "Perhaps it would be better if I left with my family once again."

However, because one of the assistant war chiefs' had believed what he had to say, he was not alone, so he decided to stay. They both had faith that one day the messenger would come, and Torewater:io would be believed.

The assistant war chief, who had believed Torewater:io, was a man of strong character, and he decided that he would be silent and wait for the messenger to come. He had originally come from the Onontaka nation whom the Kenienké people had been at war with and ended up marrying one of their influential women. He had already lost his wife in a raid by the warriors of another nation, and he didn't want the same thing to happen to his three daughters for whom he cared very much.

Meanwhile, the Peacemaker headed west to the land of the Kakwako, The Place of the Food, at the village of Kienukah. He arrived at a lodge near the great water falls, Onakara. It was situated at the intersection of the war trail that ran from the east to the west and the one that went from the north to the south. It was the lodge where Tsakonsasé lived, the neutral woman who fed and took care of the warriors. Tsakonsasé seeing the Peacemaker coming and, thinking he was a warrior on the run, said to him, "Come in. Who is chasing you?"

The Peacemaker said to her, "I understand that you have been given the job of being a council to the warriors. You not only mediate between their disputes but feed them as well."

He then told her, "Listen to me, there is a greater purpose for you and the other women. Right now, the way things are, you are part of the killing that is going on. Instead of being simply the mediator between the feuding warriors, there is a more important job for you to do. Soon there will be no need for warriors, and you must use your gift to a higher purpose; there will be a new role for you to play. Once I abolish all the *rarontaron*, war chiefs, by ending warfare, the new leaders that I choose will need someone to keep them in line. This message that I bring will need a strong backbone in order to hold it together after I am gone. It will be up to each headwoman of the different clans to choose the representatives of the people and their successors and to make sure that they do the will of the people. The women of the clans will be the ones who will crown them. They will also set the dates of the ceremonies, as they follow the cycle of Grandmother Moon. They will also name the children from the clan names that they hold. All the male leaders will look up to the head matrons of the clans and abide by their will. The head matrons get the consent of the people at the women's council. The clans will move into a new type of dwelling that will be built from the direction of the east to the west, and the Clan Matron will be its head."

He continued, "This longhouse that they will live in will represent an even greater dwelling that will include all the nations who accept the message of peace; it shall run from the nations living in the east to the nations living in the west. It will be shaped like the Sky World with an ever-growing tree in the middle. I will place something on top of the tree to watch over it as was done by Ancient Uncle, the thunder, in the Sky World before the creation of this world."

Finally, he finished by telling her, "Today is a new day and the sun is beginning to rise in the east where we will begin to build this Longhouse of One Family; when it is built, it will brighten the world. The higher the sun shines, the more people will become a part of the Great Peace and want to live in this house with us."

He continued, "There is a day when everything that I have come for will be fulfilled, and you, Tsakonsasé, should be present when it happens. The earth is something none of us can own because it belongs to everyone. The respect for it is being lost in the fighting. Sawiskera has deceived you and is gaining control of the minds of the *onkwe:honwe*. I have been sent to restore them so that they will have good minds once again."

When he had finished, Tsakonsasé warned the Peacemaker, "You must be careful because there are cannibals living in the direction that you are going."

The Peacemaker looked at her and replied, "Those are the ones that I am looking for."

He then departed, telling Tsakonsasé, "We will meet again soon when the nations of the house of one family come together. You will be the mother of all the nations from where the four white roots of the tree that I will plant will spread."

As he headed on the war trail toward the east, the Peacemaker came upon a lodge. Surrounding it were the remains of discarded human bones. The Peacemaker knew that this was one of the cannibals that Tsakon-sasé warned him about. These warrior cannibals were feared because they would cut the hearts out of the warriors they had killed and bite into them, claiming the life spirit of the victim as their own. This was said to give them great power in battle. Sawiskera had so influenced them that they had become monstrous like his creatures. These warriors roamed the earth killing anything in sight.

Upon seeing the cannibal approaching, the Peacemaker climbed to the roof of the cannibal's lodge. He could see the cannibal carrying a human body over his shoulder. The cannibal placed the body down in front of his lodge and began to dissect it, going for the heart first. He then bit into the heart of the dead warrior. Next, he cut the body up, placing some of the pieces of the heart in a wooden cauldron inside. He then boiled water in a fire outside the lodge and poured it into the wooden vessel.

The Peacemaker could see what the cannibal was doing through the smoke hole in the lodge above the wooden vessel.

Inside the lodge under the smoke hole, the cannibal began to cook a meal from the rest of the heart of the dead warrior. As the cannibal went to test his meal, he looked into the vessel and saw a face looking back at him in the reflection of the water. For a moment, he thought it might be his own refection, so he looked again. Once again a face appeared. He proceeded to do it a third time, and upon, looking into the vessel, he noticed that there was a radiance that reflected from the face.

At first he said, "Is that my face? Can I be so handsome?"

Then he became afraid, he knew that someone such as himself could not render such radiance. It was the Peacemaker's face that he saw looking down at him from the smoke hole. The image he saw in the refection before him made the cannibal awestruck.

He began to think to himself, "What kind of a life have I led—all of the killing I have participated in, all of the hearts that I have eaten? How can I change my ways? If only there were a way to stop; I promise myself, I will never kill another person again."

He then went around his lodge and began to collect the bones of the warriors to bury them properly. The Peacemaker, knowing the cannibal was truly remorseful and ready, climbed down from the lodge and appeared before him.

He asked the cannibal, "Tell me, what is your purpose in life? What are you burying in the ground?" For some reason, instead of killing this man who stood before him, the cannibal felt compelled to speak to him.

The cannibal answered, "My purpose in life so far has been to kill everyone who gets in my way. I am burying the remains of the *onkwe:honwe* I have killed and eaten."

He told the Peacemaker, "I have just made a promise to myself that I would never kill or eat the hearts of humans again." The cannibal felt remorseful for the life that he led, and he wanted to change.

The Peacemaker told him, "Do not think of the past, but look forward to the brightness of the future ahead of you. I have come to stop the warfare and killing that is going on among the *onkwe:honwe*. Until this time, your mind has been deceived by Sawiskera, the Creator's brother. When you come to understand this, you will know how to be more vigilant in your actions."

The cannibal replied, "I want to know more, so come in and enter my lodge."

After they entered, the Peacemaker said to the cannibal, "Wait for me here. I will be back shortly. I am going out to hunt a deer, and I will return soon. Make sure that you boil new water, so that we can have boiled venison when I return."

Not long after, the Peacemaker returned carrying a buck deer on his back. They both skinned the deer and boiled some venison and then proceeded to eat it. The Peacemaker said to the cannibal as they were eating, "The buck deer is a wise animal, very cautious when it comes to his family. They are also messengers to the Creator, as their name means the first to the spirit world. Whenever you hunt one of these, you must make sure that you let the first one go free. He will tell the others that you are a respectful person. When you do kill one, you must make an offering of tobacco for thanks. The buck deer will then tell the Creator about your good nature."

The Peacemaker continued, "After you have killed the deer, you will use the antlers, skin, and tendons. The meat from the deer will be sustenance for the people. There will be no more killing of humans and eating of hearts."

The Peacemaker went on to explain, "When everyone lives in peace, you will be like one family living in one longhouse facing the east to the west. The clan matrons of the longhouse of one family will choose from their clans the representatives of their people from one of the males in each of their families. Like the buck and doe deer, the representatives and clan matrons will work together on behalf of the Longhouse of One Family. Once the representatives are chosen by the clan matrons, they will have horns placed on their heads. Like the buck deer, the representatives will raise their antlers and watch over the people. The horns of the deer have power that can sense danger coming. The representatives will wear the horns of the deer in council in order to watch over the affairs of the people on the ground. They will also place an eagle feather in between the horns so that they may see far ahead like the eagle and the cap it is placed in will be shaped like the Sky World."

After the Peacemaker had relayed his message to the cannibal and just before he departed, he said to him, "Each place that I travel to, I will add something more. One day, we will all meet at the center of the Longhouse of One Family where the Great Tree of Peace will be planted."

The Peacemaker then parted from the cannibal and headed toward the east. After many days of travel and bypassing a number of villages, he stopped at an embankment, where there were some rapids below and the great Cohoes falls. He had arrived at the easternmost part of the territory of the Kenienké:haka, near Cohoes Falls at the place called Skanehtateh Kahuntah, the river below the openings. It was at this spot that the Peacemaker decided to begin to build his Longhouse of One Family; it was time for him to put up the first rafter.

This was situated about a mile from the trail that divided the Kenienké:haka from the Mahican, Wolf People. The Kenienké:haka had been known and feared as great warriors by many of the surrounding nations, including the nation of wolves that lived next to them. The wolves referred to them as Mohawkwa from their word meaning bear. Even their real name Kenienké:haka or Flint People denoted their power as fighters. Flint was also the name given to Sawiskera who had killed the first mother of the world with his sharpness of the cold. Flint was what many *onkwe:honwe* used to kill when hunting for food for it was what the arrowhead was made of. Flint could also be made very sharp, and it was used in the arrows of the warriors during battle.

The next morning the Kenienké:haka of the Anon:wara Turtle Clan, of the village of Ronakowaneh, woke up to give thanks to the first sunlight as had been the custom. They noticed smoke coming from the direction of the river. They knew that it was the custom when approaching a village that the visitors would light a fire so that the people in the village would not be afraid. The idea was that the village would then send two runners out to see who was arriving. This would ensure that the visitors were coming in peace. At that time, the Kenienké:haka had a main war chief and two assistants living in their village. Upon seeing the smoke from the fire, *oyenkonton:kowa*, runners, were sent out, and, when they arrived at the embankment overlooking the falls and the river, they noticed a strange man smoking a pipe.

He called to them, "Come over here. I mean no harm to you."

As they approached him, he said, "Allow me to enter your village, for I have come to tell your war chiefs and your people something of importance."

One Kenienké:haka warrior asked, "Who are you? Why should we listen to you? We can kill you and eat you right now."

The Peacemaker replied, "Allow me to be heard before you pull your weapons on me. Go to your *rarontaron*, war chief, and say that I want to speak to him first. If you are not satisfied with my message, you can kill me."

They said to the Peacemaker, "We will go tell him, and we will be back." They left to return to their village.

At the village they told the *rarontaron:kowa*, great war chief, about the strange man who was sitting on the embankment overlooking the river.

The war chief, now curious, said to them, "Go back and tell this man he may enter the village. I am interested in what this brave man has to say." The two runners went to get the Peacemaker, and they escorted him to their village, Ronakowaneh.

As was the custom, the great war chief made arrangements for where the Peacemaker would sit. The war chief then called for him to be brought before him. As he was brought forward, the great war chief and his two assistants gathered in front of the Peacemaker. They were all members of the Turtle Clan, as this was a Turtle Clan village. The Peacemaker was seated in front of them wondering what they would do.

The great war chief spoke out into the gathering saying, "I have been waiting to see if a man would come bring a great message for our people. I believe that this may be the man that Torewater:io told us about. Let us put up our ears and listen to what he has to say."

The Peacemaker stood up, as was the custom of the tribesmen when speaking. He told them, "I did send a message back with the man whom I met at the lake on the day that I arrived on its shores, that one day I would come to Kenienké:haka. However, I have heard that since that time you have doubted me. Because of this you have given Torewater:io a hard time. When I first met him, I asked him to go back and tell you that there is a better way of living than the way of warfare. The message, that I bring you, begins with peace."

He continued, "Peace can only come when the people have a good mind and can live together in harmony with one another. When that happens, everyone will be of one mind, and then they will become powerful. In order to have a good mind, one has to live a righteous life. The Creator is sad for what he sees happening on the earth. Many good people have passed away because of the warriors and the killing that has come from them. There are bones lying all over the ground. I have come to stop the fighting and bring back good minds to the people. Warfare will be replaced by caring, respect, and generosity."

He continued, "Many years ago Teharonhia:wako said to your ancestors that he would send someone to end the strife between the *onkwe:honwe*. Your minds have become deceived once again by his brother Sawiskera. I will warn you that once you accept my message, if you kill each other again you will suffer the consequences. There is another thing, in order to accept this message, war chiefs must be the first to throw away their weapons of war. A new leader will be chosen and once all have been selected they will become a peace chief known as a *royaner*, Tree of Equal Height. If *royaner* choose to take up the path of war, this will mean that they no longer have a good mind and must give their title back to their Clan Mother. Once they take the path of war, they may never be *royaner* again for their duty is to always try and keep the peace."

The great war chief stood up and spoke, "I like the message that you have given us. However, I still have my doubts about whether it will work."

The war chief's assistant then spoke out, "I agree with our leader. I don't trust him. Let him prove himself first. If he really is so great and was sent by our Creator he must be invincible. Here is my proposition. By the great gorge overlooking the river, there is a tree with a branch hanging over it. If this man really has been sent by the Creator, let him prove it. Let the man sit on the branch of the tree, and we will cut it down. If the man can survive the fall into the gorge, then we will consider what he has to say."

The war chief was convinced that the Peacemaker would be killed and that would be the end of the matter. It was at this same gorge that a Kenienké:haka warrior had ended his own life falling into the falls in a clan dispute over a girl.

The Peacemaker answered the war chief, "I will do as you ask, as long as all the people are witnesses to what occurs."

The next day all the Kenienké:haka of the village gathered at the gorge, including the war chief and his two assistants. They surrounded the tree and asked the Peacemaker to climb it and sit on the branch overlooking the gorge. The Peacemaker then climbed up and sat on the branch overlooking the river below. The warriors then got out their stone flint hatchets and proceeded to cut the branch down. They watched as the Peacemaker tumbled below into the river and was swept away in the strong current. Then, they all went back to the village.

The war chief said to the villagers, "The matter has been settled, and you have been witnesses to it. This man was either very brave or a fool; nonetheless, he is gone and will not be returning." The villagers then went to sleep. Both Torewater:io and the assistant war chief who believed him felt distraught and humiliated. Neither of them could sleep that night.

The next morning, one of the warriors, curious upon waking up, decided to go back to the gorge to see if he could find the body of the Peacemaker. As he began to walk toward the gorge, he could see smoke from a fire in the distance. He was frightened as to whom it might be this early in the morning; he ran back to the village to warn the war chief and the warriors. The war chief gathered the warriors together and sent two runners to see who was camping by the river.

As they approached the fire, they could see that it was the man they had placed on a branch who had been cut down into the river. They became afraid. As they were still not completely sure he was not malicious they asked him, "Who are you, and why have you come here?"

The Peacemaker answered, "I am the one that you forced into the gorge the other day. Do you have enough proof as to why I have come or do you need more? Each time you doubt me, you may cost another life."

One of the warriors said to him, "Come back to the village with us and speak to our war chief."

The Peacemaker answered, "Go back to your village and prepare the villagers for my entrance. I will not be staying long, for I still have a lot of work to do."

Before entering the village, the war chief had prepared a special seat for the Peacemaker, and the villagers waited in anticipation of his arrival. It was not long after that he appeared, and the villagers made two lines to allow him to pass through. Normally, they might have beaten him with sticks to test his bravery. This would not be necessary, for he had already proven himself to them.

The two warriors then escorted him into the council house and sat him beside the great war chief. Once there, the great war chief said to the Peacemaker, "We asked proof from you, and you gave it to us. We must therefore accept your message. In my heart I waited for you to come, yet at the same time I believe that Torewater:io had become deranged when he first told us about you. It is my belief that great changes are about to occur among us. I accept the great tidings of peace, power, and righteousness that you are bringing us."

Next, the two assistant war chiefs said, "We also accept the message of the Peacemaker." Finally, the great war chief asked the people who had gathered if they agreed. All the people answered in the affirmative.

The great war chief turned to the Peacemaker and said, "I have heard your message but would like to have a further explanation of what it means."

The Peacemaker answered, "Peace means that everyone will have a good mind and be of one voice and live as one family. When one person accepts this principle, others will follow; that is where the power will come from. Like a ball in the snow, we will let it roll; with each turn it will get larger. That is the way it will be when others accept the message that I will bring you. Peace, power, and righteousness really mean living without fear of one another. When we put our minds together, we can unite. From that unity comes strength of purpose. We will elevate a new type of representative of the people who will live by the principle of having a good mind. There will be no more war chiefs running our villages as there will be no more need for warfare among us."

He then turned to the great war chief, "You, great leader of the Kenienké:haka, will be first on the roll call of chiefs because of your position. You will put down your title as war chief, have a good mind and become a *royaner*. You will always work on behalf of the people for peace. Because you first doubted me and were not sure, I will name you and all those who will take your place in the future Tekarihokenh, He Was of Two Minds. In order to ensure that you keep the peace, I have appointed the headwomen of your clan to choose who will succeed you and the other *royaner*, peace chiefs, that will be chosen. You are to abide by the will of the council of women as well as men. It is the women who have the consensus of the community, and it is they who have the best interests of the children at heart."

Then, the Peacemaker turned toward one of the assistant war chiefs. He said, "You, great leader, who never slept while anticipating my arrival will be the second that I will elevate as *royaner* of the Kenienké:haka. From now on, you will put away all your thoughts and actions to do with warfare. From now on you will work on behalf of the Creator. I will give you a new name that you will carry until you leave this world. It will then be passed on by the women of the clan that you belong to; when your days are numbered it will go to another. I pronounce you Ayenwatha, Hiawatha, He Who Is Awoke. That is because you waited for me to come; one day you will discover a way to make sure that everything that happens here will be remembered."

He continued, "You will always be first among the *royaner* although you will be second on the roll call of chiefs. We have great work to do together. You will become my voice whenever we travel together. When I first brought the message of peace to the nations in the north, I did not devise a plan that would allow it to last for time immemorial. This will be our task that we will accomplish together in the future. We will work out a way so that we may ensure the peace remains forever. As long as the *onkwe:honwe* follow it, they will survive. Beware though; Sawiskera will try every means to fool you."

Then he turned to the other assistant war chief, he told him, "You, who doubted me as well and became confused as to what to do, will no longer be a war chief either. From now on you will have to work on behalf of your people. I will name you Shatekariwateh, Matters of Equal Height. I name you this because you could have gone either way in your decision.

Then he told them, "In the future, once we set our foundation for coming together, you three will be brothers Ahsenhninontatekenah."

Then the Peacemaker spoke to all of the assembled and said. "The Great Peace is not prejudiced against anyone; if people want to become a part of it, they may do so as long as they have a good mind. You chiefs are to make sure that the teachings that I give you will be passed on. That is your duty as *royaner*. You must never take sides on an issue for or against any group. Decisions must always be unanimous. These will be some of the roles that you must fulfill."

He then told them, "When I have got rid of the war chiefs ruling the villages, the *otiyaner*, Clan Matrons, of the families will choose the best men that they can find to fill the positions as good-minded ones. I will officially choose you first three from the Kenienké:haka war chiefs when all of the nations meet together. In the meantime Tsakonsasé and the Clan Matrons will choose the rest."

Tekarihokenh then asked the Peacemaker, "How will we be able to protect ourselves from the other nations who live near us and continue to make war on us?"

The Peacemaker answered, "I will visit those nations and bring the message of peace to them as well. When there are enough nations living together under the way of peace, you will be strong enough to ward off any attack. Instead of war you will use persuasion. You are to always use your good mind to avoid conflict, whether in council among yourselves or with others. It is Sawiskera who first killed, and it is he who influences you to kill each other even today. There will be those who will take up the path of Sawiskera, and, when they do, they will not be able to get off his path in this life or in the next."

Finally, he said, "I must depart and visit a powerful war lord who has supernatural powers and lives to the west of you. He sits on a stone shaped like a phallus by a stream overlooking a village, influencing others with his power who may one day want to listen to my message. However, first I must clear a pathway for them to walk on. One day, you will hear a cry that will echo throughout the land. It will be the war lord with the supernatural powers. Three times, you will hear him holler *"Asokane,"*—is it time? That will tell you that he is expecting us to come and do battle, and he is becoming impatient. That will be the time when all the Kenienké:haka will gather and meet at the place of the standing stone, where the Oneota:haka of that name live. Upon arriving there, we will do more of this great work."

The Oneota:haka Join the Great Peace

The Peacemaker then left the Kenienké:haka and began to travel west. The Kenienké:haka began to work the Great Peace among their people, passing the message that the Peacemaker had given them to their brothers and sisters. From the great Cohoes Falls to the place past where the little falls runs, the Kenienké:haka began to live in peace. Still they were afraid of their enemies that lived to the west of them. The hardest worker in passing the message of peace was Ayenwatha.

Ayenwatha had three daughters. Years before he had lost his wife in a raid on his village. His daughters were his pride and joy, and they were soon to be married. It was not long after the Peacemaker had left that his oldest daughter became ill. The medicine societies and herbalists tried to work their medicine, but it was to no avail. They told Ayenwatha that someone very powerful must be working bad medicine to bring this misfortune to her. It was not long after that Ayenwatha's daughter passed away. Ayenwatha was burdened with grief. He had no way of expressing it, and it soon began to quail in his throat. He could not even speak about it. The only thing that gave him comfort was his two remaining daughters.

It was not long after his first daughter passed away, that his second daughter also became ill. Once again the medicine society was called in, and they failed to find the cure. Soon she also died. Now, Ayenwatha was burdened with even greater grief. He couldn't speak to anyone about it. When others tried to console him, he wouldn't hear them. He had become deaf to what anyone had to say. The only thing that was carrying him through was seeing his youngest remaining daughter.

The people of his Kenienké:haka village became concerned with Ayenwatha's health. They decided that they would call all the men from the villages and hold a lacrosse game for Ayenwatha, in order to amuse him and lift up his spirits.

Since the beginning of time, *Tewaarathon*, lacrosse, had been played by the *onkwe:honwe* as a form of amusement for the Creator. It involved many men from the villages and was played in the fields. The fields sometimes could go on for miles. The people felt that this would surely lift the spirits of Ayenwatha and that the Creator in watching the game might be looking over him.

The men began to play the game, and all was going well. As usual, it was full contact and rough. At this time, Ayenwatha's daughter had become pregnant. She was crossing the field bringing a vessel of water to her father who was watching the game. One of the players called out to her for some water. At the same time a player threw a pass in her direction. All of a sudden, as the men were running, they heard a cry in the heavens three times. It sounded like "*Asokanee*," meaning, is it time?

Everyone turned to look up into the sky to see flying above a strange purple bird that no one had ever seen before. As they were looking up and running, they didn't notice that Ayenwatha's daughter was in their path.

They trampled over Ayenwatha's daughter. Ayenwatha stood and looked on in a state of shock. He ran to see if there was any life in his daughter's body, but he could find none. The next day, the village began to mourn her passing.

Ayenwatha was so completely burdened with sorrow that he would not look at anyone. He decided that he had to leave his village to sort out his thoughts. For many days and nights he traveled west, passing all the Kenienké:haka villages and avoiding anyone in his path. He wondered why he, who had worked so hard to bring peace to the people, had to suffer so much. "Where was the Creator to help me?" he asked. Ayenwatha then went into complete seclusion.

One day he stopped and noticed that there were some elderberry bushes along the way. He took a sapling from the bush and made a string of it. He then made a tripod on each side and placed a stick between them. Sitting in front of it, he spoke for the first time in weeks saying to himself, "If anyone was burdened with grief like me, I would make sure that someone was there to console him. I would take the skin of a young fawn and wipe away the tears from their eyes so they could clearly see hope in the future." Then he placed one of the elderberry strings over the stick.

Next, he said, "I would go talk to the person and clear their ears and take out the clogs that block them from listening to those who come to console." He then placed another string over the stick.

Finally, he said, "I would then clear the obstructions from their throat, so that they once again could speak freely about their grief." He hung up the third string.

Just then, Ayenwatha heard something in the bushes. He went to look to see who it was. It was the Peacemaker who had spoken about peace in Ayenwatha's village. The Peacemaker approached Ayenwatha and stood before the tripod. He grabbed the first string and said, "If anyone was burdened with grief like you, Ayenwatha, I would wipe away the tears from their eyes with this fawn cloth so that they could see clearly again."

The Peacemaker then took the cloth and wiped Ayenwatha's eyes. He took another string from the stick and said, "From the ears of that person, I would take the obstructions that block him from hearing these words."

He then grabbed and held Ayenwatha just below the ears and consoled him. He took a third string and said, "Next, I would clear the throat of that person so that they may speak words that are once again understandable." He rubbed Ayenwatha's throat with his hand and asked him to tell him what had made him so sad. After Ayenwatha spoke about his grief, his spirit began to be lifted.

He grabbed some more of the strings and said to the Peacemaker, "When someone is grieving like me there is turmoil in the stomach. I would give the grieving person the medicine *onanora*, sweet flag. This will relieve their stomach of grief." Then he placed another string over the stick.

He continued to say, "There is blood on the seat of the dead, and only the stains are left. With the skin of a white fawn, I would wipe away the stains forever so no one would be reminded of the pain that the person was in." He then placed a fifth string over the stick.

He continued, "When people are burdened with grief like myself, they are covered with darkness because the one they loved has passed away, and they are lost as to what to do. I would lift the darkness of the person with these kind words." He placed a sixth string over the stick.

He continued, "Those in grief, like myself, never see the sky, as their heads are always facing toward the ground. I would clear the sky so that they could look up and once again see its beauty." He put a seventh string on the stick.

He continued, "Those in grief, like myself, no longer see the light of the Sun. I would raise up the Sun so that when they turned they could see the shadow following in back of them instead of in the front. They would then know where they would be going." He placed an eighth string over the stick.

He continued to say, "Those in grief, like myself, cannot forget what might have happened if things turned differently. We keep thinking back to what might have been if the person we cared about had not died. I would go to the grave of the dead person and fix it beautifully and then cover it with elm bark. Neither the sun or rain would get through, and I would carry on with my life after that." He placed a ninth string over the stick.

Next he said, "In death the bones of our ancestors are scattered; I would bind the bones of the departed with wampum and relay these twenty matters of sympathy. I would then make a feast for the dead person ten days before the spirit parts. It would consist of all the things that the dead person liked. This I would do before we finally part our ways until the time we meet in the Sky World." He placed a tenth string over the grave.

He continued, "During this time of grief many of the *Rotyianehshon*, keepers of the faith, are also sad. The council fire has been stomped, and the logs for the fire kicked aside. I would get them to direct their minds to the Creator to alleviate the grief of all, and I would light the council fire once again." He placed an eleventh string over the stick.

He continued, "In the cycle of life each year, there are thirteen moons that are represented on the back of the snapping turtle. It was the women who first came to the earth, and they are the ones who bless the seeds and the earth so that we may continue to live. It was through the woman's sacrifice that the earth is plentiful with life, and it is the woman's cycle that we follow in life. I would rekindle the ashes of the departed who is born from a woman." He placed a twelfth string on the stick.

He continued, "The faith keeper is connected to the fire. It is up to them to make sure that the faith keeps going. If the woman faith keeper passes away, then the women must prepare the ceremony for renewal. The loss of women is great because, with their loss, the generations cannot be born. Women are responsible in making sure that the *royaner* are fed. They must guide the *royaner* when they come to their councils. In every clan there are two relations that must perform the duties of the people: a man and a woman faith keeper——a male representative of the people with a good mind and a clan mother along with his and her assistants. The clan mother's role is to make sure that the *royaner* keeps his good mind and works on behalf of the people. Her job is to make sure that the *royaner* seat is always filled. If it ever goes cold, it will mean that a great sadness is coming. It is her responsibility to make sure that the seat is warmed in three days. Both the *royaner* and the clan mother must have a good record as they must work together on behalf of the people. The assistant looks after the *royaner* as well. When one becomes a *royaner* he must follow this way. If he doesn't, his two relations will warn him. The first will be the clan mother. If the *royaner* does not hear the words, she will bring the two faith keepers to warn him. If this doesn't work, the leading *Rotiskenren:keteh*, He Who Carries the Bundle of Bones, of the family will give the final warning. If the *royaner* doesn't abide by it, he will tell the *royaner* that he is dehorned and his title will go back to his clan mother. This is how we must deal with grief." He then put a thirteenth string of wampum on the stick.

Next he said, "When people are so full of grief, they may commit suicide. During this time, they are to be kept away from certain plants that live in the swamp. They are instead to be comforted by their *athonsora,* special friend, who will condole them." He laid a fourteenth string upon the stick.

Finally he said, "When a *royaner* has departed from the world, it is important that the condolers from the other side of the fire are notified. When this has happened and they come to condole, they will return the wampum to the pouch left hanging on the pole."

When Ayenwatha had finished, he said to the Peacemaker, "I feel much better, now that I have gotten this out of me and I have found a way that we may all be able to deal with grief."

The Peacemaker told him, "You always need two people to comfort one another. Young people should choose an *athonsora* to bring their spirits up whenever they are feeling down. They will work together and comfort each other with kind words."

The Peacemaker then said to Ayenwatha, "We have to leave to go to the territory of the Oneota:haka, Standing Stone People, for now we must use this to comfort nations. The Kenienké:haka are gathering together to prepare for their journey west, and we must first make a path for them. Go to the Ohkwa:ho, Wolf Clan, village of the Oneota:haka, and I will meet you there," he told Ayenwatha. The Peacemaker and Ayenwatha then separated.

Ayenwatha came to a cornfield outside of the Oneota:haka village named Kanoalohaleh, Place of the Pole. He sat just outside of the cornfield watching a man who stood guard against any animals that might enter to eat the growing corn. On the other side of the cornfield, the man had built a small lodge so that he could rest when he was tired. He did not see Ayenwatha enter the lodge. It was not long before he saw smoke coming from a fire lit inside the lodge. The guardian of the cornfield became afraid. He decided that he should go back to the village and get help. When he entered the village, he told the *rarontaron:kowa,* great war leader, "There is someone who has lit a fire in my lodge. Do you know if anyone has left the village and may be playing a trick on me?"

The great war leader replied, "There is no one who has left the village. I will send two warriors to see who it might be and to bring the stranger back here."

The two runners arrived at the cornfield to see a man sitting by the fire. They told Ayenwatha, "We have been sent by our war chief to bring you back to our village."

Ayenwatha sat there and did not respond. Three times they asked him who he was. Still, Ayenwatha would not answer them.

An answer of importance such as this would require a person to wait three times. It had been the custom among the *onkwe:honwe* that a sudden answer may be the result of witchcraft and the person may not be speaking the truth. Frustrated, the runners decided to go back to the village to tell the war leader that the stranger would not answer them.

Upon their return to the village they told the war leader what had happened. The great war leader thought about it for a few minutes and then said, "This stranger wants something from us."

He grabbed an eagle quill and cut it up into three pieces and said to one of the runners, "Give the stranger this eagle quill and see what he does with it."

The runner took the eagle quill and set out with the other runner to find the stranger. When they approached Ayenwatha, one of the runners said to him, "Our great war chief has cut up this eagle quill to give to you. As you know the eagle has great importance, and our words are binding whenever we use him."

Ayenwatha answered, "This is the first time that anyone has asked me to do something in such a sincere manner. I will go with you to your village and visit your great war leader in three days' time." The runners thanked Ayenwatha and ran back to tell the great war chief about what had transpired. In the meantime, Ayenwatha beaded the eagle quill with the mulberries he had found.

Three days later, Ayenwatha showed up at the village. He waited as the great war chief and the people assembled in front of him. Taking the pieces of the eagle quill he passed them back to the great war chief and taught him the first three important words of the requickening address that he and the Peacemaker had first spoken when he was in remorse over the deaths of his daughters.

He said to the great war chief, "Take these three eagle quills. Whenever someone comes to visit, you will meet them at the edge of the village. There, you will speak the words that I am about to tell you. You will take a piece of the skin of a fawn. You will then tell the visitors that you want to wipe away the tears from their eyes in case they are in grief over the loss of any of their people on the way. You will pass to them one of the quill wampum. Next, you will tell them that you want to clear their throats, in case they are so choked up with grief and anger that they can't speak. You will pass the next quill to them. Finally, you will say that you want to unplug their ears so that they can hear clearly, once again, the words that have been spoken."

Ayenwatha went on, "When this is done, they will in turn pass the quills back and say the same words in return. In this way, you will be assured that there will be good relations between you both when you meet."

Upon hearing Ayenwatha's words, the great war chief and the assembled people wanted to hear more as to what he had to say. Ayenwatha told them about the Peacemaker and what had happened at Kenienké—how he had waited for the Peacemaker and how the Peacemaker, when he arrived, was tested by the Kenienké:haka. He told them about how he was given his title and why he had come to the Oneota:haka. When he had finished, everyone was very impressed with his message. They were still apprehensive about the Kenienké:haka and whether this was a trick of some kind.

The war leader told Ayenwatha, "You are welcome to stay in my lodge overnight. I have room in the back."

The great war leader really wanted to keep an eye on Ayenwatha, to see what he would do. That night the war leader slept near the opening to the lodge while Ayenwatha slept in the back.

It seemed like Ayenwatha was only asleep for a few minutes when he could hear someone at the entrance. He climbed over the great war leader, making as little noise as possible. It was the Peacemaker.

The Peacemaker said to Ayenwatha, "We will have to leave soon because the great war chief at Onontaka is getting impatient. He knows we are coming, and he is afraid. He would like to destroy us if he can. In the morning, ask the war chief to look in a southerly direction from the hills above. You will see smoke rising from the fires of those who have already heard our message and have accepted the Great Peace. They, along with the Kenienké:haka, will be arriving soon so that we can continue to spread the message. We will select two runners to gather the *onkwe:honwe* together here before we leave.

As the Kenienké:haka and the other Oneota:haka villagers began to arrive at Kanoalohaleh, they could hear the warriors coming from every direction, singing the *Hai, hai.*

This ancient song was sung by the *onkwe:honwe* whenever they moved their villages; it was based on their traditional life of crop rotation. About every ten years, the *onkwe:honwe* would move their villages when the land began to become depleted; this way they wouldn't return to that very spot for around fifty years. By that time, the earth would be restored, and they could begin cutting down and burning the bush and planting once again their three mothers: corn, beans, and squash. They would move the bones of their ancestors with them and pile them together in a special place outside the village. In this way they were ensured that their ancestors would remain with them always.

The men called *rotiskenren:keteh*, which meant bone carriers, would sing the *Hai, hai* as they walked carrying the bones of the departed that would be placed with the bones of their ancestors. They were called this because they had the responsibility of ensuring that their people made the proper transition to the Sky World.

By the time that they had moved the bones, the flesh of the departed had helped to replenish the earth with new life, and their duty in this world was finally completed, so that now they could be fully reborn into the Sky World. It was up to the *rotiskenren:keteh* to ensure that the bones were cleaned and placed together; this way the community of ancestors would continue in this life as well as in the afterlife. At the same time it was the *rotiskenren:keteh*'s responsibility to carry the knowledge of the ancestors with them, giving a double meaning to the name. As time passed, it was mostly the Wendat that had kept up this practice.

As the different villagers from the Kenienké:haka and Oneota:haka approached the wood's edge, the Oneota:haka of the Wolf Clan would greet them with the three words taught to them by Ayenwatha. The visitors would in turn reciprocate the words as they learned the protocol. When everyone had arrived at the Oneota:haka village, they heard in the air, a voice, *"Asokanee,"* is it time? They knew it was getting close to the time that they would have to leave.

When everyone was assembled in the village, the Peacemaker spoke. He said, "We, the villagers of two nations, have come together to this land of the Oneota:haka. Look around and see if we are fighting with one another. Is not this the way that Teharonhia:wako had wanted us to live? When we live in peace with one another we are living a righteous life with a good mind. This makes us stronger than when we are killing one another. Imagine if all of us could live this way."

The Peacemaker continued, "I will choose three members of the Wolf Clan family to be the first Oneota:haka *royaner* of the Great Peace. Later, when we are all assembled together with Tsakonsasé at Onontaka, she and the clan matrons of the families will choose the rest of the *royaner* from the other clan family villages.

The Peacemaker put forward the man who had stood watch over the cornfields when Ayenwatha first arrived. The Peacemaker turned to the man who had stood guard at the cornfields and said to him, "Come forward. I will name you Rotatsheté, The Quiver Bearer. You will be the first on the list of *royaner* for the Oneota:haka, because you were the first Ayenwatha met while you were guarding the cornfield. You will now stand guard on behalf of your nation."

The Peacemaker called another member of the Wolf Clan and asked him, "What do you do besides fight?"

The warrior answered, "Whenever I am not in battle, my job is to look after the corn for the women."

The Peacemaker turned to him and said, "You will be *royaner*. From now on you will be called Kanonkwenyo:ton, He Looks After the Corn. Whenever there is an assembly, you will gather the people in the same way you gather the corn."

The Peacemaker then asked the war chief to come forward. He said to him, "When Ayenwatha first arrived, he told you to look for the fires burning in the morning of those who now believe in the Great Peace that is upon us. You were the first one to get up in the morning and look. I name you Teyohakwenteh, He Looks Through the Opening. You will always be vigilant toward your people in working to maintain the peace."

The Peacemaker then said, "I leave you three to begin your work. Never argue with one another. You must always have one mind, head, and body whenever you make decisions. It will not be like before. You have no authority over your people. You are there to serve them, and this means you will always have fewer possessions than the rest of the people."

Then he told them, "In the future, once we set our foundation for coming together, you three will be three brothers Ahsenhnihondadekenah."

He then spoke to the *onkwe:honwe* of the two assembled nations, the Kenienké:haka and the Oneota:haka. "If we work together, we will have more power. This is a new day, and the Sun is beginning to climb in the sky. Each day it climbs a little higher and gets a little brighter. The Great Law of Peace is about to arrive, and, when the Sun reaches its zenith in the sky, all the surrounding nations will be living in peace. Soon, you will be able to walk without having any fear. As more people join, it will be like a ball rolling in the snow. With each spin forward, it gets bigger and bigger."

The Peacemaker continued, "We now have six *royaner*, Trees of Equal Height, with good minds who will work on behalf of the *onkwe:honwe*. We will now appoint two runners to go to the land of the Kaokwa:haka, Mucky Lake People, who live around the long lake, to inform them that we are coming."

The Kaokwa:haka Join the Great Peace

The *onkwe:honwe* then chose their quickest runners to head for the Kaokwa:haka country. They had to be careful and keep out of sight, because they would be passing through the territory of the Onontaka:haka, the People of the Hills, where resided the most powerful war chief. Alone, the Kenienké:haka and Oneota:haka would not be powerful enough to face him at Kanata:kowa village of the Onontaka:haka and convince him that it would be better to live in peace.

They traveled on the along the upper trail, and, when they arrived at the northern part of the lake where the marshes are near the salt spring, they searched for the great war leader of the Kaokwa:haka. They made camp, lit a fire, and waited for the Kaokwa:haka to send some runners to them. The runners arrived and welcomed the Oneota:haka villagers to their village. Once they had arrived at the Kaokwa:haka village and had been accepted by the warriors, they found the great war leader bending down and staring at the dirt.

The great war leader sat the two runners down beside him and looking at the way they wore their feathers, he knew that one of the runners was a Kenienké:haka and the other an Oneota:haka *onkwe:honwe*.

He said to them, "Already I know why you have come here. You have come to bring me a message that there is a cool breeze that is coming through during these hot times. This breeze will cool down the warriors, and we will live in comfort together. My people have already been prepared for this, for it has already reached our ears what has happened. We are tired of war. Next to us, living to the east, the powerful war chief of the Onontaka:haka lives, and situated to the west is the most powerful nation of all—the Sonontowa:haka, Great Mountain People, who can put together twice the warriors as any of us. We are tired of the killing and being in the middle of it. Look to the south of the great lake where the cliffs are, and you will see the fires lit by our people who have already accepted the Great Peace." The runners looked down the lake; there was a small river that lead from the Kaokwa:haka camp to the lake's opening, and the shore was visible on each side. They could see the campfires of the Kaokwa:haka who had already accepted the Great Peace lit in the distance.

After the runners had heard what the great Kaokwa:haka war chief had to say, they ran back to inform the Peacemaker and the others who were waiting for them in the Oneota:haka village that it was safe to move on.

All of a sudden, they heard a shout three times pass them like a great wind, *"Asokanee,"* is it time? The Peacemaker said to the Oneota:haka and the Kenienké:haka, "It is the powerful war chief calling, and he is getting impatient with us. We will bypass him and his village for now. It is important that we get the Kaokwa:haka and the Sonontowa:haka on side with us before we visit him."

With the Peacemaker and Ayenwatha in the lead, the Oneota:haka and the Kenienké:haka began to walk toward the west through the rest of the Oneota:haka country. As they came to the Oneota:haka village of Tsuténang.

Rotatsheté said, "Maybe we should wait a while longer. The weather is getting cooler, and we should wait until the autumn has begun before we leave. In this way, there will be plenty to eat along the way." At the time, there was much arguing as to what they should do. It was like a log had been put in the road not allowing them to pass.

Finally, the Peacemaker said, "Maybe Rotatsheté is right; if we are going to succeed we must be in a good mind and have unanimous consent. We will remain here in Oneota territory until the three hunters in the sky shoot the great bear, and the leaves turn the color of blood." From that time on they said that Rotatsheté had placed a log on their path. This took place in a valley between two hills on the southern side of Oneota:haka country.

They then went back to their villages and harvested the crops to prepare for winter. Finally, they looked up and saw the Great Bear at its lowest point in the sky being hunted by the three hunters. They then met once again at Tsuténang and proceeded toward the country of the Kaokwa:haka, bypassing the main Onontaka:haka village.

In order to avoid detection they traveled south, passing the Shell Lake—Tully Lake—and then they moved toward the settlement of the Kaokwa:haka on the south side of Kaokwa Lake—Cayuga Lake—where the cliffs were. As they got to the main trail, they could see the cliffs on the south side of the path that lead into the lake. They then approached the village of Káiakaanah singing the *Hai, hai,* instead of carrying the bones as was done in years past, they added a roll call of the *royaner* who were chosen by the Peacemaker to the chant. Once they had entered the village, the great war chief was waiting for them. He brought out his pipe, and they each smoked from it.

Then the war chief began to speak, "We the Kaokwa:haka of the lower side of the lake where the cliffs are had heard you were coming. We believe in the thing that you are trying to accomplish, although we don't quite understand the full meaning of it as yet. As you can see, our nation is already united in belief and in council. We think that this can be extended with other nations."

The Peacemaker answered, "From now on, you, who are of great faith, will be called Takaheyonh, He Looks Both Ways, of the Bear Clan Ohkwa:ri. That is because you anticipated that we would be coming and were watching on the cliffs above to see when we would arrive.

The Peacemaker then said, "Now, there are three nations that have accepted the Great Peace. The Sun is rising even higher, and the world is getting brighter. We will now send runners to the other Kaokwa villages so that they may join us when we travel to the Sonontowa:haka nation."

Runners were then sent out to the other Kaokwa:haka villages until they came to the village of Kanokeh. There, the runners saw all the canoes lined up along the shore of the lake. The *onkwe:honwe* in this village were called the Big Canoe People. Upon entering the village they were presented to the great war chief.

The runners said to the great war chief, "We have come on behalf of the message of peace. The one who has brought us the message is waiting near the cliffs at the end of the lake. He wishes that you would join him and the rest before they cross into the territory of the Sonontowa:haka nation."

The great war chief replied, "Go back and tell them that I will arrive shortly."

Three days later, the great war chief of the Kaokwa:haka showed up with his people at the village of Káiakaanah by the cliffs of lower Kaokwa lake. There, they were greeted by the Peacemaker and the others.

The Peacemaker said to the gathering of *onkwe:honwe*, "Now there are three nations that have accepted the Great Peace. The Sun is getting brighter each day." He turned to the great war leader of the lower village of the Kaokwa:haka, and said, "You will be known as Tsinontawerahonh,

He Crawls on His Knees, of the Deer Clan Ohskenon:ton, because you sat here looking on the ground at bugs as you waited for me to arrive and had already accepted my message of peace even before I had arrived."

Then he said, "Both you and Takaheyonh are *Ratitsistanon*, fire keepers of your nation, and are to be like *Kahsenhon:weh*, two sons, to one another."

He continued, "In the future, when this message of us coming together reaches the Kaokwa:haka villages in the northern region, there will be two prominent Kaokwa:haka nations that will sit together: those of the lower house and those of the upper house. This is the way it will be for all time."

The Peacemaker then said, "We will wait for the powerful war chief of the Onontaka:haka to yell three times and then it will be time to visit the Sonontowa:haka." It was not long after that he had told them this when, in the air above, they heard the yell, *"Asokanee, Asokanee, Asokanee"* is it time, is it time, is it time?

The Sonontowa:haka Join the Great Peace

The Peacemaker then gathered everyone and said to them, "The Sonontowa:haka are a very powerful people. Only the Kaokwa:haka of the lower lake have had interaction with them over the years. We will remain here and let Takaheyonh and his people visit the Sonontowa:haka who live by their great lake."

The village of Kanuntasakia, at the west end of Seneca Lake, was only a day's journey away through the hills and onto the northern trail by another great lake. It was the easternmost village of the Sonontowa:haka. They lit their fires at the eastern shore of the lake and waited for the Sonontowa:haka runners to arrive. When the runners arrived, one of them said to Takaheyonh, "The warriors are waiting and ready for battle. We have notified our other villages as we have heard that you have joined with the Kenienké:haka and the Oneota:haka from the east."

Takaheyonh said to the runners, "Tell your great war chief and his assistant that we have come in peace and not for war. We will return to our village to tell the others that you have not let us pass. We mean you no harm, but instead come as one body in a search to extend peace so that our bodies will be whole."

Takaheyonh then left with his people to tell the others that the Sonontowa:haka were not ready to listen to peace. Upon returning, he explained what had happened at the lake.

The Peacemaker told everyone, "Do not be discouraged; I will go myself and try to resolve this by persuasion." Upon arriving at the lake, the Peacemaker set up his fire.

Not long after, two runners approached from the Sonontowa:haka village. They asked the Peacemaker, "What is your purpose in coming here?"

The Peacemaker answered, "I have come with the Kenienké:haka, the Oneota:haka, and others to stop the warfare, and I bring a message of peace based on the laws of our Creator. I want to restore the natural order that was given to us by Teharonhia:wako."

The runners said, "Since you are alone and can do us no harm, we will allow you to enter our village." They then led the Peacemaker into the village of Kanuntasakia where he was met by the great war chief and his assistant.

The war chief asked, "Why have you come here, and what is the purpose of your visit?"

The Peacemaker explained, "I have traveled a long way, from the Wendat nation in the north to the Kakwako:haka west of you, then back to the country of the Kenienké:haka to the Oneota:haka and on to the Kaokwa:haka. Each time I have added something more to the Great Peace, and now there are many who are beginning to see the power that can come from living in peace with one another. I am creating a longhouse that will travel from the east to the west. In this longhouse, the *onkwe:honwe* will live as *kanonsioné,* one family, together. Anyone who lives in this longhouse will live in peace. I want to extend this longhouse west, so that you may live with us in peace."

The *rarontaron,* war chief, said, "We had a council after you sent the two runners. There are many of you, and we know that if you came waging war against us, there would be much bloodshed. My assistant and I accept your message of peace. However, we cannot speak for the two war chiefs who live west of us at the Kanunkakwa and Teonuntakahah villages. The most populous village, Teonuntakahah, is in the great valley of the Geneseo. We have sent runners to them, and they have not sanctioned the peace."

The Peacemaker said, "We will take care of that business later on. Now we will get down to the business of adding another *wahatinah-stashonteren,* rafter to the longhouse. Since you have accepted the peace, you will put away your war club and become a *royaner* and work with a good mind on behalf of your people. When we first met, you were looking over the lake as if you were trying to figure something out. I will name you Skanyiatar:io, Beautiful Lake of the Anon:wara, Turtle Clan, because you were gazing at the lake, thinking on whether to join."

The Peacemaker asked Skanyiatar:io, "Where is your assistant?"

Skanyiatar:io replied, "He is looking from the top of the great hill to see whether there are any warriors who are coming to attack us."

The Peacemaker said, "Tell him not to fear, and bring him here."

Skanyiatar:io sent a runner to fetch the other war chief. When he had arrived the Peacemaker said to him, "Because you were looking from the mountain to look for our army and saw nothing coming but the sky, I will give you the title, Shatekaronias, Skies of Equal Height of the *Tawis Tawis,* Snipe Clan. Both you and Skanyiatar:io will be cousins."

The Peacemaker then said to everyone assembled, "We must hurry. If you look up, you will see the Sun becoming brighter, and each day, the Peace is becoming more powerful."

At that moment, they heard in the sky a voice yelling three times, "*Asokanee,*" is it time?

The Peacemaker told them, "We must head to the territory of the Onontaka:haka nation. Before we cross the lake to the shaman's village we will wait for Tsakonsasé, the mother of nations, to arrive. It is through her and the women that the peace will prosper for they will be the backbone of the nations."

The Onontaka:haka Join the Great Peace

The Onontaka village of Kanata:kowa was a three-day journey from Kanuntasaka. Upon arriving at Onontaka Lake, they waited for Tsakonsasé. As they waited, they discussed how they would approach the powerful war chief of the Onontaka:haka who lived in the main village.

Everyone began to argue with one another. The arguments were becoming so intense that there were fears that the Peace would be broken.

The Peacemaker yelled, "Stop! We four nations must begin to speak with one voice if we are to convince the fifth to join. We will create a means where everyone will have a chance to speak. We will divide the nations up in two halves who will sit across the fire from each other. Whenever the four come together to council, the Kenienké:haka and Sonontowa:haka will sit on one side of the fire. On the other side will sit the Kaokwa:haka and the Oneota:haka. If there is a resolution to be discussed, it will be discussed by the Kenienké:haka first, who will in turn pass it to the Sonontowa:haka. When they have resolved the issue, it will be passed back to the Kenienké:haka who will in turn pass it across the fire to the Kaokwa:haka. They will then turn it over to the Oneota:haka, who will pass it back to the Kaokwa:haka, who will turn it over to the Kenienké:haka for a final resolution. If we do it this way, everyone's voice will be heard." He continued, "In order to make sure everyone understands one another, we will make the Kenienké language our common language when discussing issues during council." They all agreed that it was a good idea.

Just then Tsakonsasé arrived from the neutral Kakwako nation. She saw the men who had been warriors now being advocates of peace. There were many canoes lined up at the western shore of the lake Onontaka. She then went and took her place at the head of the women.

Upon receiving Tsakonsasé, the Peacemaker said, "Now that we are all together, we will show the *Rarontaron:kowa*, great war chief, the power that can come from living in peace."

Ayenwatha said, "This is great; we are now one mind, one voice, and one body."

They all got into their canoes with the Peacemaker, Ayenwatha, and Tsakonsasé in the lead, and they began paddling across the lake. Suddenly, the clouds began to darken, and, like the sound of the thunder beings, they heard a voice travel through the air saying *"Asokanee,"* is it time? Everyone dropped their tobacco into the water in order to appease the spirits of the lake as it began to swell. All of a sudden, they saw the Peacemaker wave his hand, and at that moment the waters began to calm down. Two more times they heard the cry *"Asokanee."* Every time the waters became rough, the Peacemaker would wave his hand, and the water would calm down. Finally, they reached the other side safely.

They parked their canoes and took a path that led up a hill. Sitting on a rock, with all of his warriors waiting to do battle, was the great war chief of the Ohkwa:ri, Bear Clan. His mind had become so twisted that there appeared to be snakes coming out of his head. When he saw all the men from the different nations surrounding him and his warriors, he appeared to be intimidated. Even he knew that if they battled he would probably lose. However, he put up a brave face. He knew that the way to avoid annihilation depended on everyone remaining at peace.

The powerful war chief said to them, "I know why you have come. My warriors and I are ready to do battle with you."

The Peacemaker replied, "We have many potential warriors here on both sides. If we do battle with each other, then many will be killed. Remember, once the killing starts it will not stop. This is why we must remain at peace with one another. If we live together in peace, we will continue to grow stronger to take up the hatchet against one another. Then no one will ever want to do us harm. The potential for war, to take up the hatchet against one another is always there for us. If we continue to do so, our enemies will know that we are weak. We have to open ourselves to them so that they will never attempt to destroy us. Through the power of numbers, we can be examples of righteous living and always live in peace with one another and with others as well."

The powerful war chief said, "If we accept to join your Great Peace, what is in it for me and my people?"

The Peacemaker answered, "The four nations that are here have formed a council for resolving disputes. The Kenienké:haka and the Sonontowa:haka sit on one side of the fire, while the Kaokwa:haka and the Oneota:haka sit on the other side of the fire. There will be times when new resolutions will be put forth *wahatinahstashonteren*, extending the rafters of our nations and laws. We shall sit you in the middle, above the fire. When all the rest have counseled, you will be given the final voice to decide the issue."

The Peacemaker continued, "The central fire for all the nations will be here at Kanata:kowa. Our territory from the east to the west will be a reflection of the Sky World. Even our lodges that we will live in will be based on the sky world. Here at Kanata:kowa, we will plant a great tree of peace that will travel into the sky, just as the tree exists in the Sky World. Skarenhesehkowah, The Great White Pine, will represent the heart of the five *onkwe:honwe* nations. Anyone will be able to breathe in safety once they reach it. The tree will spread its *oktenrakenrahkowah,* white roots, to the four corners of Turtle Island. Anyone who chooses to follow the roots may do so, and they will find peace, charity, protection under the long leaves at the tree's source."

The Peacemaker then said to the great powerful war chief, "You will have more *royaner* than the other nations. That is because you will have to keep the central fire alive at all times."

Before the powerful war chief could answer, the Peacemaker began to sing, *"Aee, Aee yai."* So peaceful was the song that everyone soon joined in.

The powerful war chief and his warriors were overwhelmed by it. It was said that the Peacemaker had learned it from listening to a bird during a moment of reflection, when he was contemplating what to do next while in the forest.

Just then Tsakonsasé and Ayenwatha moved toward the great war chief. The powerful war chief had been known to be an abuser of women. It was said that he sat on an enormous phallus. Like the keeper of the Tree of Light in the Sky World, he was a destroyer of the generations to come, but could add new life if he could change.

The Peacemaker pointed toward Tsakonsasé and said to him, "There is the mother of all our nations. Go and abuse your mother."[3]

The powerful war chief looked down in shame and said, "I cannot."

The Peacemaker replied, "Women are the mothers of the future generations to come of this Longhouse of One Family. They are to be respected from now on and held in the highest esteem."

Just then, Tsakonsasé took the war chief by the hand, and she rubbed away the aggression from his warrior's body. Then Ayenwatha spoke soft words, as Tsakonsasé helped comb the snakes from his hair. This meant that his mind was cleared of violence and anger. In fact, so moved was he that he became completely subdued by all that had happened to him.

The war chief then replied, "I accept the Great Peace."

The Peacemaker said, "Now that we are all together, we will call it *Kanonsioné*, Longhouse of One Family, and others will know us as Rotinonshonni, Longhouse People."

He then told Tsakonsasé to step forward, and he said to her, "Tsakonsasé, mother of our nations, it is time to put the *onah:kara*, antlers, on the head of this powerful war chief whom will always be known as Atotarhoh, the Entangled, of the Ohkwa:ri, Bear Clan.

He continued, "It is now time to put the antlers on the other *royaner* chosen."

Tsakonsasé picked up the deer antlers and placed them on the war chief's head. As she was doing this, the rest of the warriors and women stood in a *teyotiokwaonhahston*, circle, and sang the peace hymn. Tsakonsasé then told the great war chief, "You will now perform your duty as a *royaner*, that is to keep the peace inside the territory of the Longhouse of One Family."

The Peacemaker said to the great war chief, "You will always be known as Atotarhoh, the Entangled, in remembrance of this moment when the snakes were removed from your head. Whenever another is chosen in your place, unlike the other *royaner*, a council will take place to choose a successor from the best men. Yours will be an open title that will be reserved for the best representative of the Onontaka:haka of the Longhouse of One Family. You will not be chosen by the clan matrons from a specific clan like the others, but by all of the clan mothers of your nation and thus you are cut from the umbilical cord tying a person to only one mother."

He continued, "Now that you have the duty of a *royaner*, the Sun is getting brighter all the time, and the darkness is being lifted from our eyes. When nations come to the trunk of the great tree, you will oversee them. I will place an eagle on top of the tree to be your eyes. Like the uncle Akatuni:heno, the Great Dew Eagle, who sat watching the children in the Sky World, the eagle will watch over his children here on the earth. That is because the eagle can see far distances. Whenever it is required that all the nations are to meet at the central fire, it will be your duty to send the wampum out and they will come. This will be your duty; however, you will not have any more power than other *royaner*. You *royaner* will all be known as trees of equal height. Whenever you council, you will speak one at a time; you will deal with one issue at a time until you speak with one voice. Only when everyone has come to a consensus will the issue be resolved. Those who represent their nation must speak on behalf of the nation and not for themselves. To ensure that everyone remains at peace with one another, councils will meet until midafternoon, and if the issue has yet to be resolved, it will be put under the pillow until the next day. Then the mind will be fresh the next day."

The Peacemaker Relays the *Teyotiokwaonhas:ton*, Laws of Peace, to the Five Nations

The Peacemaker then said to everyone, "It is time to make the *katsistah*, sacred fire, and this fire will remain lit forever. The smoke will be seen by all nations. What I have told you is only the beginning of the *Kayeneren:kowa*, Great Laws of Peace, that you will live by. Tsakonsasé will be the mother of our nations, and the women will hold the titles and elevate and place the *onah:kara*, horns, upon the heads of the *royaner*. They will be the backbone of the nations. It is here in the Onontaka:haka territory that we are bestowing the name of the titles of the *royaner* with the antlers, and it is here that they will all meet the Onontaka:haka who will always be known as the name bearers."

After Atotarhoh was crowned by Tsakonsasé, the Peacemaker called Tekarihokenh of the Kenienké:haka forward and said, "Tsakonsasé place the antlers upon this *royaner*'s head." Tsakonsasé picked up the antlers and placed them on his head.

The Peacemaker then said to Tekarihokenh of the Anon:wara, Turtle Clan, "You are now a representative of the Kenienké:haka nation and will be responsible for the generations to come. You will work on behalf your nation."

Next, he said, "Ayenwatha of the Anon:wara, Turtle Clan, step forward." Tsakonsasé then crowned Ayenwatha. As this was occurring, the Peacemaker said, "You both will always work together and respect one another."

Next, he said, "Shatekariwateh of the Anon:wara, Turtle Clan, step forward." Shatekariwateh stepped forward, and Tsakonsasé placed the crowns upon his head.

The Peacemaker told the three, "You will resolve your differences, and when you speak it will be with one mind as *ahsenhnihontatekenah,* three brothers."

He continued, "You will also be *onerahsehtsen,* cousins, to the next three Kenienké:haka *royaner* chosen from the Ohkwa:ho, Wolf Clan."

Next, the Peacemaker went to the Oneota:haka and said, "Rotatsheté of the Ohkwa:ho, Wolf Clan, step forward." Rotatsheté stepped forward and Tsakonsasé placed the antlers on his head.

Then, the Peacemaker said, "Kanonkwenyoton of the Ohkwa:ho, Wolf Clan, step forward." Tsakonsasé placed the antlers on his head.

Next he called, "Teyonhakwenteh, step forward." Tsakonsasé placed the antlers on his head. Then he said, "You will be *ahsenhnihontatekenah,* brothers, to one another and *ronarasehtsen,* cousins, to the next three Oneota:haka *royaner* chosen by the clan mothers from the Anon:wara, Turtle Clan."

The Peacemaker said to the six *royaner* who had been chosen by him personally. "You are crowned to work on behalf of your people to bring out the good mind. You will have no more or no less power than another. You will be trees of equal height. Like the buck deer, you will protect the offspring, and, like him, you will have ears that will listen in case there is danger to the people."

The Peacemaker then called the two Kaokwa:haka *royaner* to come forward. "Takaheyonh of the Ohkwa:ri, Bear Clan," he called, "Come forward." Tsakonsasé then placed the deer antlers on his head.

Next he called, "Tsinontawerhonh of the Ohskenon:ton, Deer Clan, come forward." Tsakonsasé then placed the deer antlers on his head.

He then said," You both will be *Ratitsistanon,* Fire Keepers, of the nation and be *Iitahtawa,* sons to one another as well as *Ronwatikowah:nen* elders of your nation".

Next, the Peacemaker called the two Sonontowa:haka *royaner,* but, before they came forward, he said to those assembled at Onontaka, "I have only convinced two of the Sonontowa:haka war chiefs to accept the peace and become *royaner.* There is still some unfinished business to settle with the two remaining war chiefs who are farthest west."

He then called out, "Skanyiatar:io of the Anon:wara, Turtle Clan, step forward." Tsakonsasé placed the deer antlers on his head.

Then he called out, "Satekaronias of the Tawis Tawis, Snipe Clan, step forward." Tsakonsasé then placed the antlers on his head.

He then told them, "You will be Snipe Clan cousins to one another."

When this was done, the Peacemaker told them, "You will oversee any bad that may be coming your way and cultivate the good minds of the nation. Like a young tree, the good mind will grow."

Then he said to them, "Now that we have elevated the great war chief, Atotarhoh of the Ohkwa:ri, Bear Clan, into a *royaner:kowa*, we can truly call ourselves *Kanonsioné*. The *royaner* of the *Kayeneren:kowa* are now almost complete."

The Peacemaker continued, "There is still an important matter that has to be taken care of before we elevate the other *royaner*. On one side of the fire will sit the Onontaka:haka, Kenienké:haka, and Sonontowa:haka *royaner*. On the other side of the fire will sit the Kaokwa:haka and Oneota:haka *royaner*. The Kenienké:haka Turtles, being the first to accept the message, will council first, and then it will be passed to the other Kenienké:haka *royaner* for a resolution. Once it has been discussed, the resolution will then be put in the well. It will then be taken up by the Sonontowa:haka *royaner*. When the Sonontowa:haka are able to speak with one voice, it will be passed back to the Kenienké:haka. They will in turn pass it over to the Kaokwa:haka *royaner*, and when they are finished will turn it over to the Oneota:haka *royaner*. From there it will travel back to the Kaokwa:haka, who will pass it back to the Kenienké:haka. During all of this, the Onontaka:haka *royaner* will be listening. Tekarihokenh of the Kenienké:haka will then pass it to Atotarhoh, who will see if there are any mistakes in interpretation or objections. If he doesn't agree with the process after discussing it with the other Onontaka:haka *royaner*, it is put back into the well for further discussion."

He continued, "However, as a final point, all Kenienké:haka *royaner* must be included before a resolution is passed."

The Peacemaker continued, "When the other *royaner* are crowned we will develop this constitution even further. However, first there is still an important matter that has to be settled. There are still two Sonontowa:haka war chiefs who live in the western part of their country who have not accepted the Great Peace. Since we are all together, we will make this the first order of our council."

At that time, the five nations got together in council as the Peacemaker had showed them, and they discussed what they should do. When they were finished discussing the matter, and Atotarhoh had given it his approval, Ayenwatha approached the Peacemaker and told him what was decided.

He said, "We have now counseled and have a proposition for the two war chiefs. Since they have many warriors with them, we will propose to them that they be given a special duty. We will put an entranceway on the western side as well as one on the east. We will ask them to be the keepers of the western entrance. The two war chiefs will protect that entrance, and when someone enters the territory they will have to pass through that entrance. They will be the ones to check to see the intentions of the visitors. If the strangers come in peace, they will be led into the territory through the black entrance where they will be reborn into the light of the Great Peace. If the stranger comes with ill will, they will be prevented from entering by a long black pole that will be used to protect the Longhouse of One Family. The *royaner* will try their hardest to make them accept the Great Peace. If this doesn't work and they slip through, we will put the bark of the slippery elm by the entrance. There, they will slip on the elm bark and be helpless. Then they will be slid out along the bark. This is the only time that the two *royaner* may keep their title as war chiefs."

The Peacemaker liked the plan that was proposed, as well as how the council had resolved their first problem. He asked Ayenwatha, "Do you still have the elderberry wampum?"

Ayenwatha answered, "I still have it."

The Peacemaker told the council, "Ayenwatha will send runners with the wampum of the eagle feather quill to the two war chiefs at the western entrance and invite them to come here."

The council then said, "Why do we not send Ayenwatha personally to fulfill this important matter."

Ayenwatha answered, "I will agree to go, as you will need my skills of diplomacy."

Ayenwatha had to travel as far west as the Geneseo Valley to find the village of Teyonuntakaha, where the war chief and his assistant war chief lived. Upon arriving outside the village, he set up camp and lit a fire, waiting for the Sonontowa:haka runners to come. After they arrived, they led Ayenwatha to their war chiefs. Once there, Ayenwatha told the war chiefs, "I have come to deliver a message from Kanata:kowa village where the Onontaka:haka live. There are many of us waiting for you to join us in the Great Peace."

The war chief asked Ayenwatha, "What is in it for us if we join?"

Ayenwatha answered, "You will have to come and see for yourself. However, if you come, I promise it will be worth it to you."

He then pulled out the eagle quill wampum and handed it to the war chief.

The war chief was impressed as this was the first time anyone had asked him in his way.

He answered Ayenwatha, "Wait for us, we will gather our warriors and be there in three days' time."

The war chief then sent runners throughout the village to gather the men. A soon as they were assembled, they headed back with Ayenwatha.

Upon arriving at the outskirts of Kanata:kowa village , the war chiefs and the warriors of the Sonontowa:haka waited outside the village for Ayenwatha to inform the others that they had arrived.

Ayenwatha told the Peacemaker and the others, "The war chiefs and their warriors will arrive when the Elder Brother, the Sun, hits the midpoint in the sky tomorrow."

The next day, as the Elder Brother, the Sun, hit the midpoint and stopped to take its daily break, the Sonontowa:haka war chiefs arrived with their warriors.

Ayenwatha said, "Everyone has arrived. We will now let the Peacemaker speak."

The war chief of the Sonontowa:haka said, "I will surround all the chiefs with my warriors and protect them. Once we are seated, we will sit down and listen to this Peacemaker."

The Peacemaker stood in the middle of the warriors. He said to them, "Now that we are all together, the Sun is higher than ever. In fact, it is brightening the world. You are the last that we have waited for. If you join us, we will be complete. We will combine ourselves into one power living in one longhouse. You will be the keepers of the western entrance. Inside the house, we will be all related in mind, body and belief. We now wait for your answer."

The Sonontowa:haka war chief answered, "I am interested. However, I want to know what we would do if anyone comes and attacks us from the west. How would we defend ourselves?"

The Peacemaker answered, "I have already visited many nations, and the message of peace has traveled even quicker than I have. When nations hear about the Great Peace, they will want to put down their weapons. The more who join, the more there will be who will want to be a part of it. In order to keep peace in the Longhouse of One Family, you will guard the entrance to the western door."

He then asked the war chief, "What clan are you from?"

The war chief answered, "I am from the Ohkwa:ho, Wolf Clan."

The Peacemaker then said, "You will be the keeper of the entrance for the nations who enter our extended longhouse. In fact I will name you *Teyonhninhokarawenh* of the Ohkwa:ho, Wolf Clan, He Who Holds the Flap Open."

Tsakonsasé then moved forward and placed the antlers on his head.

The Peacemaker then turned to the assistant war chief and asked him, "What clan are you from?"

The assistant war chief, answered, "I am from the Tawis Tawis, Snipe Clan."

The Peacemaker then said, "I will name you Kanonkerihtawih, Hair Burnt Off.

"Because you were stripped of your hair like the bark of an elm tree in the war, you shall stand by the entrance; if anyone tries to pass through unnoticed, they will slip over you and fall. Therefore, you will be the one to place the bark of the slippery elm tree at the entrance of the longhouse so no unwanted parties get past."

Then he said you two will be the last *royaner* and sit as two of four Snipe Clan cousins.

He continued, "When this Longhouse of One Family is built, there will always be room for others. We will *whatitinahstanonteron*, extend the rafters of the house, to let them in. We are not here to coerce them into anything that they don't want to do. Therefore, they will have their own councils to decide on their issues. When we all need to come to a consensus, they will speak their voice, and we will listen to them through the younger brothers. We should not try to make decisions for them. The purpose of this Great Peace is to end the bloodshed and to find a way to reason with each other. It is the will of the Creator that everyone may walk without fear of killing and bloodshed."

He continued, "The warriors who surround us will be the symbol of what you stand for. They must put away their weapons, as they are the ones who must carry the bones of the ancestors on their back and become *rotiskenren:keteh*, Bone Carriers. The bones do not decompose like the rest of the body. It is up to them to make sure that the knowledge here does not rot away. This will ensure that the Great Peace never ends. From now on, whenever they meet one another on the path that leads through this extended longhouse, they will greet each other by saying, 'Are you still living in the Great Peace?' If the person answers, 'I am in peace,' you will know that he is your friend."

The Peacemaker then said, "Now then, in order to make this come to pass, we will surround the Great White Pine Tree here at Onontaka. We will uproot it, so that there will be a cavern that will lead to a river that has streams that travel under the four white roots. We will cast all these weapons into the *tyohnawatehtsi:hon*, strong current of water. There, they will travel with the streams to the four corners of the earth, never to be taken up again. In fact, all the *royaner* will be known as trees of equal height, and once they throw out their weapons they will never be able to take the war trail again. If they do, their antlers will be removed forever."

He continued, "Whenever the *royaner* of the five nations come together, they will be one great power. No *royaner* can say that they have more power than another."

He continued, "The *Otiyaner*, clan matrons, will also be of equal height and carry the same power as one another. In fact, all the women in each clan will deal with their own problems and not interfere with the doings of other clans. Each clan will have its own government to decide on issues. Among the Kenienké:haka, it will pass from the Turtles to the Wolves and the final decision will be made by the Bears. Their decision will pass on to the men's and *Otiyaneh:shon*, women's council, of each village. From there, it will go to the council of each nation where the fire is lit. Among the Kenienké:haka, for instance, the nine *royaner* and nine *otiyaner*, clan mothers, will resolve the issue. Their decision will then be passed to the national council at Onontaka. Every five years there will be a meeting at Onontaka to confirm your continued allegiance in the Great Peace. However, a national council can be called anytime in times of crisis that concerns the whole confederacy. Otherwise, local issues may be resolved internally. The same will go for the Oneota:haka."

He continued, "The Kenienké:haka, Sonontowa:haka, and the Onontaka:haka will be divided internally in the way that the young man who brought the first clan system divided the clans along the long river before they migrated to their territories. Every *royaner* will have an equal voice on behalf of their nation when in the great council. They will be the *akatuneh*, uncles, to their *kheyatahwenh*, offspring or nephews, the Oneota:haka and the Kaokwa:haka, who sit on the other side of the council fire."

The Peacemaker then said, "Now we will be thankful for what has been achieved. However, we are not a full power as of yet because there are still many war chiefs who have to have the antlers of the *royaner* placed on their heads. They also must receive their title names. Before we do this, we will all sing the song of peace to confirm the binding of the five nations together. The song begins by singing, 'I greet the Great Law.'"

When the Peacemaker said this, everyone began singing the peace song: *"Aee, Aee/ Aee/ Aee/*, 'We greet the Great Law.'"

After the song was sung, the Peacemaker gave the thanks Teharonhia:wako had taught the *onkwe:honwe* many seasons before. He began by saying, "We give thanks because the power of peace comes from the Creator. We are grateful for coming together here on our Mother Earth. We thank the things that the Creator planted. Our mothers came from the bloodline of the first mother who resides in the earth. We give thanks to the grasses and medicines. We give thanks to the Little Water

Society for the cures that come from the medicines. We give thanks to the trees, especially the maple who gives us sustenance. We give thanks to the first fruits of the earth, the strawberries and the others. We give thanks to the corn, beans, and squash, for they allow us to live. We give thanks to the lakes, streams and rivers, for they are the blood of our mother. We give thanks for the thunders who freshen the earth and the water. When we hear them coming from the west, we know we will be refreshed. However, if they ever stop, we will know that we are near the time of the great purification. We give thanks to our Elder Brother the Sun in the east and our Grandmother the Moon who comes from the west. We give thanks to the stars who show us our life duties when they rise in the night. Most of all, we give thanks to the Creator for breathing life into our bodies."

The Peacemaker then said, "We are now ready to make our *ronatetsis-tan,* capital fire. From there, the smoke will rise, and everyone will be able to see it. The fire will burn forever."

He continued, "It will be up to Atotarhoh to make sure that the fire continues to burn. He will be the one to summon the general council, and he will be the one to open it with the giving of thanks. Once this is done, the *onkwe:honwe* will be united in one mind in themselves and with the rest of the creation."

He continued, "In fact, Atotarhoh will be given another title, Name Bearer. This doesn't mean that he will rule others, but, like the goose when he flies, he will take the lead. The names of the *royaner* will be used only when in council. They are not to be used in common."

The Peacemaker then said, "We will now plant the *Skaronhesekoh:wa,* Great White Pine, at the place of the central fire, at Kanata:kowa village with the Onontaka. This Tree of Peace will light up the world once again. We choose the Great White Pine because it is an evergreen that never dies or changes its color. The five needles on each branch will symbolize the Five Nations. From this great tree, roots will spread out into the four directions. Our words will spread from the trunk to the roots and travel into the four directions. Anyone who chooses to follow our words back up the roots to its source may join in the peace. They will then be protected under the *Rotenhnon:teron,* Long Leaves of the Great White Pine. There, they will be shaded when it becomes too hot. If ever one needs to cleanse themselves, they may burn the needles and spread the smoke over their bodies. If a nation decides to join us, we will refer to it as extending the rafters of the Longhouse of One Family. The Oneota:haka will be the nation that will formally bring then in while the Kaokwa:haka will be the nation who will adopt them under their bosom."

He continued, "I have something to tell you about the future. There may come a time when you may forget what I am saying. If that happens you will say aloud 'Someday, our ancestors will say what you have established. Our generations will be crying. The law will be old. We hope you are listening to us, our ancestors, that we are poor in knowledge. It is the responsibility of the elders to teach us. If they forget, we will all suffer.'"

He then said, "If there ever comes a time when you fight with one another, when you do not listen to your *royaner* or clan matrons, or when the *royaner* become war chiefs again, you will suffer as their will be no means to keep the peace."

He continued, "There will be two entrances into the Longhouse of One Family. In the west, the entrance will be guarded by the Sonontowa:haka. Anyone coming from the west or south will have to travel through that entrance. Those coming from the north and east will have to travel through the entrance guarded by the Kenienké:haka. Every nation, with good intentions has the right to enter through either entrance. That is because the *onkwe:honwe* have the responsibility to take care of the land in the territory. They will ensure that the generations of unborn will one day have the right to its use. However, no one can own the land, as it belongs to the Creator and our first mother. You cannot sell your mother from whom your bodies were created. Your first mother gives herself to the generations to come, so that they may use her in the future."

The Peacemaker said, "You will all have equal hunting rights. We will take out a dish and place the tail of a beaver into it. When we eat from the dish, we will use no sharp objects. We will eat only with our fingers. That means when we go to another nation's territory for food, there will be no blood spilt. However, you should notify them of your needs first. They can then tell you where the animals are more populated. If ever we see someone hungry, we will share what we have with them. We will bring them into our lodges and feed them if we have to. There is enough for everyone, as long as you do not waste anything. When you go hunting and you have too much meat, you will try it to ensure that it is not wasted. You are to kill only the bucks and not the does while with child. If you kill the does, you kill future generations, and you will one day go hungry. If you look at your Grandmother the Moon, she will tell you the season when there will be an abundance of a type of food. Your ancestors, the stars, will point to the time when you are to begin and end your activities."

He then told them, "During the midwinter moon, Kahiyatah:kowa, when the female deer are great with young, the hunters are not to take the female. The moon after Konrahtah:kah is the time that you see the buds of the trees on the snow and know that winter is coming to an end. This will be a time of famine, and you should have supplied yourselves during the autumn. The third moon after Kanuskwah:kah is the time when you hear the frogs and the crows. It is the time to tap the maple trees and build canoes. The next moon Kanuskwahta:kowa is the time you can see the grasses appear and the animals come closer to graze. The seven dancing brothers will begin their descent at this time, and there will be hunger. The fifth moon, Kahnakaht, is the time the flowers appear in the woods. It is the time to begin to plant the seeds of the corn, beans, and squash. Fish is used for fertilizer as this is the time when the fish are plentiful. The next moon, Oyiakneh, is the berry moon. This is the season when the berries are pounded and placed into the cornbread. It is the time to prepare the strawberry medicine. During the moon after the berry moon, Sahtekekenhahenh, the summer is divided, and one can expect the thunders to arrive in force. The next moon, Tsayskihkah, is the season to fish and dry food for future use. It is also the time when frost may first appear. The moon, Tsayskihneh, is the time when green corn is roasted and the husks pulled back. It is the time to dance the green corn dance. The fall moon, Kasahkinéhah, is the time when the hunting season begins, and the Great Bear in the sky is shot in the sky by the three hunters. You will then see the trees turn red from the blood. The next moon, Kasahkineh, is the moon of the falling leaves and the beginning of the cold. It is the time when the *onkwe:honwe* say farewell to any visitors until after the winter. The last moon, Tsohtonh, is the month of great cold and long nights. This is the time when storytelling occurs. All of these things have been given by the Creator to you to live. These are the natural laws of creation. This is why we continue to give thanks to the creation."[4]

He went on, "It is the responsibility of the young to hunt and provide for the old. They are to consult with their elders when they make decisions about the welfare of the *onkwe:honwe*. The elders have the experience as well as the knowledge and language."

The Peacemaker then said, "When the fur of the animals is changing, the meat is no good. The stars will tell you that the hunting season will begin when the leaves turn red from the blood of the Great Bear in the sky. This will last until the time of the midwinter moon. Medicines are also not to be picked during the two moons after the berry moon because they also must renew themselves."

He then said to the *royaner*, "You are the wisest of the *onkwe:honwe*. You will have to have good minds. It will require having skin *tsatah:nyionionkarakeh*, seven spans, thick. If any sharp objects or words are thrown at you, they will bounce off you and won't pierce your heart and give you too much pain. You and the elders are the teachers of the children, and it is your duty to ensure that the elders are respected."

The Peacemaker then said, "Now we will place Atotarhoh under the Great Tree. We will then take some thistle downs and make a mat out of them for Atotarhoh to sit on. The white of the thistle will represent having a good mind. Atotarhoh will also have a *skaweyesokoh:wa onera-hohnsta*, seagull wing, placed next to him. If there is a problem, he will sweep it away by using the seagull wing. He will sweep around the fire and Great Tree to ensure that it is clean of any obstructions that may get in the way of having a good mind. If there are any bugs that crawl on the mat that may cause trouble, he will sweep them away. If that doesn't work, he will use a pole and knock the creature down. He will notify the Sonontowa:haka door keeper to ask his assistant to lead the obstruction out of the Longhouse."

He continued, "The next thing that we must do is to place the eagle on top of the Great White Pine Tree. Like the uncle in the Sky World who looked after the children and later offered to bring light to the earth when Teharonhia:wako asked him, the eagle will be our eyes. He will warn us and let us see if there is any danger approaching. If there is a danger to the entrance, all of the *rotiskenren:keteh* will assemble at the entrance. The *royaner* will try to reason with those who pose a danger to the Great Peace. During this time the *onkwe:honwe* will tremble under the Great Tree lest the Great Peace be broken. They will do everything they can to prevent bloodshed. Woe to all if blood is spilt and weapons are taken up again."

The Peacemaker then said, "The best way to prevent the taking of weapons is to be as strong as we can be. If we are united in peace, others will not want to force our hand. They will rather join us. The taking up of weapons is wrong. We must show others that it is in no one's interest to take weapons. I now ask that each of the five nations represented here bring me an arrow."

A representative of each nation brought forward an arrow. First there was Ayenwatha who brought the Peacemaker an arrow; next it was Rotatsheté; then it was Atotarhoh; then Takaheyonh; and then Skanyiatar:io.

The Peacemaker took the arrows and said to them, "Each nation has a power, and he pointed to the arrows. If we put these powers together, we will be one great power and speak with one great voice. If a nation pulls out, we will be easily broken like this individual arrow." He pulled an arrow out and snapped it. He continued to say, "If that happens, we will all suffer. In fact, I predict that one day this will happen. There will come a time when a great white wind will blow through the territory of the Longhouse of One Family. When this happens, you will have to decide if you will stand together or be divided. If you divide your power, you will be broken apart."

The Peacemaker then said, "Now our minds are together and one in purpose. I will put the arrows under the tree. It will be up to the *royaner* and clan matrons to ensure that you remain sitting under the tree in unity."

He then said, "Now you *royaner* and others, stand up! We will circle the tree and the central fire. You will guard the tree and fire and support Atotarhoh."

Then he said, "Tsakonsasé, stand here. The *onkwe:honwe* will stand behind you to support you in your task. You must never break this circle. Inside will be all your beliefs: the *teyotiokwaonhas:ton*, Laws of Creation, the clan system created by the young man, and the *Kayeneren:kowa*. In the future, there will be even more."

He continued, "If any of you *royaner* leave this circle, your horns will drop in the middle. You cannot leave this circle to represent your people. Your allegiance is to the members here. Not only will your horns drop, but your name and title as well."

He went on, "This goes for everyone as well. Every clan has a set of names that belong to that clan. No one else can use those names. If ever someone is taken in from the outside, they will be given a name from the clan. The names are to continue always. They will be given a necklace to wear that will represent the clan and the name from that clan. As long as they have an allegiance to the clan and nation they have been adopted into, they may wear the necklace. If they go against the Longhouse of One Family, they will forfeit their name and clan. The same goes for those children of a nation who have received their clan name. If they step out of the circle, they will forfeit their clan name and have to live outside the circle. It will be up to the clan matrons to keep a record of the names and to give them out. They will be the ones to comb the tangles from the heads of those who receive a clan name, just as Tsakonsasé did with Atotarhoh. Once they are ensured of having a good mind, then they may join us."

The Peacemaker then warned them again, "In the future, a high wind will come from the east. The tree will bend and almost fall. It will be up to you *royaner* to link each other by the arms and catch it before it hits the ground. If you don't, the tree will rot and the fire will go out. Then the language and the culture will disappear. The power that is here will be no more. Once again there will be arguing over how to do the ceremonies and who should lead them. The heads of the Rotinonshonni will begin to roll aimlessly. Other nations will remember that at one time you were great. You will be at the edge of a cliff dangling by the feet. There will be suicides among you. Others will find shelter under the Oka:ratsikowa, Great Swamp Elm Tree, in a faraway land and be happy for a little while until the Elm Tree is killed. You will see warriors like you have never seen before fighting in great wars. They will want to lead the *onkwe:honwe* instead of the *royaner*. That is because Sawiskera will have kept his promise to try to deceive you. It will be up to you to pray and ask for Teharonhia:wako to help you. I will be listening and if I hear you cry out my name three times, I will come and guide those who believe in me. It is up to you to make sure that the tree is raised to its full height. You will have to nurture it in order for it to do so."

The Peacemaker continued, "Today we are united. You will have to respect one another. Whenever you leave your lodges, you will put a stick in front of the entrance. That will mean that no one is there and you can't enter. If strangers come to your lodge, you are to bring them in and feed them. There should always be enough food for guests. No one should go hungry."

The Peacemaker then said, "Now then, we will take a break for three moons. Then we will return here all together. The reason for this is that it will give you time to tell the rest of the *onkwe:honwe* what has happened here. You will then return with all your people. The clan matrons in the meantime will select the rest of the candidates for the position of *royaner*. When you return, I will name them, once the clan matrons tell me about why they were selected. This will be the same way that the clan matrons selected the clans from the animals—when the great young man first put together the clan system, except they will be selected by merit. We are now going to take the clan system one step further."

The *royaner*, the clan matrons, and their followers then dispersed to their nation's territories to inform the people about the *Kayeneren:kowa*. Ayenwatha went back with the rest of the Kenienké:haka *royaner* and clan matrons to his village. They then spread the news about what had taken place at Kanata:kowa village of the Onontaka:haka. After several moons had passed, the *onkwe:honwe* gathered in their villages to begin the journey back to Kanata:kowa village. They would be coming from the east and from the west.

As the Kenienké:haka had met the Oneota:haka, they approached Onontaka:haka territory together. At the time that they rested together before entering Onontaka territory, Ayenwatha decided to head south for about a half day's journey. He wanted to be alone to contemplate what was happening before he entered Kanata:kowa village. There seemed to be so much to learn and to remember. It seemed that whenever the *onkwe:honwe* had been taught anything, they would forget in time and revert back to their former ways. Ayenwatha wanted to find a way that would remind them for all time about the *Kayeneren:kowa*.

As Ayenwatha sat beside a small lake thinking about the things that happened, he noticed a flock of ducks swimming close to the shore. As he stood up to get a closer look, the ducks spotted him and began to swim off. As they ran to take off, they splashed their feet. Ayenwatha spotted something white at the bottom of the lake bed. He moved into the shallow water and with his hand scooped up some earth. In the earth, he picked out a lake water clam shell. It was white on one half and dark on the other.

He thought to himself, "If there was a way to drill into the shell, we could use this to bead with. Perhaps, a pump drill, like we use to make fire could be used. It would need a hard point to get through the shell without breaking it. A fine flint point might do it."

Ayenwatha then found a flint stone. He then pounded it down with a rock until it was fine and thin. He made a pump drill out of some wood he found, placed the flint in a groove in the front of the drill, and tied it with twine. He then placed the shell and began to drill into its side using his hands for friction. As he tried to drill into the shell, the shell would crack open. He tried two times to do this but did not succeed.

He thought to himself, "It seems like the end of the drill gets too hot, and results in the shell cracking. Maybe, if I drill it in the water, there won't be as much heat from the friction." He took the shell into the shallow part of the lake and began to drill. This time he was able to drill into the shell; the water prevented the friction.

He said to himself, "I will make belts using the two parts of the shell. On these belts we will remember everything that has taken place. As long as these belts are kept, the teachings of the *Kayeneren:kowa* will continue to exist. The two parts of the shell, the dark and the white, will represent the duality in the creation of all things, just like the twins. The fact that the shells come from the water means that they are pure. We will place our words into these shells, and when we need to hear them again we will pray and listen for our words to come back to us."

Ayenwatha then went back to Onontaka to meet with the others. When he arrived, he went to Atotarhoh's lodge to tell him about the shell wampum he had discovered.

Upon seeing the wampum, Atotarhoh answered him, "This new recording device will be used for sanctioning marriages, deaths, councils, *royaner, Otiyaner,* and everything that is important to us."

He and Ayenwatha then walked back to the assembly together to tell the Peacemaker about the wampum. The assembly at Onontaka included members of all the nations. The Kaokwa:haka and the Oneota:haka sat on one side of the assembly, while the Kenienké:haka and the Sonontowa:haka sat at the other end of the assembly. The Onontaka:haka sat at one end of the assembly while the Peacemaker stood in the middle. The *royaner* and the clan mothers sat in front of their particular nations.

Upon being told about the wampum, the Peacemaker told the assembly, "This wampum brought to us by Ayenwatha is both black and white. It will be held by the clan matrons. Whenever a *royaner* dies, they will take the black wampum to the condoling nation to notify them of the death. If the death occurs among the nephews who are mourning, the wampum will be sent to the clear-minded nation, the uncles who will condole them during a great ceremony that will be held."

He went on, "As the condoling nation approaches the village of the mourners, they will sing the *Hai, hai,* or the roll call of the *royaner* as they approach the wood's edge of the mourning nation. They will then hear the three bare words by the mourning nation that were first said when Ayenwatha lost his daughters. They will clear the eyes, the ears, and the throats of the condolers in case any grief happened to them on their journey. They will give the condolers the white wampum of the deceased *royaner* to hold until a new *royaner* is chosen."

He continued, "The clear-minded condoling nation will then say the three bare words back to the mourners to relieve some of the grief of the mourning nation. The mourners will then take the clear-minded nation by the arms and bring them back to a great council house that we will build together. Once again, the clear-minded will sing the roll call as they are led into the council house. A deer skin will be placed between the clear-minded and the mourning nations. This is the same as is done at Tsakonsasé's lodge by the war road when she mediates between nations. The clear-minded will then sing the six songs of farewell that come from the song of peace that we all sang to Atotarhoh, to disentangle the disruptive thoughts that were within him."

He continued, "The clear-minded will then take out the wampum belts that Ayenwatha is devising for us to help remember and recite the things that have occurred when we formed this league. When they are finished, they will then recite the last twelve condolences that were made between myself and Ayenwatha, and pass the strings of wampum that were first made between us to the other side."

As the Peacemaker spoke, some of the assembled got up and began to leave. The tension of what was happening was too much for some of them. They needed a break to think things over. All of this was new, and there was confusion as to whether this would work.

The Peacemaker seeing that some of them were becoming agitated said to them, "Don't leave! Take a break and compose yourselves. Come back and let me finish. In fact, this is the way it will be in the future. The condolers will leave to compose themselves, and then they will be called back by the mourners to finish. In fact, condolences will be held in either the fall or spring when it is neither too hot nor too cold, to ensure that we are not affected by the weather."

He continued, "Upon their return, the mourners will then speak the twelve words back to the condolers. Then they will show the face of the future *royaner* who will hold the title of the departed. The clear-minded will then recognize the *royaner* by acknowledging him and charging him with his duties."

He continued, "When all this is done, the mourners will hold a feast, and we will clear our throats of the tobacco that has been burned here. Then, there will be cries of joy on both sides, and we will dance with our *royaner*, rubbing their antlers together ending the period of grief once and for all."

The Peacemaker then said, "We have still left something unfulfilled. That is, we have to fill all the titles of the *royaner* as well as show how they will be related to one another."

He then asked Tekarihokenh of the Kenienké:haka, "Have the clan matrons chosen their representatives."

Tekarihokenh answered, "They have chosen the rest of the representatives for the Kenienké:haka nation."

The Peacemaker then said, "We will first elevate the rest of the *royaner* from the Kenienké:haka. Let us have the representatives of the Ohkwa:ho, Wolf Clan, stand up.

A clan matron then stood up, "I represent the Ohkwa:ho, Wolf Clan. We have chosen three representatives from the Ohkwa:ho, Wolf Clan, just as there were three chosen from the Anon:wara, Turtle Clan, before."

She continued, "The first who was chosen was done so because of the great respect that we have for his wisdom and strength." She then presented the man for everyone to see.

The Peacemaker said, "You will be known as Shorenhoweneh, a Great Tree with Branches Out, because of your being like a stout branch that spreads out; therefore, you have earned your people's respect."

The clan matron then placed the antlers on the *royaner*, Shorenhoweneh.

The clan matron then said, "The second man who was chosen was done so because of what he has provided for us. Although he is very old, he is among the wisest of the men."

The Peacemaker then said, "Your title will be Teyonhenkwen, Double Life. This is because throughout your life you have sustained us like the plants on our mother."

The clan matron then placed the antlers on Teyonhenkwen.

The clan matron then said, "The third who was chosen was done so because of the way he looks after his people."

The Peacemaker said, "Your title will be Orenrhe:kowa, A Great White Eagle, because of the way you watch over others."

The clan matron then placed the antlers on Orenrhe:kowa's head. The clan matron of the Ohkwa:ho, Wolf Clan, then sat down, as that was all who were chosen.

The Peacemaker, them told the three that they were to be *ahsenhnihontatekenah*, brothers, to one another and Snipe Clan cousins to the next three from the Ohkwa:ri, Bear Clan.

Next, the clan matron of the Ohkwa:ri, Bear Clan, stood up. She said, "The first that was chosen was done so because of his wisdom in resolving any issues in the clan." She then brought the man forward.

The Peacemaker replied, "Due to your great wisdom in solving any problems that may arise in your clan, you will be known as Tehenakarineh, Double Horns, for double the wisdom."

The clan matron then placed the antlers on Tehenakarineh.

Next, the clan matron brought another man in front of the assembly. She said, "This man was chosen because of the way he was noticed by others whenever he entered a lodge."

The Peacemaker said, "Your title will be Agstawenserontha, He Holds Up the Three Rattles."

The clan matron then placed the antlers on the head of Agstawenserontha.

The clan matron then presented another man to the assembly. She said, "This man was noticed for the way he reasons things out whenever there is something that needs to be done."

The Peacemaker then told the man, "Because you are in the forefront whenever something needs to be done, your title will be Shoskoharowaneh, Great Drift of Wood."

The clan matron then placed the antlers on the head of Shoskoharowaneh.

The clan mother then said, "This is all the *royaner* that we have chosen. There will be nine all together, three for each clan."

The Peacemaker finalized by saying, "You three will be *ahsenhnihontatekenah,* brothers, to one another and Snipe Clan cousins to the previous three."

The Peacemaker said, "Will the Oneota:haka clan matrons please stand up and bring the men they chose forward?"

The clan matron of the Oneota:haka Turtle Clan stood up and said, "We have chosen this man from the Anon:wara, Turtle Clan, because, whenever anyone needs a place to stay, his place is always open to them."

The Peacemaker replied, "Because you are so generous and have opened your house to others who want to join the Great Peace, you will be known as Shononses, Extended House. You will have a further duty once a nation is adopted in; you will represent them in council."

The clan matron then placed the antlers on the head of Shononses.

The clan matron then said, "The next man who was chosen was done so because of his powerful oratory skills."

The Peacemaker replied, "Because you can project your voice in every direction, your title will be Tehonahokenah, Two Forks in the Water. You will speak on behalf of your nation."

The clan matron then placed the antlers on Tehonahokenah.

The clan matron then presented her third man and said, "This man was chosen because of his ability to allow others to go before him."

The Peacemaker said, "You will be known by the title, Hahtyatenentha, He Lowers His Body."

The clan matron placed the antlers on the head of Hahtyatenentha.

The clan matron of the Anon:wara, Turtle Clan, then sat down while the clan mother of the Ohkwa:ri, Bear Clan, took her place.

The Ohkwa:ri, Bear Clan, matron said, "We chose this one because of his great ability to listen to others."

The Peacemaker said, "Then we will give him the title Tewatahontenyon, Two Hanging Ears."

The clan matron stepped forward and placed the antlers on the head of Tewatahontenyon.

The clan matron then presented another man and said, "We chose this one because he speaks slowly, so that everyone will understand everything he says."

The Peacemaker said, "Then his title will be Kanyataghshayenh, He Swallows Slowly."

The clan matron then placed the antlers on Kanyataghshayenh.

The clan matron of the Ohkwa:ri, Bear Clan, then stood up her third man and said, "We chose this man because of the way he is able to get things done without notice to himself."

The Peacemaker said, "Then we will call him Ronwahtsatonneh, He Is Buried in the Mist."

The clan matron then placed the antlers on Ronwahtsatonneh's head.

The clan matron then said, "This is all we have chosen. Including the three Ohkwa:ho, Wolf, *royaner* that were first given their antlers by Tsakonsasé, there are now nine in all. There will be three *royaner* for each clan from now on and they will be *ahsenhnihontatekenah*, brothers, to one another and Snipe Clan cousins to the others."

The Peacemaker said, "It is good, as we now have two nations who have all their *royaner* chosen. Next, I will ask the Onontaka:haka clan matrons to bring their men that they have chosen close to the front."

The Peacemaker said, "We will now choose the rest of the *royaner* from the Onontaka:haka nation. Atotarhoh, will you inform the clan mothers of the Onontaka:haka nation to come forward and stand up their representatives?"

The clan matron of the Tsiennis:to, Beaver Clan, got up and said, "We have chosen this man because, whenever there is something that needs to be finished, this man will make sure it gets done."

The Peacemaker said, "Your title will be Onehsenghhen, He Stretches the Hide, because you get business taken care of. This means that you will take a place beside Atotarhoh as a special advisor to him; therefore, you will be a Snipe Clan cousin to him."

The clan matron then placed the antlers on the head of Onehsenghhen.

The same clan matron said, "We have chosen another from the Tsiennis:to, Beaver Clan, because of the way he is able to see things before they happen."

The Peacemaker said, "You will be called Tehhatkatos, He Looks Both Sides, because of the way you anticipate things. You will also work as an advisor to Atotarhoh on the other side of him; therefore, you too will be his Snipe Clan cousin."

The clan matron then placed the antlers on the head of Tehhatkatos.

The clan matron of the Tsiennis:to, Beaver Clan, sat down and a clan mother of the Ohkwa:ho, Wolf Clan, stood up and said, "We have selected this man because of the way he twists his words to make his point."

The Peacemaker said, "Your title will be Skanyiatajiwak, Bitter Throat, for the way you use words."

The clan matron then placed the antlers on the head of Skanyiatajiwak.

The same clan matron said, "We have chosen this man and called him Karhakonha, Sharp-Skinned Hawk, because of the way he looks to see that everything has been taken care of after a council is over."

The Peacemaker said, "From now on your title will be Awenkenwat, The Edge of the Water."

The clan matron then placed the antlers on the head of Awenkenwat.

The clan matron of the Ohkwa:ho, Wolf Clan, called another man forward and said, "We have selected this third man because, although his father was from another nation, he is now one of the most dedicated of us all."

The Peacemaker said, "Your title will be Tehayatkwayen, Red on the Wing."

The clan matron then placed the antlers on the head of Tehayatkwayen.

The Peacemaker said, "You three will be *ahsenhnihontatekenah*, brothers, to one another."

Another clan matron got up from the Ohkwa:ho Wolf Clan and said, "I am from the Ohkwa:ho:kowa, Big Wolf Clan. We have chosen this man because of the way he is able to compose himself in difficult situations."

The Peacemaker said, "The first time I saw you, you were throwing beach chips in the water as you were thinking things through. The fact that you are able to compose yourself so well means that you should have a special duty to perform. Your title will be Hononwirehtonh, He Conceals Something. Your duty will be to wait until the last minute in council, and if you see anyone getting out of hand, you will stand up and put them back into order."

He continued, "You shall also be *Hochustanona*, Keeper of the Wampum. You will be alone with two relations on each side of you.

The clan matron of the Ohkwa:ho:kowa, Big Wolf Clan, then put the antlers on the head of Hononwirehtonh.

The clan matron of the Big Wolf sat down and the clan mother of the Ohskenon:ton, Deer Clan, stood up. She said, "We have chosen this man because of the way he speaks for the women."

The Peacemaker said, "Because you speak for the women council, we will name you Kowennenserontoh, Her Voice Is Suspended." He continued, "You will be an *akatuneh*, uncle, to the Ohkwa:ho:kowa and sit on one side of them."

His clan matron then placed the antlers on Kowennenserontoh.

The same clan matron then said, "We chose this next man because of the way he can get information across to many people."

The Peacemaker said, "We will give you the title Harirronh, The One Who Scatters Matters."

The clan matron then placed the antlers on Harirronh.

The Peacemaker then said, "Harirronh will also be an *akatuneh*, uncle, to the Ohkwa:ho:kowa and sit on the other side of them."

The clan matron of the Deer sat down and the clan mother of the Eel stood up. She went up to the front and said, "The clan mothers of the Okonte:na, Eel Clan, have chosen this man because resolutions are placed before him."

The Peacemaker said, "Because you have so much ability, you will be called Honyunhnyennih, It Was Made for Him."

The clan matron then put the antlers on Honyunhnyennih.

The same clan mother said, "We have chosen this next man because he will reprimand those that don't listen after three warnings."

The Peacemaker said, "Your title will then be Shotehkwaseh, He Clubs Them."

The clan matron then put the horns on the head of Shotehkwaseh.

The clan matron then said, "We have chosen this next man because he is always visiting everyone to see how they are feeling."

The Peacemaker said, "We will give him the title Shakokenhen, He Saw the People."

The clan matron then put the antlers on the head of Shakokenhen.

The clan matron of the Okonte:na, Eel Clan, sat down.

The Peacemaker then said to the five that they would all be *wiskhnihontatekeneh*, brothers, to one another.

Next, the clan matron of the Ohskenon:ton stood up.

She said, "The man we have chosen was done so because of the way he is able to handle the hatchet. Many are afraid of him, and we think that if he became a *royaner* he would be able to put the ways of war away."

The Peacemaker replied, "There is always a risk in having someone who is proficient in warfare to lead the people. However, some of the *royaner* were war chiefs already, and they now have good minds. We will call this one Shehhawih, He Wears a Hatchet. We hope he uses it on trees and not people from now on."

His clan mother then put the antlers on his head. The Shehhawih title would pass from the Anon:wara, Turtle, to the Ohskenon:ton, Ball Deer Clan, when he went back to war.

The clan mother then said, "The next who we have chosen was done so because he is always willing to travel and would be good in council."

The Peacemaker said, "We will give this one the title Skanawatih, The Other Side of the Marshes."

The clan mother then placed the antlers on Skanawatih's head.

In the future, there would be confusion between Skanawatih's and Shehhawih's title. That is because Skanawatih would be the first *royaner* to take up the hatchet of war again. When he went to war, he would use the title given to Shehhawih and become Anon:wara, Turtle Clan. He would extend the rafters of the Kayeneren:kowa, such as the laws concerning warriors and war chiefs. He would take two titles, one of a war chief and the other a peace chief; this went against the original plan of the Peacemaker. He would say that the assistant to the *royaner* should be a war chief to make sure that he did the will of the warriors. This went against everything the Peacemaker had tried to achieve, and the *onkwe:honwe* would one day become confused again about the meaning of the Great Peace. These would be called Skanawatih's Laws of War.

The Peacemaker, then said, "You two will be *yatatekeneh*, brothers, to one another. Furthermore the Onontaka:haka will be *akatuneh*, uncles, to their Kaokwa:haka *kheya:tawenh*, offspring. Fathers are less important, as uncles always look after their sisters' sons.

There would be fourteen Onontaka:haka *royaner* chosen in all. The clan mothers of the Onontaka:haka then sat down, and the Peacemaker began to speak.

The Peacemaker said, "It is now time to elevate the *royaner* of the Lower Kaokwa:haka."

The clan matron of the Ohkwa:ri, Bear Clan, stood up, and said, "We have chosen this man because of his resolve, as he never gives up."

The Peacemaker said, "It is good that we change the strongest-minded into a good-minded *royaner*. From now on his title will be Katarakwara-son, He Was Bruised."

His clan matron then put on the antlers of Katarakwarason.

The clan matron of the Ohkwa:ri, Bear Clan, sat down and the clan matron of the Ohskenon:ton, Deer Clan, stood up.

She said, "We have chosen this next man because of his bravery."

The Peacemaker said, "We will give you the title Soyouwes, His Guts Are Long, because of your bravery. Instead of having guts, you will carry a long wampum belt for your nation, which will keep you in peace."

His clan matron then placed the antlers on his head.

The clan matron of the Ohskenon:ton, Deer Clan, sat down, and the clan mother of the Anon:waron, Turtle Clan, stood up.

The clan matron of the Anon:waron, Turtle Clan, said, "We have chosen this man because of his great memory and the way he can repeat whatever has been said after hearing it once."

The Peacemaker said, "You will be known by the title, Watiaseronhneh, He Piles It On, and it will be your duty to memorize and repeat what has been said in the council if anything is forgotten."

The clan matron then put the antlers on the head of Watiaseronhneh.

The Peacemaker then continued, "You three will be *ahsenhnihontatekenah*, brothers, to one another and here we will divide the *katsistah*, fires, and *kahwatsireh*, titles, between the lower and upper Kaokwa:haka.

The clan matron of the Anon:waron, Turtle Clan, sat down and the clan matron of the Ohkwa:ho, Wolf Clan, stood up.

She said, "We have chosen this man because of his devotion to Teharonhia:wako and our ancestors in the Sky World."

The Peacemaker replied, "Because you are such a spiritual person and always burn tobacco in your prayers, you will be known as Teyohronyonkoh, He Reaches the Sky. It was across the marshes at the northern part of the lake you first heard the message of peace."

His clan matron then placed the antlers on his head.

The clan mother of the Ohkwa:ho, Wolf Clan, then said, "We have chosen this next man because of his ability to remain steadfast in every situation and hold his emotions."

The Peacemaker said, "You will hold the title, Teyothorehkwenh, Cold on Both Sides, for the way you compose yourself."

His clan matron then placed the antlers on his head.

The clan matron of the Wolf sat down, and the clan matron of the Tawis Tawis, Sandpiper Clan, stood up.

She said, "We have chosen this next man because of his great knowledge of the culture."

The Peacemaker said, "You will be given the title, Tewenhethon, Two Things Happen, because you have twice the knowledge as the rest."

The clan matron of the Tawis Tawis, Sandpiper Clan, then placed the antlers on his head.

The Peacemaker then said that you three will be *ahsenhnihontatekenah*, brothers, to one another.

Once again, the clan mother of the Ohkwa:ho, Wolf Clan, stood up and said, "We still have one more to be chosen. We choose this man because of the way that he is always first to get anything done."

The Peacemaker said, "In council, you will be the first to speak for the Kaokwa:haka; you will be given the title, Watontahherhah, He Crowds Himself In."

His clan matron then placed the antlers on his head.

The clan matron of the Ohkwa:ho, Wolf Clan, sat down, and the clan matron of the Ohkwa:ri, Bear Clan, stood up once again.

She said, "There is still one that we chose who is left. We choose this man because of his patience when getting anything done."

The Peacemaker said, "You will be given the title Teskaheh, He Rests on It, and, whenever a resolution is made by the Kaokwa:haka, the decision will rest on you to finalize it. Not only that, but it will be through you that other nations are adopted in; they will then be represented by the Oneota:haka at the council. However, they must first enter through the western entrance guarded by the Sonontowa:haka if they are to remain."

The Kaokwa:haka clan matron then placed the antlers on Teskaheh's head. She said, "We have chosen ten men to be *royaner* who will sit for us in council." She then sat down.

The Peacemaker said, "You two will be Snipe Clan cousins to one another."

The Peacemaker said, "Now we are almost full. There are only the Sonontowa:haka left to finalize this process. I have elevated four, and it is time for the clan matrons to elevate the rest."

The clan mother of the Karhakonha, Hawk Clan, stood up and said, "We have chosen this man because he is a great thinker."

The Peacemaker said, "Because you are renowned for the way that you can reason things, you will be given the title, Shakenjoweneh, Great Forehead."

His clan matron then placed the antlers on his head.

The clan mother of the Karhakonha, Hawk Clan, sat down, and the clan mother of the Anon:waron, Turtle Clan, stood up.

She said, "We have chosen this man because of the manner in which he speaks. His voice is so strong that people begin to tremble when they hear him."

The Peacemaker said, "Because you have such a strong voice when you speak, you will be given the title Kanokareh, He Threatens Like an Arrow. Those who try to get in through the western entrance without notice will hear your voice and tremble."

His clan matron then placed the antlers on his head.

The Peacemaker then said, "You two will be Snipe Clan cousins."

The clan matron of the Anon:waron, Turtle Clan, sat down, and the clan matron of the Tawis Tawis, Snipe, stood up.

She said, "We have chosen this man because he speaks with such eloquence; when you hear him, the day passes by quickly."

The Peacemaker said, "From now on his title will be known as Teshayenah, The Day Falls Down.

His clan matron then put the antlers on Teshayenah, The Day Falls Down.

Next, the clan mother of the Ohkwa:ri Clan said, "We have one more man that we think should have a title. We chose him because of the way he retains information."

The Peacemaker said, "You will be the one to remember what the Sonontowa:haka have said in council. If anything is forgotten, you will remember it. Your title will be Shotyenawet, He Holds onto It."

The clan matron of the Ohkwa:ri Clan placed the antlers on his head.

The Peacemaker said, "That you two and the first two chosen by the Peacemaker will be Snipe Clan cousins to one another."

The Peacemaker then said, "There are now fifty *royaner*, Trees of Equal Height, to sit in council and fifty *Otiyaner*, clan matrons, behind them to ensure that they fulfill their duties. If a clan matron is informed that a *royaner* has not fulfilled the wishes of the people in council, she may give him a warning. If he still does not abide by the will of the people a second time, she will give another warning through the faith keeper. If he still does not abide by will of the people, the men of the clan will gather, and, after the third warning, the *royaner* assistant will take away his horns, and he will be removed from office forever."

One of the men asked the Peacemaker, "Why do we not kill him instead?"

The Peacemaker said, "The whole purpose of this coming together is to live among each other in peace. Did you not understand everything that has just happened? The taking away of the *royaner*'s antlers is a much tougher punishment to face than killing him. He will have to walk among the people in humiliation. Remember, if we start to kill one another, the peace will come to an end, and the unity we have will melt like the snow in the spring. If anyone takes up the path of war and kills a *royaner* or an *Otiyaner*, clan matron, they will cough up blood."

He continued, "If ever you become weak in your resolve, you are to burn tobacco and pray to the Creator to give you guidance. If ever there are not enough men to fill a clan, you may borrow a man from another clan to fill it. You should not lend a clan title to another clan, lest it becomes lost to the original clan forever."

He continued, "You must ensure that the fifty titles of the *Rotiianeh:son*, combined lords, remain filled. You have been taught the process on how to do this. Now is the time to begin. We have completed our longhouse from the east to the west, and our house is now full; we are all related."

He then said, "Now that we are a house of relations, there will be no intermarriage between those of the same clan anywhere in this house.

That is because you will need your family to take care of you when you travel."

He continued, "It will be up to the clan matrons to ensure that the lineage remains secure. They will be responsible for marriages. They will all have equal power and will be given three days to select a new *royaner*. They are also to arrange the funeral rites by preparing the burial of the *royaner* who has passed away."

He continued, "The clan matron will hold two strings of wampum, one black and one white. If a *royaner* becomes sick, his clan matron will keep an eye on him. She will notify her nation that there is a problem. The *royaner* will then be dehorned by his assistant and his horns placed beside him. The black wampum will then be hung near him. Special words will be said as he is dehorned."

The Peacemaker then said the words to be used, "'Now then, the Creator put you here for so many days to become a *royaner*. Today, I must dehorn you. If you recover, it is up to the Creator to give you more days. Your nation has made you *royaner*. Since you became *royaner* you were guided by the Great Laws of Peace. You held your title for life. Right now your clan mother is watching you to recover. If you recover, you will resume your duties and your clan mother will take back the black wampum that hangs near you. Your colleagues will come and elevate you again so that you can fulfill your duties. We will then be thankful.'"

The Peacemaker said, "No *royaner* will take his horns with him to the grave. If a *royaner* does die, the *royaner* from his nation will send runners to notify the other *royaner* of the death. During the time of condolence, if it is an *Akatuneh*, Our Father's Kinsmen, *royaner*, the clan mother will pass the black wampum to the *Kheya:tawineh,* Our Offspring, until a new *royaner* is raised. The same will be done if it is a *royaner* from *Kheya:tawineh* who is being condoled. They will pass it to the *Akatuneh*, Our Father's Kinsmen. Once the new *royaner* is elevated, the wampum goes back to his clan matron."

He continued, "clan matrons who die are not dehorned, they will be chosen from their clans. This must be done in three days' time after death and can be done in a small condolence within the nation. They will then be confirmed during the big condolence."

He continued, "The white wampum that the clan matron holds will only come out during a big condolence and will go across the fire at that time. This will occur only in the autumn after the harvest is in. If there is an emergency, you will hold the condolence in the spring. However, the rivers are high and the paths muddy. The autumn is the best time for it to be held."

He continued, "Mourning will not be longer than a year. Then there will be a feast held for the dead to end the period of mourning. The belongings of the deceased will then be spread among the clan family."

He continued, "If someone dies in an accident far from the village, you will take some corn soup, burn some tobacco, go to the place where death occurred, and lead the spirit back to the village. If it is a *royaner* who dies, his clan mother must retrieve the spirit."

He continued, "In order for people to be chosen as a *royaner*, Tree of Equal Height, or *Otiyaner*, clan matron, they must have shown the responsibilities in having a family. They will be judged according to parenthood. If they cannot take care of their children, they cannot take care of their nation."

He continued, "If a clan matron dies, a small condolence will take place in her village. At some point they would meet together in the council house of the grieving nation where a new *royaner* or *Otiyaner* would be officially recognized to replace the person lost."

He continued, "If a clan family dies out, the title will be held by the nation until a new family is found and the titles can be restored."

He continued, "If there are no clan matrons left for some reason. A *royaner* may borrow a clan matron from another clan to replace her until the clan is replenished."

He continued, "Assistants to the *royaner* who do not fulfill their duty can also be replaced by the clan matron."

He continued, "Neither murderers, thieves, nor abusers of women and children can become *royaner* or *Otiyaner*, clan matrons."

He continued, "It is the duty of the clan matron of the deceased *royaner* to make sure that a feast is ready for the condolence. She will be helped by the other clan matrons, and it will be up to the *royaner* to ensure that there is deer meat."

He continued, "When a bereaved nation is to be condoled, a fire is made for them. A man will then sing the roll call of the now fifty *royaner* in the order that the clan matrons placed the antlers on them. Then the six Songs of Peace are to be sung by all. Then the speaker will summarize all the points of the Great Law of Peace using Ayenwatha's wampum belts as a guide."

He continued, "Those who are the condolers will ask the condoled across the fire to bring forth their future *royaner*. The clan matron will then stand and present him in front to face the nations. Behind them will be the assistants to the *royaner* and clan matron, as well as two faith keepers, a man and a woman. The clan matron of the new *royaner* will send the white wampum across the fire. A speaker will then speak on behalf of him. The wampum will then be inspected by all the *royaner* and clan matrons on the other side. A speaker will then tell the future *royaner* of his duties, such as being honest and good to others. Also being generous is important, for to be a *royaner* means often to have less than others. The white wampum will then be sent back to the condoled side once they acknowledge the choice. The future *royaner* will then be asked to make a *tehontatenonhtsawah:khon*, pledge, into the white wampum by the *royaner* in his nation to fulfill his duty in the best way that he can. Then all the other *royaner* will make a pledge into the wampum to confirm his words. Once this is done, the other side will say to the new *royaner*, 'Everything is complete, and never forget your pledge. We now elevate this new *royaner* into your nation.' The clan matron will then place the antlers on the *royaner*'s head."

"The condolers then will say, 'Let us now dance and socialize and bang our antlers for we have completed the matter and everyone is content.'"

Everyone listened to what the Peacemaker had told them. They realized that the laws had been formed by the events that had happened as the Peacemaker had visited each one of them. Each time a little more had been added. The great tree had been planted once again and the sky world would be restored in the shape of the Longhouses and the territory of the

Longhouse of One family. By following the Great Law of Peace, it would be up to them to ensure that it continued.

Finally, the Peacemaker said, "If you are ever in doubt and need me to guide you, go into the bush and fast and call out my name three times. You may not think so, but I will hear you and I will answer you, in my own way when the time is right."

They all watched as he walked away, circled a tree, and disappeared.

4

Sawiskera Gains Control

The Coming of the Light-Skinned Beings

After the Great Peace, the *onkwe:honwe* felt safe to travel anywhere without having to worry about being killed. Some of the onkwe:honwe including Wendat, Kenienké:haka and Onontaka:haka had moved to the north, to a great river that led into the sea. There they resided for many years, living in peace. They built villages all along the river where they hunted, fished, and grew their three mothers—corn, beans, and squash. The main village of the northern onkwe:honwe was on an island where the great river divided into two. The village was situated by a mountain on the island and was the place where the northern onkwe:honwe had their council fire. They became known as the *Otsiré:laka*, the People of the Council Fire.

The south river had rapids and a lake on one side, which led into Great Lakes that were like oceans and a few days' journey away. The first of these lakes was situated above the territory of the Onontaka:haka, Kaokwa:haka, and Sonontowa:haka. At its most western part, it divided the country of the Kakwakoh where Tsakonsasé resided, between the first great lake and the second great lake by the falls named Onakara. The Wendat had moved above the third lake, the latter being situated in the north. Their cousins the Teyonontateh lived near them. For many changes of the seasons, the *onkwe:honwe* remained at peace with one another. In fact the *Skarenhesehkowah*, White Roots of Peace, had spread across Turtle Island to many nations.

Another people, who spoke a different language and had different customs than they the *onkwe:honwe*, lived near the great ocean to the east. These people were more proficient at hunting than the *onkwe:honwe* and were therefore better in the use of the bow and arrow. The *onkwe:honwe* referred to them first as atsha'kahnha and then as Atirontok Bark Eaters and as they moved west as Tehakanus, They Speak a Different Language. They referred to them as Atirontok because of the designs they made with on tree bark with their teeth. Like the anen:taks porcupine, they appeared to eat bark. These people also lived in abundance with all their needs taken care of.

The Atirontok spiritual leaders had great spiritual powers and could communicate easily with the ancient ones in the Sky World. Some of these ancient ones were good, while others could do harm if asked. One day, their spiritual leaders began to have dreams about a terrible calamity that would occur if they remained where they were. While they were communicating with the ancient ones, as was their custom, it was said that seven spiritual beings came out of the ocean to warn them and tell them what they were to do in order to survive.

They had been told that they would have to leave their lands one day and move west if they were going to continue to survive. If they didn't, they would suffer like they had never suffered before.[1] Some of them decided to leave, while others stayed behind. Slowly they began their journey toward the west. They would have to travel through northern onkwe:honwe country. Both the northern onkwe:honwe and the Atirontok had known of each other; however, they had remained out of each other's way after the Great Peace. In fact some of their leaders had been taken to the Rotinonshonni, People of the Longhouse, Grand Council to learn about it.

The northern onkwe:honwe had always let the Atirontok hunt in their territory as was the custom under the Great Peace. The Atirontok never really respected the Kenienké:haka and the other *onkwe:honwe who lived there*, because they felt that they were not true men—not good in war and not having enough power. The Atirontok felt that the northern onkwe:honwe women had too much power for the men to be useful. Nonetheless, they traded with one another. The northern onkwe:honwe would trade their tobacco, corn, beans, and squash for the furs and meat of the Atirontok.

It was at that time that Sawiskera blew some of his islanders over the water to Teharonhia:wako's island. In a short time, Sawiskera sent a great white wind from one end of Teharonhia:wako's Turtle Island to the other. So powerful was his wind that many of the cousins of the *onkwe:honwe* were destroyed by disease, warfare and alcohol. Many were left with doubts about who they were, and they turned against the things that Teharonhia:wako had taught their ancestors.[2]

A young girl had visioned in a dream a strange event that was about to happen. One day, some of the cousins of the Atirontok named the Migmaa saw three trees on an island, with bears climbing from ropes sailing down the great river. When they landed, it was found out that they were not bears or trees at all, but rather men with light skin who sailed in a great canoe that had wings that seemed to allow it to fly through the water.[3] The girl's dream had come true.

As it sailed down the great river, one of the onkwe:honwe *royaner* went out to meet the light-skinned strangers, just as these strangers were putting up a post that pointed to the four directions.

The *royaner* pointed to the sign and asked the strangers, "Why are you putting up that post?"

A man named Jacques answered using sign language, "There is no harm; it is only a beacon for our ship so that others can come and trade with you."

The two men shook hands and became friends.

The *royaner* who represented the *Akoyanneh*, women's council, didn't know that Jacques had claimed the land for his great war and spiritual leaders; the marker meant that they now thought that they possessed the land.

The *royaner* said to Jacques, "Come to our village." *Kanata* was the term he used for the village.

Jacques thought to himself, "This country must be called Canada. When I go back I will tell my King that I have discovered Canada and that the people must be called Canadians."

The *royaner* introduced the strangers to his village and cured them of a terrible sickness with the boiled leaves of a Cedar tree.

One day, Jacques said to the sons of the *royaner*, "Would you like to see our ship?"

The two sons were thrilled to see the great sailing ship and replied, "Yes, we would."

As soon as they boarded the vessel, they were captured and put in chains. Jacques and the two sons then sailed away.

The *royaner* thought he would never see his sons again. However, many moons later, the great canoe with wings returned with his sons safe inside.

Upon their return, the sons said to the *royaner*, "Father, we have been to far-off lands where a war-like people live. They are very powerful, with some having great wealth while others are starving to death."

The *royaner* thought to himself, "How can they let their own people starve?"

The *royaner* could have killed the strangers with the light skin. However, he knew it was wrong to kill, for he believed in the Great Peace. Instead, he fed them and looked after them through a harsh winter. One day, he believed he was safe after all he had done for the strangers.

Jacques said to him, "We will be leaving soon. We would like you to come on board our ship for a final get-together."

The *royaner* replied to Jacques, "I will miss you when you are gone."

As soon as Jacques and the *royaner* boarded the vessel, the *royaner* was captured; they sailed off.

The northern onkwe:honwe men, seeing what had happened, tried to stop the great canoe by yelling, *"Akoyaneh, Akoyaneh."* This was an old Turtle Clan title for the *royaner* who wore the antlers of the deer.[4]

That was the last that they saw of their *royaner*. However in the future, they would be warned that there were strangers who did not understand the meaning behind the Great Peace.

Not long after that time, more strangers arrived who made camp close to the ocean where the great river ended. The Atirontok who lived near the ocean began to die off from strange maladies for which they could find no cure. They decided to heed their spiritual leaders' warning and began to travel west in large numbers. As they traveled, they entered the territory of the northern onkwe:honwe. They referred to the northern onkwe:honwe as *Muntua*, or People Who Were Very Spiritual.[5]

They decided that they would have to fight the onkwe:honwe if they were to live in this country. They concluded that they would attack during the early morning before the sun appeared, as they knew that the onkwe:honwe would never prepare themselves for an attack at that time. Onkwe:honwe never did anything when the sun was down as it was believed it would bring them bad luck. In the mist of the dew of the early morning, they struck at the village by the mountain, taking the northern onkwe:honwe by surprise. There, they killed many of them and captured many others.

For the first time in a long time, the onkwe:honwe had to fight to survive. They hid their women in pits as they defended their land. Some escaped, while others were adopted into the Atirontok Martin Clan and made into warriors while others fled as far as Ktaranto, Where the Logs Are Placed in the River—the land of the Wendat who then made peace with the powerful coalition of Atirontok who now surrounded them. Those who remained were forced to pay tribute, sometimes giving their wives as payment.

The rest of the *onkwe:honwe* of the Longhouse of One Family thought about what they should do. If they took up the weapons of war, they would be breaking the Great Peace; still, if they didn't do something, they might all come under the subjugation of the peoples they called Atirontok. It would be the captured Kenienké:haka and Onontaka:haka faction of the onkwe:honwe women who would decide the issue.

Things remained the same for quite a few seasons. The Kenienké:haka and Onontaka:haka men were continually made fun of for their weaknesses in hunting and the fact that women were such an authority in their councils.

One day a party of Atirontok and northern Kenienké:haka were out hunting on their shared grounds on the north shore opposite the island in the traditional manner with six men to each party. It had been a harsh winter that year, and there was little food to eat. For some reason the Atirontok spiritual leaders failed to find any game. It was decided the two hunting parties should split up.

The Atirontok had little success while hunting. Meanwhile, the northern Kenienké:haka hunters had come upon many caribou and had plenty to eat. When the two hunting parties met up, the Kenienké:haka showed the Atirontok their great success. The Atirontok became jealous and were afraid that they would be made fools of when they returned to the village. They decided that they would kill the northern Kenienké:haka hunting party and tell their people that they waited for Kenienké:haka but that they did not know what happened to them.

That evening as they slept, they clubbed the northern Kenienké:haka hunting party to death. When they arrived back at the main village on the island where the northern Kenienké:haka and the Atirontok lived, they carried back the meat that had been killed by the northern Kenienké:haka and said it was theirs.

Tekarihokenh, the *royaner* of one of the northern villages, asked the Atirontok hunters, "What happened to our men?"

They answered, "We don't know. We think they may have become lost somewhere. We tried to find them but could not."

Tekarihokenh replied, "We will have to send out a search party to find out what has happened to them."

Not long after, the northern Kenienké:haka men went searching for their friends. They followed the Atirontok tracks back to where they had come from but could not find any evidence of their men.

As they were about to head back, one of the northern Kenienké:haka men said, "Look over there. It seems like something has been buried."

The men began to dig out the snow. They then came upon the bodies of the six hunters and figured out what had happened. They returned to the village to tell Tekarihokenh what they had found.[6]

Immediately, Tekarihokenh confronted the Atirontok war chief. "What did your men do to our men?" he asked.

The war chief yelled to his warriors, "Take these men and tie them up." Tekarihokenh was now a hostage.

The Great Way of Peace had made the Kenienké:haka and other onkwe:honwe a peaceful people up to this time, and they were not known as fighters. However, this was seen as the last straw by them. For years they had asked Teharonhia:wako to help them, and now it was time that they put their trust back into him.

One evening, the women decided that they had to do something. They held a council. The clan mother of Tekarihokenh said, "We have had enough. We have to break this bondage that we are under and release our men. Does anyone have an idea?"

A young woman stood up and said, "I have an idea. We will hold a feast and invite the Atirontok chiefs to come. Since we are in the maple syrup season, we will offer them some food. When they are seated, we will fling the hot maple syrup in their faces. The rest of us will release the prisoners. We will then make our escape by canoe. Instead of paddling on the south river that leads toward our brothers in the southern country, we will head west along the great river and turn down into Oneota:haka country. We have a better chance of escaping this way. We will need decoys to travel down the southern river to lead the Atirontok away from the elders and children."

The clan mother said, "It sounds like a good plan."

The women boiled the syrup and prepared the feast. They invited the Atirontok chiefs, as planned, to the feast. When they arrived, the women sat them down and brought them their hot meal. As the women approached the war chiefs to offer them food, they flung the hot syrup that they were carrying into their faces.[7]

There was much commotion, and, as the Atirontok men rolled on the ground, the women stuck their knives into them. Some of the elder men and young boys jumped Tekarihokenh's guards and released him and the other men. They had hid their canoes near the lake at the west end of the river. They hoped that they would get away in time, before the Atirontok warriors could gather themselves and attack them. A few of them headed east of the island to divert the warriors away from the rest.

As they paddled away, they were spotted by some of the Atirontok warriors who had heard the commotion. They yelled to the rest of their warriors that the Kenienké:haka and Onontaka:haka were escaping at the lake that was at the head of the rapids. They got their war clubs and bows and arrows and made their way to their canoes.

The northern Kenienké:haka and Onontaka:haka had their children and elders with them; this slowed them up. The women meanwhile shared the paddling with the men. They decided that their only route of escape would be to travel down the great river as far as the first great lake, Kanontario, and head south, doubling back along the Oswego River to their southerly Kenienké:haka and Onontaka:haka villages. They would then be in the heart of Rotinonshonni territory and would feel much safer. Even the Atirontok would not be foolish enough to follow them that far into Rotinonshonni territory.

As they traveled, they kept watching and hid during the day; then at night, they traveled down the great river toward the Great Lake. When they came to the Great Lake, they went south as far as the Oswego River. They then began to travel down the Oswego and believed that they were safe. Suddenly one of the women pointed, "Look!"

The Atirontok war canoes were not far behind them. It looked like they were going to be overtaken by the Atirontok warriors and be killed.

Tekarihokenh started to give the words of thanks. He yelled, "Teharonhia:wako and our grandfathers, help us."

Just then, out of the west, the sky began to darken, the sound of the grandfather's thunders were heard, and the Great Dew Eagle appeared flapping his wings. A storm hit the Atirontok canoes head on, overturning them. Some of the Atirontok drowned, while the rest of the Atirontok warriors returned to their village.[8]

The northern Kenienké:haka and Onontaka:haka made their way back to safety with the northern Onontaka:haka joining their brethren at Kanata:kowa village, while the northern Kenienké:haka crossing at the Oneota:haka carrying place, named Woods Creek, to the Kenienké:haka river. Tekarihokenh settled into a village, naming it Ossesneron. The Kenienké:haka would later move across the river and call their village, Kahnawaké—after the river rapids near the village they had left behind. The villages were west of the original village Ronakowaneh at Cohoes Falls and Teyotonakeh village between two mountains. That is how a Turtle Clan village ended up west of the Wolf Clan village at Schoharie Creek. Later on, there would come a time when another Tekarihokenh and some of his people would return to their former village near the mountain divided between two rivers, naming it Kahnawaké once again.

It was not too many seasons after that the Kenienké:haka learned that more light-skinned men had landed and were now staying at the place where their old village was situated on the island near the mountain. These white men referred to themselves as French. They had befriended the Atirontok, who now resided there with their remaining captives who had not escaped with Tekarihokenh.

One of these captives was known as Iroquet, now an Atirontok war leader. His people had blended in with the Atirontok and were known as the Little Nation. They lived near Kanesetaké along the Kichesippi Great River of the Algonquins.[9] Iroquet was one of the Kenienké:haka survivors who had been adopted into the Martin Clan of the Atirontok.[10]

The Kenienké:haka wanted to remain at peace, in spite of all that had happened to them. After all, they had relations who were still living around the island who had not escaped with them. They didn't want to have to go to war with their relative Iroquet.

One day, they heard that one of these light-skinned Frenchmen was coming down a river that led into their country with a group of Atirontok. They were not sure if they were coming for war or peace. The Kenienké:haka held a national council to decide what to do.

The *royaner* Ayenwatha said, "Let us greet this man and befriend him. We will choose one *royaner* from each of our clans to head the delegation. We will meet him at the wood's edge, near the head of the lake *Kaniyateri karunteh,* Doorway of the Country."

All the *royaner* agreed, and they chose Ayenwatha, Shoskoharowaneh, and Teyonhenkwen to lead the delegation. They would all wear their ceremonial headdresses as befitted a special occasion.

The three Kenienké:haka *royaner,* one from each clan, camped out with their men not far from the Atirontok camp near the edge of the river at the shore of the lake. That night, the men called back and forth to each other between the two camps. They played their ceremonial drums to one another.

What the Kenienké:haka men didn't know was that the light-skinned man named Champlain had destructive weapons that they had never seen before. He planned to hide some of his men with their weapons under boats by the river.

The next day, the three Kenienké:haka *royaner* went out to meet the light-skinned man to say the three clear-minded words given by the first Ayenwatha and to wipe away any grief that might have occurred to them on the way. They wore their ceremonial headdresses as was befitting dignitaries. As they approached the clearing to greet the visitors, Ayenwatha held some wampum in his hands. He faced the light-skinned man and began to say, "We take away any pain that may have befallen you while on your journey here. We wipe away the tears from your eyes."

Suddenly the light-skinned man began to yell something. The men whom he had hid under the boats suddenly sprang up with sticks that shot fire from them. Instantly, Ayenwatha and the other *royaner* fell to the ground. Soon, many others fell as well. The men ran in every direction in panic. They had never seen such thunderous power before coming from sticks that shot out fire and death. As they retreated, they tried to get their wounded, but it was to no avail. That day they lost fifty men, including their three *royaner*. This was devastating to the Kenienké:haka, as many had come from one village nearby.[11]

That same year, another light-skinned man sailed up a river that joined the Kenienké:haka river at Cohoes Falls. The remaining Kenienké:haka were at first wary of him.[12]

The man got out of the ship and brought out one of the fire sticks. He said through a translator of the Wolf People, the Mahican, "I have come here to trade with you. I will trade one of these fire sticks for fifty beaver skins."

The Kenienké:haka *royaner* Shatekariwateh said to him, "This is quite excessive." However, Shatekariwateh knew that they needed the fire sticks if they were going to defend their villages from the French.

That night, Shatekariwateh held a council with the clan mothers and *royaner*.

He told them, "If we don't accept the fire sticks, we will be killed off by the Atirontok and their new friends."

The next day, Shatekariwateh told the man. "This is what we agree to."

He then took out a *kuswentah*, wampum belt, that a newly condoled Ayenwatha had made; it had *tekani teyohatateh*, two rows, that ran down it.

He said to the light-skinned man, "You and your people represent one row, while my people and I another. We will live and trade, side by side one another. Neither of us will interfere with the affairs of the other, our way of life, beliefs, and trade. This is the way it was set down by our forefathers whenever anyone enters into the Great Peace with us. You may rest here for a while, but don't stay too long."[13]

The light-skinned man agreed. These people were called Dutch, and their leaders would later be known as Corlear. This was because Corlear, a Dutch official, laughed one day when the Kenienké:haka placed tobacco to appease the water spirits of a lake. Corlear drowned that same day on the lake.[14]

Not long after, the light-skinned Dutchmen brought out what looked to be water in a vessel. He said to a Kenienké:haka man, "Drink this, you will enjoy it."

The Kenienké:haka man took a drink; it burned when it went down his throat. Soon the man began to feel good, and he asked for more. In the future, the Dutch promised that they would bring more each time the Kenienké:haka came to trade at the trading post that they would set up.

When the Dutch set up their trading post, they placed Jacob Elkens at its head. He remained a friend of the Kenienké:haka until he was relieved.[15] The Dutch traders learned that, when the Kenienké:haka were under the influence of alcohol, the Dutch could make them do what they wanted. Pretty soon, they were offering more and more alcohol to the Kenienké:haka. The effects were devastating; the Kenienké:haka began to be cheated by the Dutch, for they often didn't remember what they had done the night before. They then would return to the villages with alcohol and no other trading items. The women would hide out of fear of being beaten when this happened. The Kenienké:haka could do little about it because it was believed that a person who was out of his mind could not be judged in the same way as a person who was sane. Sometimes a murder would take place, and there would be forgiveness because the person was under the influence of the deadly spirit that lived in the drinking vessel that they called the mind changer. Sawiskera was gaining control of their minds though the mind changer.

In spite of this, there were important decisions that had to be made, and everyone had to be at their best. One of those decisions was: Would they have to go on the war trail or would they try and remain at peace?

They counseled with one another but could not come up with a final resolution. A few seasons later, the issue was decided not by the Kenienké:haka but by the keepers of the central fire, the Onontaka:haka.

The same light-skinned man Champlain, who was French, attacked an Onontaka:haka village.[16] He had come by the same route that the Kenienké:haka had taken when they escaped from the Atirontok many seasons before. He laid siege to a village, killing the *royaner*, Shehhawih, and many others. He had been led there by the Wendat, who were close cousins to the Rotinonshonni. The Wendat now had guns and had joined the Atirontok in a war against them.

The Revival of the War Chiefs

A grand council was called at Kanata:kowa village in Onontaka territory. Representatives from all the Five Nations of the Rotinonshonni attended. The issue at hand was whether they should accept the weapons of war to defend themselves and possibly take the war trail once again. Most of the *royaner* had chosen peace. However, Skanawatih was incensed at what had happened.

When it was his turn to speak, he said to the council, "It is time to change some of the things that occurred during the Great Peace and extend the rafters to allow us to defend ourselves. Things are not the same now since the coming of the light-skinned men, and perhaps it would be better if weapons were once again allowed to be taken up."

Many of the young men who stood behind their *royaner* nodded their heads in agreement. Even some of the *Otiyaner*, clan matrons, who had suffered from the attack by the Frenchmen agreed.

Skanawatih said, "I want revenge for Shehhawih. My clan mother is willing to allow me to carry the name of Shehhawih, Axe Handler, when I go to war. This way I can keep both the peace and go to war. It will appease Shehhawih's spirit."[17]

As Skanawatih's resolution was brought up in the council, Tekarihokenh stood up and said, "I agree with Skanawatih. Things have to change or we will be all killed."

What had really brought the issue to the forefront was an attack by the Wendat on the main Oneota:haka village. So devastating was the attack that the Oneota:haka clan matrons had to plead to the Kenienké:haka clans for men to replace their losses.[18]

When it was the Oneota:haka's turn to speak, Rotatsheté said, "We have lost too many of our men because of the fire sticks that the French give to the Wendat. I agree. I am ready to take the path of war."

There was confusion in the confederacy council, for the older *royaner* knew that they were losing support to the younger generation, many of whom wanted revenge. The younger generation agreed with Tekariho- kenh, Rotatsheté, and Skanawatih's position. The council wanted to pre- vent a division from taking place in the council and the communities. They knew that they could not prevent individuals from going to war.

Atotarhoh stood up and said, "We have decided to extend the rafters by making a new resolution, if Skanawatih goes to war, he would have to take off his title of *royaner*. When he returns, he may retain his title. There will also be a new type of representative of the people who will be selected by the clans. This is so some of the younger generation can sit in council, and we may hear their voice. His title will be based solely on merit. They will be called a *Wakehnetoh:ten*, Pine Tree Chief. We will also reinstitute the *rarontaron*, war chief, who will now stand behind the *royaner* to represent himself on behalf of the warriors. We must make sure what happened to the three Kenienké:haka *royaner* and Shehhawih does not happen again. From now on, we will send our war chiefs to speak for us. They are more able to defend themselves than we are."[19]

This resolution seemed to appease the younger members of the coun- cil and the young men who backed them. It seemed like they were now being sanctioned to go to war. The Kaokwa:haka were the most opposed to the new resolutions.

Tewenhethon stood up and said, "This goes against the *Kayeneren:kowa*, Great Way of Peace. I want to make a resolution that these new ideas remain separate from the *Teyotiokwaonhas:ton*, Laws of Peace. They should be called Skanawatih's Laws of War. This is so there will be no confu- sion in the teachings of the Great Peace. These teachings will govern the responsibilities of those who go to war and not those of the *royaner*."[20]

Tewenhethon's resolution went around the council, and everyone agreed. The Kaokwa:haka, however, lived farther west than the others and were not as exposed to the dangers as the others were. They also had the powerful Sonontowa:haka next to them at the western door.

Skanyiatar:io stood up, "If we are the keepers of the western door, we will need all the help we can get. The Sonontowa:haka agree that something has to be done. We accept the changes."

The *Rotenhnon:teron,* Confederacy Councilmen, then began to choose the war chiefs. The Kenienké:haka *royaner* said, "We select Ayonwaks to be our *rarontaron,* war chief. "

Then the Oneota:haka *royaner* said, "We select Kahonwatiron to be our *rarontaron.*

Next, the Onontaka:haka *royaner* said, "We select Rayentes to be our war chief."

The Kaokwa:haka relented and said, "We select Wennehs to be our war chief."

Finally, the Sonontowa:haka said, "We select Kanenoton to be our war chief."

The Sonontowa:haka had heard rumors that the light-skinned Frenchmen had traveled as far west as their country and were making arrangements with nations living west of them. They were also becoming fearful.

Conciliation with one another was the most important thing to occur if the confederacy was to survive. Cracks were already starting to occur within its structure. What they didn't know was that something so devastating would occur to all of them that it would shake their belief in Teharonhia:wako, as well as the very foundations of the confederacy.

It was not long after that many of the *onkwe:honwe* began to fall ill. Their faces and bodies would boil and blister, and they would then succumb to its effects.

The worse hit were the Kenienké:haka and the Oneota:haka. They began to lose many of their elders who were the most knowledgeable in the culture, as well as the young who would be the ones who would learn from them. This left a great void in the spiritual beliefs in their cultures. It seemed like every day there were other condolences taking place and more losses. The strain of all that was happening was becoming too much to take.

To replace their losses and appease the grieving *otiyaner*, clan matrons, the Kenienké:haka men started going out in war parties to capture enemy men. They were adopted into their villages to replace losses and to calm the grieving mothers and widows. The other nations began to follow suit. In time, it seemed like there were more adopted and captives living in the villages than there were original members of the village. Instead of people following the roots of the tree to its source, they were now being forcefully absorbed as members.[21]

Some of the adoptees were Wendat and Atirontok who had already been exposed to the new religion called Christianity. They had asked that they continue to be allowed to practice their new religion even after being held captive. There were also traditional Wendat who volunteered to join the confederacy and were incensed at the French Black Robes who would only trade with those Wendat who had become Christian.

It was decided at a national council of the Kenienké:haka that they should make peace with the French and their native allies—the Atirontok and the Wendat. At the council, the newly chosen Ayenwatha said, "We will send Kiosaeton to represent us in the peace. He is brave and a great orator. This way, if anything happens, the *royaner* will be safe." Everyone agreed as Kiosaeton was an excellent orator. Kiosaeton went to the council at the village where the French now lived. He brought a wampum belt and said:

> "*Onontio*, lend me your ear. I speak for my whole country. I ask that you listen to what we the Kenienké:haka of the Rotinonshonni have to say. I come with heartfelt good intentions. There are only good songs that come out of my mouth. We have many war songs that have been placed under the tree in the ground. We have only songs of rejoicing left within us." *Onontio* meant Mountain, and that became the name for all the French leaders thereafter.
>
> He took a second wampum belt out and said, "I want to thank you for saving *Tokrahenehiaron*'s life. However, I want to admonish you for sending him back to us alone. If something had happened to him and he had drowned, we would have accused you of killing him. If he were in my country and if he were your nephew, I would not have let him take

a canoe and return to Quebec alone." He was mentioning the fact that *Tokrahenehiaron* had been released as a prisoner and left to fend for himself to get back to Kenienké:haka territory.

He took a third wampum belt out and said, "This belt signifies that our allied nations have accepted the presents that you gave them to put away their hatchets."

He then took out a fourth wampum belt out and said, "This belt signifies that we have put away our grief for our people who have been killed."

A fifth belt was taken out, and he said, "This is to clear the river and drive away any of your enemies' canoes."

A sixth belt was taken out, and he said, "This is to smooth the rapids, waterfalls and strong currents that occur in the rivers on which one must travel to reach the country of the Kenienké:haka."

A seventh belt was taken out, and he said, "This is to still the waters on the Great Lake, *Kanontario*."

An eighth belt was taken out, and he said, "We will clear a path of all obstructions, so that you may move freely into our country."

A ninth belt was taken out, and he said, "There will be fires in our lodges lit all day to keep you warm if you decide to visit us."

A tenth belt was taken out, and, taking a Frenchman and an Atirontok by the arms, he said, "Here is the knot that binds us together, and nothing can separate us."

An eleventh belt was taken out, and he said, "Come to our homeland and eat with us. We have many provisions that we could all share together."

He took out a twelfth belt and said, "This is to clear the clouds so that everyone can see that our hearts have hidden nothing."

A thirteenth belt was taken out, and he said, "It has been five years since the Wendat came with pouches of wampum beads and other presents. Why then have you come here now?"

He took out a fourteenth belt and said, "You Wendat should not be shy to come into our country alone without the French and the Atirontok."

He took out a fifteenth belt and said, "We have always accepted the Black Robe, named Jogues,[22] to return to our village. We do not know where he went."

He took out a sixteenth belt and said, "This belt is to protect us during the time that we visit you."

Finally, he took out a seventeenth belt and said, "This is for one of our captured men who was spared by you."

Kiosaeton then told them, "I am going to my country to celebrate this occasion; however, I am afraid that the Wendat may not be as peaceful as they say they are."[23]

There were further negotiations and another council the next day. It appeared that peace had finally come to the Kenienké:haka. In order to keep the peace, they knew they would have to let the Black Robe, Isaac Jogues, return to their village.

When Jogues entered the Kenienké:haka village of Ossesneron, a council was held. The nine Kenienké:haka *royaner*, the *otiyaner* and *rarontaron* attended. There were also representatives from Onontaka as well as two Atirontok envoys. Jogues had been here once before and had learned the Kenienké:haka language. He had been taken in by a family who came to love him and adopted him as a son. However, one day he decided to escape and return to New France. Now, he was returning at the request of *Onontio*.

At the council, Jogues began to make demands right away. He said to the council:

> "I am pleased that there is now peace between our peoples. I want to thank the work that Kiosaeton did to bring about the peace." He continued, "I have a payment of 10,000 wampum beads for the release of the Wendat prisoner, Therese *Oionhaton*, and a captive Frenchman that I am told you have."
>
> A speaker of the council stood up and replied, "Tell *Onontio* that we will release the Frenchman with this necklace of 2,000 wampum beads that was the bond that held him captive. The girl will be released shortly, and we offer 1,500 wampum beads with her return."
>
> Jogues then said, "I now give these 2,000 wampum beads to the Onontaka:haka representatives to inform you that we will be arriving in your country by three roads: the road that leads to the lands of the Kenienké:haka; the road that passes through the first Great Lake we call Louis and you call *Kanontario*; and finally by way of Wendat country."

The Kenienké:haka speaker replied, "Those other two roads are dangerous. We ask that you come through our country first, as there is peace there and the road is clear."

Jogues said, "I don't think we need to go through Kenienké:haka territory to visit the other nations." He then handed the gift to the Onontaka:haka to the displeasure of the Kenienké:haka."[24]

The Kenienké:haka did not trust Jogues, they believed he was trying to divide the nations. Since the time of the *Kayeneren:kowa*, it had been protocol that nations coming from the north or east travel through the eastern door. Jogues also had brought a small box with him; some of the warriors were suspicious of its contents. They knew the power of the priests to bring disease among them.

After the council was over, one of the warriors said to Jogues, "Open the black box that you brought with you."

Jogues opened it and said, "Look inside, there is nothing here."

For the time being, the warrior was satisfied. It was not long after that another epidemic hit the village. As well, there was an infestation of worms that destroyed the crops, resulting in a famine. The same warrior who mistrusted Jogues had lost more of his family, and he blamed Jogues for their deaths.

He was a member of the Bear Clan. The men and women of the Wolf and Turtle Clans pleaded with him not to kill Jogues. One of the men said, "If you kill Jogues, that will mean war for us once again. There will be more killing than what has taken place now. Leave him be, or kill us instead."

The warrior shook his head. No one was sure if he agreed or not.

Jogues had been away, and upon his return he was led to the lodge of the Bear Clan. Waiting for him was the distraught warrior with a hatchet. Another warrior, named Ronatentiateh, put out his arm to ward off the blow. As the warrior swung his tomahawk, he said, "This is to appease the spirits of the ones whom you killed."

As he swung, he cut the arm of Ronatentiateh, but it was to no avail. Jogues lay dead on the ground. Ronatentiateh left the village distraught. It was his family that Jogues had been adopted into. Eventually, he would leave the Kenienké:haka and move in with the French. He died in France and was known by them as the Berger or lover of the French.[25]

The Christian Wendat, although the minority, were becoming wealthy and powerful at the expense of the other Wendat, who also had become depopulated. The traditional Wendat told the Kenienké:haka and the others of how their powerful nation had become depleted by disease brought by the Black Robes. So that they could survive, some of them asked to join a war party to kill off all the Black Robes and Christian followers.

A council was held between the Kenienké:haka and the Sonontowa:haka. It was controlled by the warrior element.

One of the Kenienké:haka *rarontaron,* war chiefs, said, "We will help the traditional Wendat be rid of the Christians. Although they have done much harm to us, they are now one with us."

The Sonontowa:haka war chiefs agreed and said, "As long as the Christian Wendat receive fire sticks to attack us, we are most vulnerable. We will join this war party."

The *royaner* had not been informed of this at the confederacy council at Onontaka. In fact at the time Skanawatih was visiting the Wendat trying to make a truce with them. No one was sure of what mantle he was wearing, that of a *royaner* or that of a war chief. The distinctions in some cases were becoming less and less clear.

He told the Wendat chiefs, "I can promise you that the *royaner* of the Onontaka:haka have vowed to never allow an attack on you if you accept peace with us."

It was while he was resting with the Wendat that the attack began by the Kenienké:haka and the Sonontowa:haka warriors. They were led into battle by traditional Wendat. Many of the Christian Wendat were killed, while others were absorbed into either the Kenienké:haka or Sonontowa:haka warriors. They even killed the Black Robes, knowing it would incense the French.

Skanawatih was distraught over the attack, as he had given his word to the Wendat that there would be no attack. As a result, he took his own life.[26]

The remaining Christian Wendat set off for an island on the third Great Lake that would be named after them one day. Others were absorbed into the Rotinonshonni, and they would later become known as Wyandot, Floating Islanders, when they were amalgamated with the Kakwako, Neutrals, and Teyonontateh, Tobacco People.

Not long after defeating the Wendat, the Sonontowa:haka set out against the Kakwako who were known as the Neutrals. This was because of Tsakonsasé's position as mediator for the tribes had been compromised.

Tsakonsasé's title had continued throughout the many cycles of the seasons that had passed. Even after the Peacemaker arrived, she was still considered a mediator for the many nations even though there had been no more warriors to look after. Now there was war once again. One day, a Sonontowa:haka *royaner,* while hunting north of his settlement, was killed by two Mississauga warriors from the northern tribes. The Mississauga were called Tehakanus by *onkwe:honwe.* This meant speakers of a different language. They were also related to the Atirontok and had moved west with them during the migration from the east coast.

The Sonontowa:haka warriors chased them as far as Tsakonsasé's lodge where inside they found refuge.

The Mississauga warriors said to Tsakonsasé, "Help us escape. We will always be in your debt if you do."

The Sonontowa:haka warriors entered her lodge. They were angry with what had happened to their *royaner.*

One of the warriors said to Tsakonsasé, "Give him to us to kill."

Tsakonsasé said, "I cannot, as this would only escalate things among you."

She continued, "I have to let them go free so that there won't be a war between your nations."

The Sonontowa:haka warriors were really angry. One of them said, "If you let them go, you will pay a heavy price for it. We will consider you an enemy to be subdued. It is not right that you give refuge on your land to warriors who kill *royaner* on ours."

When Tsakonsasé wouldn't relent, the Sonontowa:haka warriors left to tell their people what had happened.

The Sonontowa:haka held a national council where the *rarontaron,* war chief, who now had a stronger voice in council than ever, said, "Our *royaner* has been killed by the Tehakanus, and Tsakonsasé has let the murderers go. We must attack the *Kakwako* before they further prevent our doing our duty. It is now time they sit under our council fire under our watch. If we allow the Mississauga to use the *Kakwako* land to do what they want, more of us will be killed. It is time to make sure that this doesn't happen again."

The warrior element all agreed. Each day it seemed that the *royaner* were losing more and more of their voice in council.

Soon after, a thousand Sonontowa:haka warriors set out onto the lands of the Kakwako. They killed many and absorbed the rest, including Tsakonsasé and her title. They now had control of the land that separated the two great lakes, in case the Tehakanus further encroached upon them.[27]

Tsakonsasé, along with the rest of the Kakwako, would now have her lodge close to the Sonontowa:haka village of Kanuntaok.[28]

It was important that the confederacy expand into areas that were far from their villages. The farther they were thought to have expanded their power base, the more likely that their villages would remain safe. They needed a buffer zone to ensure their safety.

In spite of this, Onontio, The Mountain, did not stop attacking the Rotinonshonni villages. He sent for fresh troops from his country France, situated on Sawiskera's island. Then they sent for ambassadors from the Rotinonshonni to see their military power. These ambassadors had arrived with the intention of suing for peace. Upon their arrival the commander of the French army, De Tracy, said to them:

> "We want to have peace with you as well. However, your lands are our lands now. We claim it on behalf of the discoveries of Champlain and the Black Robes who visited your villages. You will have to obey our laws and stop your attacks on our allies."[29]

The ambassadors convened and returned the next day. They said, "On behalf of the Onontaka:haka, Sonontowa:haka, the Kaokwa:haka, and the Oneota:haka, we accept the terms of peace in that there should be no more killed. We cannot speak for the Kenienké:haka. We will return in four moons' time to ratify the agreement."

The French once again prepared to attack the Kenienké:haka. They tried to destroy the Kenienké:haka villages and were forced back by winter and by starvation. They then regrouped and again attacked in full force. They did little damage to the Kenienké:haka themselves but did manage to burn their much needed food supplies.

It was one thing to fight in a battle, and it was another thing to burn food. The Kenienké:haka were appalled by the actions of the French. They were tired of the continual incursions into their territory. Many lives had been lost on both sides, and so the Kenienké:haka and the light-skinned people, known as the French, decided once again to make a truce with one another. In the truce, it was decided that the Kenienké:haka would leave some of their people behind with the French, and in return they would accept some of the French to come live among them. This was ancient protocol among various nations of the area to ensure that a treaty stood up. In this way each would marry among one another, and they would have family relations in each of their villages.

The French sent representatives who had no intention of marrying with the Kenienké:haka. That was because they were the black-robed male spiritual leaders who did not have unions with women. Upon arriving at a Kenienké:haka village of Tyonontoken, the first thing that the Black Robe named Fremen said to the Kenienké:haka was: "You must stop your warfare and be men like us by becoming Christians. If you kill any Frenchmen, you will be hanged like the wampum belt I have put up on that pole."[30]

To show his authority over them, the Black Robe Fremen had taken a wampum belt and hung it on a pole for everyone to see. To say the least, the Kenienké:haka of the village Tyonontoken were not impressed.

Upon their arrival in the Kenienké:haka community of Kahnawaké, the Black Robes Fremen, Bruyas, and Pierron, began to secretly foment divisions between the Christian adoptees and their traditional adopters, as well as with some Kenienké:haka who were having doubts about the power of Teharonhia:wako over the Christian god. The Black Robes had told them that they were being punished by the Creator for not being Christian and that was why so many of them had died from disease. Soon after this, the villages were hit by new diseases killing more Kenienké:haka. The Black Robe Fremen told them: "The country has been really afflicted with disease. It is a fever so malignant in character that it would kill in five days. It is ever so sad to see many brought into the village dying."[31]

The Black Robes then told the Kenienké:haka converts, "Where we live, we do not suffer to the same extent from disease; there is no mind changer to destroy the villages, and the people did not die so easily."

One of those who listened to the Black Robe was the wife of Tekari-hokenh, a Wendat adopted into the Turtle Clan. She and others wanted to return with the Black Robes to the French. This caused great pain among the Kenienké:haka, as they now loved their new spouses. However, stopping them from leaving would require that they kill the people they cared for the most, and they could not.

For others, it was even more deeply rooted. They believed that the Christian converts went to a different spirit world than the traditionals. The only way that they could ensure an eternal union together was if they became Christian. Soon after, some of them began to leave for the island with the mountain by the great river, where the French now lived. One of these was Tekarihokenh, who also knew that the former Tekarihokenh and his family had lived there many seasons before.

Those who had been left with the French during the peace treaty had already been Christianized and had set up a mission. Tekarihokenh converted to Christianity, and his family decided to move to the new village. He would have to remove his antlers, and the Kenienké:haka would have to find another clan family to replace him. This was no longer easy, as there were so many dying in the villages. After several moves, when Tekarihokenh arrived with the others, they named their new village Kahnawaké as a reminder of their own village they had left behind.[32]

Although the Black Robes had spoken of being peaceful, the first thing that they did after the Kenienké:haka arrived was to choose a civil chief and a war chief. Soon they were asking the Kenienké:haka converts to war against the other Kenienké:haka who remained in the valley. Most refused, but some said that they would scout against the Sonontowa:haka.[33]

At around the same time, a new light-skinned people had taken over from the Dutch. They were a powerful people who seemed to be at war forever against the French. An agreement was made between the traditional Kenienké:haka and these new people called English. At Fort Orange, later Albany, near Cohoes Falls, the Kenienké:haka brought out a wampum belt. It showed two men holding a chain.

The Kenienké:haka *royaner* Ayenwatha said to the English, "This is our wampum belt to confirm our treaty with you. Like the Two Row Wampum, each will have our nations on separate sides, retaining our own beliefs and traditions. However, we will hold a chain, and if anyone tries to get through it, they will be repelled by it. Every once in a while we will meet here and polish the chain to keep it bright."[34]

The alliance between the two was a mutual one. The Kenienké:haka would be supplied with fire sticks, and the English would have a powerful ally against the French. This however did not prevent the French from invading the Kenienké:haka territory. That was because, whenever the Kenienké:haka asked the English for support, they either did not come or arrived after the Kenienké:haka villages were destroyed.

The French sent an army against the Sonontowa:haka villages. The men were out hunting when they struck, and the children repelled the French army by bluffing that they were much stronger than they were. The French had used Kenienké:haka converts from the missions to scout for them. They pulled out of the battle when they discovered that the French planned to burn all the villages and food supplies.[35]

The Kenienké:haka from the valley had captured one of the Kenienké:haka who had participated in the raid.

A Kenienké:haka war chief asked him, "Why did you help the French attack the Sonontowa:haka. Were you not ashamed to do so?"

The Catholic Kenienké:haka replied, "The priest forced us to go, by saying we would be imprisoned if we did not."[36]

This angered the Onontaka:haka. They called a council to be held at a place where both parties would be safe. The Kenienké:haka converts were invited to a council to discuss their participation in the raid. The Onontaka *royaner*, Onenwirehtonh, chastised the Catholic Kenienké:haka by saying to them, "Because you have chosen to fight against us, you can no longer be a part of the confederacy. You must now walk your own path and be considered an enemy of us."

A Catholic Kenienké:haka warrior replied, "We are free men and make our own choices. We do not listen to the council of the Onontaka:haka. When we meet in the field, you do so at your own risk."

A Kenienké:haka from the valley said, "We will never fight against our brothers from Kahnawaké. They are our blood relations. If you harm them, you harm us."

Some of the Onontaka:haka and Kenienké:haka warriors almost came to blows. It left a bad feeling between the Onontaka:haka and the Kenienké:haka.[37]

Not long after, the Sonontowa:haka retaliated by attacking the French in their great village on the island. They killed and captured many of the French but left the Kenienké:haka converts for the most part alone. They knew that there were only a few of the Kenienké:haka who had taken part in the raid against their villages. They were not going to kill all the Kenienké:haka because of the actions of a few. Besides they needed them to mediate between them and the French, who were continually making inroads with the nations, especially the Tehakanus to the west and the north of them. Besides, they didn't trust the English, believing that the English were too powerful to ever keep their word.

Onontio once again sent an army against the Kenienké:haka. They burned the three main villages on the north side of the river, and, from that time onward, the Kenienké:haka moved their villages to the south side of the river.

Up to this time, the losses had been so great that the Oneota:haka chose a French Black Robe named Millet to represent them in council, as Rotatsheté. The role of the *royaner* was becoming so undermined that even Christian leaders were becoming *royaner*. The new Rotatsheté had been a spy for the French, relaying information about the workings of the Rotinonshonni.[38]

It was not long after that a great treaty was made between the French, their allies, and most of the Rotinonshonni. The Kenienké:haka under pressure from the French arrived at the last minute. The treaty also included the Atirontok nations and their cousins west of them, the Tehakanus, as well as the Wendat. A wampum belt was made between the Rotinonshonni confederacy and the northern nations. It looked much like the covenant chain with two blocks on each end tied to a chain. One block represented the far nations and the other the confederacy. They promised that they would never try to destroy one another again. However, an even greater contingent of Rotinonshonni had headed for Albany, ready to polish the covenant chain with the English.[39]

From then on, relations between the French and the Sonontowa:haka became better. Within a few years, the French had representatives in all Rotinonshonni territory except the Kenienké:haka's. This put more pressure on the unity of the confederacy.

Soon thereafter, the French and the English began to fight several wars against one another. The Sonontowa:haka were inclined to support the French who had forts near them, while the Kenienké:haka supported the English who lived next to them. This caused dissension among the Rotinonshonni Nations. By this time, the *Wakehnetoh:ten*, Pine Tree chiefs, and *rarontaron*, war chiefs, were taking over the confederacy councils. They began to refer to the *royaner* and *Otiyaner* as old men and women. Many of them had become powerful in trade. Some of the Kenienké:haka and Oneota:haka war chiefs had become Christian. They became Church of England Protestants as opposed to the Kenienké:haka Catholics who lived near the French. There were divisions among the Protestants, as well as with the Catholics in belief; this baffled those who remained traditional. They had believed that all Christians were the same and, that because converts were Christian, they must believe in the same thing.

It was at this time that the Skaroo'ren, People of the Hemp, joined the Rotinonshonni. They were also known as Tuscarora, for the shirts they wove from the hemp. The Skaroo'ren had moved to the east of the Great Turtle's back near the great water that divided Teharonhia:wako's island from Sawiskera's island. One day some of the English Christians also landed near the Skaroo'ren territory.

> One of the Christian leaders told the Skaroo'ren, "We are hungry and desperate. Could we stay here for a while?"
>
> The Skaroo'ren representative of the people replied, "You may stay here. We will bring you our three mothers that come from the earth; the corn, the bean and the squash."
>
> Not long after, more and more of the English Christians began to take the land. One of them said to the Skaroo'ren, "We are Christians

and have been given the right to take any land that we need. We are the chosen people to spread the message, and your land is our promised land."

Soon after, they began to take the land by force. When they captured the Skaroo'ren, they made them slaves. Eight times the Skaroo'ren sent wampum belts to the Christians as a symbol of peace.

The first wampum belt was sent by the women; they asked that there be friendship with the Christian people, so that they could fetch wood without being killed.

The second belt sent was for the children and the children to be born, asking that they be allowed to run and play without fear of death or slavery.

The third belt sent was so that they could go out and hunt meat for their families, without fearing being killed or enslaved.

The fourth belt was sent by the elders. It was for a long and lasting peace, so that all men could walk without fear.

The fifth belt was sent by all of the Skaroo'ren, asking the Christians to be peaceful.

The sixth belt, the chiefs sent, was for seeking peace. This was because the minds of the Skaroo'ren were full of fear and anxiety.

The seventh belt asked that the Christians stop murdering and enslaving everyone, so that the Skaroo'ren would not have to fear the sounds that come from the forests, with men waiting to enslave and kill them.

Finally, an eighth belt was sent. The Skaroo'ren asked for a continuing dialogue of peace with the Swiss, German and English Christians who were killing them.[40]

Finally, after defending themselves the best they could, the Skaroo'ren moved with what was left of their people to the Rotinonshonni lands. They asked the Kaokwa:haka if they could enter the territory of the Longhouse of One Family. The Kaokwa:haka let them in, and they were adopted by them into the Oneota:haka.

The Sonontowa:haka *royaner*, Teyoninhokara:wenh, said, "As the gatekeeper of the territory of the longhouse, I have to object. The Tuscarora have entered our territory through the side door and have not come through the western door as they are supposed to."

Atotarhoh replied, "The Sonontowa:haka are right. What we will do is allow the Tuscarora to come and stay with us for a period of four years. If they accept the ways of the Great Peace, they may stay among us."

Everyone agreed with this, and the council was closed with the Skaroo'ren given land to live on by the Oneota:haka. From that time on, it was said that the Rotinonshonni had six arrows.[41] The Skaroo'ren leaders Sakwaritha, Nehaweniha, Tyokwawaken, Nakayendoh, Tekgwateha, Nechanenakon, Neyonkaweha, Nayonchakten, Thanatakwa, Karenyenta, Nehnokaweh, and Nehkahehwatheah would council among themselves and then be represented by the Kaokwa:haka in council.

Soon after, some of the Kenienké:haka war chiefs began to sell land for personal wealth. In the past, the clan matrons had been the only ones allowed to make transactions, as they were the true keepers of the land. These Protestant war chiefs no longer recognized the authority of the women over the land. Like the Catholic Christian Kenienké:haka of Kahnawaké, they were told by the Priests that only men were dominant. It was solely the traditional *royaner* and their followers who still respected the role of women.

The war chiefs of the Rotinonshonni also began to belittle the Lenape and the Shawnee. They not only sanctioned the selling of their own land but the selling of Lenape and Shawnee lands to the English.[42] However, they had difficulty negotiating with the English because the English remained so divided in their own colonies. One day, an Onontaka:haka war chief named Kanasehtekoh spoke to the English representatives of the thirteen arrows. He said to them:

> "We heartily recommend union and a good agreement between you and our people. Never disagree, but preserve a strict friendship for one another, and thereby you, as well as we, will become stronger. Our wise forefathers established union and amity between the Five Nations; this has made us formidable; this has given us a great weight and authority with our neighboring nations. We are a powerful confederacy; and, by your observing the same methods our wise forefathers have taken, you will acquire strength and power; therefore, whatever befalls you, never fall out with another."[43]

Kanasehtekoh was a war chief and interpreted the meaning of the Great Peace, the way warriors had wanted. What he didn't realize was that he was paving the way for English warriors to unite so that thirteen arrows united would be stronger than the now six arrows of the Rotinonshonni.

A Fracture within the Great Peace of the Rotinonshonni

In the final war between the French and English, the Kenienké:haka of Kahnawaké fought a battle against the Kenienké:haka of the valley. They had tried to avoid this for almost a hundred years. The Catholic Kenienké:haka tried everything to lead the French away from the Kenienké:haka of the valley. Leading the Kenienké:haka of the Valley was the noted Christian war chief, Hendrick. Suddenly from the side of the road, the Catholic Kenienké:haka popped their heads out of the forest and surrounded Hendrick and both his Church of England and traditional Kenienké:haka warriors.

> One of the Catholic Kenienké:haka from Kahnawaké rose and asked, "Who are you and where are you going?"
>
> Hendrick answered, "I am a member of the Rotinonshonni, the greatest of all the *onkwe:honwe* that live on Turtle Island."
>
> A Kahnawaké Kenienké:haka, replied, "We are from the Seven Nation confederacy,[44] and we come with our Father, the King of France, to fight against the English; we have no quarrel with you. We therefore ask that you keep out of the way, lest we end up fighting one another."
>
> Hendrick replied, "The Rotinonshonni have come to assist their brethren, the English, against the French who are encroaching on our lands in the Ohio. The Kahnawaké should join us in this worthy cause against them or keep out of the way."[45]

Just then, an overexuberant Kenienké:haka warrior from the valley fired at the Kahnawaké Kenienké:haka. In a few minutes, forty Kenienké:haka from both sides fell dead, as they began to kill one another. They were fighting for the light-skinned beings in their own wars. The light-skinned being had divided them against one another and now the Kenienké:haka were killing each another. The Kahnawaké women, who were waiting in the bushes, caught Hendrick as he fled the battle and helped to kill him.[46]

Teharonhia:wako looked down from the Sky World. He knew that the Rotinonshonni were soon going to suffer in a way that had never happened before. He had sent his own emissary to bring a message of peace to the warring nations. Now, nations were even killing their own people in the wars brought to them by the Sawiskera islanders. The Great Peace was becoming more and more of a shell of what it had meant to represent. Sawiskera was truly at his worst, by influencing the *onkwe:honwe* to kill one another in a war that wasn't of their making.

After the English had won their war against the French, they began to abuse the nations who traded with the French in the west. These nations rose up and, with the help of the Sonontowa:haka, defeated many of the English forts. This angered the Kenienké:haka who were in favor of the English whose army was at the eastern door of the Rotinonshonni; the French army was at the western door. The Sonontowa:haka did not want to fight a war against their cousins who lived in the north and west and who favored the French.

When the war was over, a great treaty was called that divided the land at the foothills of the Allegheny Mountains. The English leaders had promised that no light-skinned person would ever move across the mountains and take the lands away from the Rotinonshonni and their cousins. This angered the English Christians, who believed that any land that they touched belonged to them automatically. They said that if their English leaders didn't do something, they would revolt and take the lands by force anyway.

> The Kenienké:haka had a friend named William Johnson who had married into the Kenienké:haka Turtle Clan. They had named him *Ouirrakh-iakeh*, He Who Does Great Things. He was the representative of the great English leader who lived on Sawiskera's island. Johnson had been influential in getting the Kenienké:haka to fight with the English against the French. Johnson called for a council at his home named Johnson Hall. He wanted to meet all the *royaner* of the confederacy. When the *onkwe:honwe* of the different nations arrived, there were no *royaner*, only *rarontaron* war chiefs. Johnson asked, "Where are the *royaner* to represent you?"

A war chief for the Sonontowa:haka stood up and answered:

"The reason that you do not see many of our *royaner* here is because the weather and the roads are bad. They are not able to travel like we can. Therefore, negotiate with us, for it is we who are the leaders of consequence who manage the affairs of our people. Our *royaner* and *Otiyaner* are a parcel of old people, who say much but do little. It is we who have the power and ability to settle matters with you, and we are determined to answer you honestly from our hearts to the fullest."[47]

By this time, the *rarontaron*, war chiefs, were in complete control of the confederacy. Johnson knew that if he ever needed them they would be more easily manipulated than the wise *royaner* of the confederacy who would try and stay neutral. With the French defeated, the English knew that the Kenienké:haka were at their mercy. They asked Johnson for more land to live on; it was Kenienké:haka lands as well as those of their southern neighbors that were wanted. Soon after, Johnson called for a large council to be held at Fort Stanwix, near the lands that were divided between the Oneota:haka and the Kenienké:haka nations.

At the council were the following: commissioners for the various English colonies; Christian religious leaders; as well as approximately 3,000 warriors from various Indigenous nations, such as the Lenape, Mingoes, Shawnee, and the Rotinonshonni representatives of the Six Nations.

Johnson opened the council by saying, "The Rotinonshonni are the masters of all the other Indians. They therefore have the right to sell any of your lands. You will be compensated for your losses with presents."

The Lenape, Shawnee, and Mingoes shouted aloud, "No!"

He then said, "The Kenienké:haka will also forfeit some of their lands to retain the peace."

Not long after, the English delegation, along with their Christian spiritual leaders, began arguing as to who would get which lands. During the night, Johnson invited the war chiefs of the Rotinonshonni to a council. He said to them, "The English in the colonies want more land and are willing to fight you for it. If you give up your southern lands up to Woods

Creek, as well as that of the Lenape and Shawnee in Pennsylvania, you will be left in peace."

The Rotinonshonni war chiefs thought about it overnight. The next day, they said, "We accept the selling of our southern territories up to Woods Creek."[48]

The leaders of the Lenape and Shawnee sat and listened in dismay. They left, feeling bitter that the Rotinonshonni had sold off their lands to protect their own. They would remember this time in their stories and never support the Rotinonshonni again. It was not the first time that they had been humiliated by the Rotinonshonni. During the loss of the Lenape lands in Pennsylvania during the walking purchase, a war chief of the Rotinonshonni had said to the Lenape. "A long time ago, we put dresses on you and now you are our subjects."[49] He then sanctioned the selling of the Lenape lands. It was true that the Lenape were said to wear dresses. At the time, they were considered the grandfathers of all the Atirontok and therefore were the mediators of peace, the women's role. Now the role of women was becoming so undermined that it was being used as justification for selling Lenape lands.

It was not long before the thirteen arrows decided to break away from their mother country England, situated just off Sawiskera's island. They wanted the unrestricted use of Indigenous people's lands to the west. By this time, the *rarontaron,* war chiefs, were almost in complete control of the Rotinonshonni. Some of them had been educated by the light-skinned beings. The *royaner* did not want to participate in the war; however, their voices as well as the *Otiyaner,* clan matrons, had been silenced. Soon the great white wind would blow through the territory of the Longhouse of One Family as had been prophesied by the Peacemaker.

A young man Tyendináka, Two Sticks Together, had been given the name Joseph Brant. He had been befriended by Johnson, who had married Brant's sister Molly. Brant hated the English of the thirteen arrows.

One day, a man named George Klock had gotten some Kenienké:haka drunk and had them sign a deed for their land and their village of Canajoharie. He then tried to evict the Kenienké:haka from their village. Brant knew that there would come a time when he would have to deal with men like Klock.[50]

Johnson had Brant educated by English missionaries so that he could read and write like the English. This put Brant in a powerful position as a negotiator between the Rotinonshonni and the English.

At Johnson Hall, the Rotinonshonni warriors had come to speak to Johnson. Johnson had made Johnson Hall the central fire of the warriors of the confederacy. There were few *royaner* who would ever visit it.

At the council, a Kenienké:haka war chief asked, "Why are your people entering our lands in the Ohio from the south?"

Johnson replied, "We are doing everything to keep them out. Your only hope is to remain loyal to the English."[51]

Suddenly Johnson fell down. He had suffered a heart attack and died. There was no one now to mediate between the English and the colonists who were breaking away.

The Shawnee were now being killed by the colonists of the thirteen arrows who were entering the Ohio region. They sent emissaries to the Rotinonshonni warriors asking for help.

When they arrived, they said, "At Fort Stanwix you took it upon yourselves to give the colonists our lands in Pennsylvania. If they are your lands, are you willing to stand by us and fight for them in the Ohio?"

The warriors knew that they didn't have the power to save the Shawnee lands. They answered, "We cannot help you right now. You will have to fend for yourselves until we call a grand council."

The war chiefs knew that they were humiliated and had made mistakes; things were now getting out of control. A grand council was held at Kanata:kowa village in Onontaka territory to turn over the decision process back to the traditional *royaner*. There the *royaner* chastised the war chiefs.

Atotarhoh asked, "Are you ready to listen to us before it is too late and we lose everything?"

The *rarontaron,* war chiefs, nodded their heads and one said, "We will promise that from now on any decisions that are made will first come back here to the grand council to be discussed by the *royaner* and the *Otiyaner,* clan matrons, as had been done in the past."[52]

William Johnson's nephew took his uncle's place after he died. He called for another council at Johnson's Hall with the warriors. He knew that he had to solidify an alliance with them if they were to beat the colonists who now called themselves Americans.

He said, "My brothers, do not be afraid. The Great King in England will protect your lands from the colonists. You will have to remain loyal in order for him to do so. We ask that you remain at peace while we settle this matter between the colonies and the Great King."

A Kenienké:haka warrior brought a wampum belt forward and said, "Here is the covenant chain between us. Let us polish it so that it shines bright into the future."

All agreed and the covenant chain was renewed.

A Grand Council was held at Kanata:kowa village shortly after. Atotarhoh brought up the resolution of remaining at peace. It went through all the nations.

Tekarihokenh stood up and said, "The Kenienké:haka wish to remain at peace."

Skanyiatar:io stood up and said, "The Sonontowa:haka want to remain at peace."

Takaheyonh stood up and said, "The Kaokwa:haka want to remain in peace."

Ronwahtsatonneh stood up and said, "The Oneota:haka and Tuscarora want to remain at peace."

Atotarhoh then stood up and said, "Be it resolved; we will not interfere in the dispute between the thirteen arrows and the Great Father the King."

While this was going on, the Christian leader Kirkland was trying to gain the Oneota:haka's support for the thirteen arrows. One of his most devout converts was the war chief Skenantoh, The Deer.

The Oneota:haka had made their intentions known through the words of a *rarontaron*, war chief. He told Kirkland and some other representatives of the thirteen arrows, "We are unwilling to join on either side of such a contest, for we love you both, old England and new. Should the great King of England ask us to go to war, we will not. If the Colonies ask us, we will refuse."[53]

It was not long after that the Kenienké:haka had become so discouraged over the losses of their lands that they appealed to the Oneota:haka for land.

One of the Kenienké:haka warriors asked the Oneota:haka, "We have no home any longer. The colonists have taken everything away from us, including our villages."[54]

Kirkland said, "The people of New York have done inexpressible hurt in the interest of religion among the lower tribes by taking away their lands and have made the other tribes angry."[55]

The Kenienké:haka's only hope of keeping some lands was to maintain good relations with the King of England. Joseph Brant was the key to that relationship. The great white wind that had been predicted was already beginning to blow through the Kenienké:haka lands. Kenienké:haka were already responding by taking up their hatchets and sheltering themselves against the wind. This meant some of them choosing to fight the colonists from the thirteen arrows.

A council was held at Onakara Falls by the English. They had built a fort there to gain more support from the Rotinonshonni. The English would do anything to prevent the Rotinonshonni from being neutral. Their emissary Butler spoke on behalf of the English King:

> "Your father, the Great King, has taken pity on you and is determined not to let the Americans deceive you any longer. Even though you were foolish to listen to them last year and believed their wicked stories. They mean to cheat you; if you should be so silly to take their advice and they conquer the King's army, their intention is to take all your lands from you and destroy your people, for they are mad, foolish, crazy and full of deceit. They told you last fall at Pittsburgh that they took the tomahawk out of your hands, buried it deep, and transplanted the Tree of Peace over it. I now pluck up that tree, dig up the tomahawk, and replace it in your hands with the edge toward them that you may treat them as enemies."[56]

Kakonkaukawetah, a *rarontaron*, war chief, of the Sonontowa:haka, answered:

> "You have called us here to break the peace with our American brethren and to ask our help to fight them. We have lived in peace with them a long time, and we resolve to continue to do so as long as we can. When they hurt us, we will strike back. It is true that they have encroached on our lands, but of this we will speak to them. If you are so strong,

Brother, and they so weak, why ask our assistance? It is true that I am tall and strong, but I reserve my strength to strike those who injure me. You have plenty of warriors, powder, lead and goods and they are so few. Be strong and make use of them. You say that their powder is rotten. We have found it to be good. You say they are mad and foolish, wicked, and deceitful. I say you are; they are wise, for you want us to destroy ourselves in your war; they advise us to live in peace. This advice we intend to follow."[57]

At the same time, a number of Oneota:haka warriors were becoming angry, because of the way a Kenienké:haka war party treated a delegation from the thirteen arrows who had gone to arrest John Johnson, William's son.

Meanwhile, Joseph Brant, having previously married into Skenantoh's family, went on a mission to keep the Oneota:haka in alliance with the Kenienké:haka and the English. The commander of the colonists, in turn, opened a trading post for the Oneota:haka who were in need of supplies to feed their families. So destitute had they become that they were becoming beggars in their own land.

The Great Peace Crumbles

Another grand council was to be held at Kanata:kowa village in Onontaka territory to keep all the warriors in line. Just then another pestilence hit. The Onontaka:haka *royaner* sent a message through the Oneota:haka saying:

> "We have lost from our town ninety members, including three *royaner*. We, the remaining Onontaka inform our brothers that there is no longer a council fire at the capital of the Rotinonshonni. However, we are determined to use our feeble endeavors to support peace through the confederate nations, but let this be kept in mind that the central fire is extinguished and can no longer burn."[58]

With the central fire out, the war chiefs would now resume control over confederacy matters.

Butler, soon after, called for another council at Onakara. When the Sonontowa:haka warriors arrived they were told. "Go to the storehouse and take anything that you want. There are barrels of rum waiting for you there."

The Sonontowa:haka women had come along with their men believing that it was a trick to get them to fight, but it was to no avail. Just then a ship docked with every present imaginable, thousands of beads and trinkets that the women valued. Brant at the same time was telling the Sonontowa:haka and the others. "We must fight for the English. Look at everything they have to offer. We cannot lose."[59]

At the same time, the colonists' missionary to the Oneota:haka, Samuel Kirkland, who had a long standing policy against the use of the mind changer, told the Oneota:haka warriors. "There are two barrels of rum; go help yourselves as there will be more where that came from."[60]

The Sawiskera's mind changer had completed his work.

Soon after, Brant and his Sonontowa:haka warriors were taking up the hatchet and fighting the Americans at Fort Stanwix. The American general Herkimer was on his way with a relief force. At its head were Honorary Toxtator, Thawenkarakwenh, Blatcop, and Henry Cornelius and three Oneota:haka warriors, along with sixty other Oneota:haka and some Tuscarora. Hiding in the bushes at Oriskeny Creek were Brant, the Kenienké:haka, and the Sonontowa:haka warriors, one of whom was Sakayowatha, Red Jacket.

As the Americans approached, Brant and the others began to attack from the rear. Blacksnake, a Sonontowa:haka warrior, would later say, "I have never seen so many dead bodies in my life. There was so much blood running down that it was like a stream."

Blatcop fought bravely, swinging his war club and knocking down one and then another Kenienké:haka. Thawenkarakwenh was wounded in the wrist. Brant fought ferociously from the rear, killing Americans and Oneota:haka alike. Red Jacket and two others ran from the battlefield. Some say it was cowardice. Perhaps, he had no stomach to kill Oneota:haka in a Whiteman's war. He did the right thing according the Great Way of Peace.[61]

Once again, Teharonhia:wako looked down on his children. Now they were killing one another on their own land in a war that was made by the Sawiskera Islanders. He knew now that his children would truly suffer. The Peacemaker had told them that if they ever shed blood on their own land against each other, they would lose it.

Soon the great white wind passed through their villages, destroying many of them. His name was Washington, and he sent his army to punish those who supported the English. He would forever be known as the Rana-takarias, Town Destroyer. Then the English King left the Kenienké:haka, Kaokwa:haka, Sonontowa:haka, and Onontaka:haka on the battlefield to fend for themselves. Finally, at a treaty on Sawiskera's island, he gave the territory of the Rotinonshonni to the American victors while members of the Kenienké:haka fought on.

Many of the *onkwe:honwe* sought refuge at Onakara until they could acquire land from their old enemies the Tahakanus Mississauga who had moved there not long before and replant the tree where the *Oka:ratsikowa*, Great Elms, stood. There, some of the remnants of the Five Nations of the Rotinonshonni remained, as was prophesied by the Peacemaker.

The Sonontowa:haka and Kaokwa:haka were sent further west, away from their homelands.

The Oneota:haka, as a gesture of thanks, were given thirty-two acres of land of their five million to live on by the thirteen arrows who called themselves Americans. Others would live under or near the Elm Tree with the rest of the confederacy, while still others would move far to the west and then forced south to live with their cousins.

The Skaroo'ren would be given land near Onakara falls where the Kakwako lived, while others would join those near the Great Elm trees.

Some of the Kenienké:haka would join the Kahnawaké and Akwe-sasne Kenienké:haka, while others would move back to the place where the Peacemaker was born, even though they had become Christian.

The Onontaka:haka would be allowed to return to their homes to rebuild Kanata:kowa village if they promised not to help their brothers and cousins in the Ohio. This was said to be a great treaty, and it was for the thirteen arrows.

When the *royaner* were sent for by the Town Destroyer to speak at Albany, they were asked why they had fought against the colonies. A *royaner* answered:

"Times are altered with us *onkwe:honwe*. Formerly the warriors were governed by the wisdom of their uncles, the sachems, but now they take their own way and dispose of themselves, rebuilding their village without consulting the *royaner*. While we wish for peace, they are for war; brothers they must face the consequences."[62]

It appeared that Sawiskera had gained control of the whole territory of the Longhouse of One Family. He had turned them away from Teharonhia:wako and the teachings of the Peacemaker. The clan system brought to them by the great young man was slowly being lost. They had fought in wars against one another on their own territory. There was darkness that was taking place that had never been seen before on Teharonhia:wako's island. After the war, the Rotinonshonni territory was given away to the Sawiskera Islanders of the thirteen arrows. Christians, like Kirkland, took most of the lands for themselves. The Town Destroyer paid his soldiers with the lands of the Rotinonshonni. Others who had become Christian, such as the Kenienké:haka warrior Brant, either sold or had stolen most of the newly acquired lands where the Great Elm trees stood to the Sawiskera's Islanders with whom they had fought with. These Sawiskera's Islanders, called Loyalists, would then claim for themselves most of the lands where the Great Elm trees stood with pitchforks. They chased the *onkwe:honwe* and their adopted Tutelo friends including both women and children across the river that had been given to them. Then, they took the town that Brant built and made a law that no *onkwe:honwe* could live within eight miles of a Whiteman's town.

To add insult to injury, the thirteen arrows, now bound together as one, would plant the *Skarenhesehkowah,* Great White Pine Tree, at Philadelphia. There they would place the eagle on top. They would then let the four white roots, which had turned black, spread to the four corners of Turtle Island. They would follow these roots to every corner of the Teharonhia:wako's island, destroying all the cousins of the *onkwe:honwe* and taking their lands. Sawiskera was using the things that Teharonhia:wako had given the *onkwe:honwe* to gain control of the rest of the island. It seemed like the Rotinonshonni were spiritually and culturally finished. However, Teharonhia:wako had another plan for them.

5

The *Kari:wio* of Skanyiatar:io

Teharonhia:wako Sends Four Messengers
to Restore Order and Peace within the Longhouse

Teharonhia:wako had seen his children war against one another and lose
their land. He felt sad inside but knew that he could not return any longer.
If he appeared in full form, then so would his brother. They would then
fight one another and destroy the world. The *onkwe:honwe* were falling
like leaves to the mind changer. They seemed to have no purpose in life.
Many of them were no longer practicing the ceremonies given to them
by Teharonhia:wako. Sawiskera seemed to be in control of their beliefs.
Almost all the Kenienké:haka and Oneota:haka were Christian. There
were still some Onontaka:haka, Kaokwa:haka and Sonontowa:haka who
were still doing the four ceremonies.

Teharonhia:wako said to himself, "My children are becoming farther
and farther apart from me than ever before. They bring the mind changer
into their ceremonies and all-night feasts, and then they kill one another. I
have brought them the four ceremonies, a clan system, and a Peacemaker
to help them live. What more can I do for them?"

He continued, "I will send the four spiritual beings who live in the
direction of the four winds to visit them. They will tell the *onkwe:honwe*
how they should conduct their lives. Their territory for the ceremonies will
be confined to the size of a longhouse until the time when there will be a
great change that will take place to mother earth. There, they will continue
their way of life. I will choose an *onkwe:honwe* who is beyond redemption to
be visited by the four messengers, so that the *onkwe:honwe* will know that
anyone can be redeemed if they choose to follow my teachings once again."

There was a Kenienké:haka *onkwe:honwe* who seemed to be the ideal person to pass the message. He was a person afflicted by the mind changer. He began to have visitations by three of the messengers. Soon he was preaching about the things that he saw. It seemed that wherever he went, no one would listen to him. They thought he was crazy. The man then began to take the mind changer again, and he died in the mist walking in the valley of the Kenienké:haka. He was alone when he died, for there were no more Kenienké:haka living in the valley. It was said that you could see steam coming from his body that was left in the cold in the valley. From that time on, it would be hard for the Kenienké:haka to accept the message. Only a few would. Sawiskera would make sure that the original Good Message would be influenced by him, and this would turn the Kenienké:haka and others away from it.[1] However, in the end all who would follow the traditional teachings would practice in the new Longhouse way brought by the four spiritual beings even though they would continue to disagree among themselves as to their meaning.

The four messengers had tried the eastern door of the Kenienké:haka first; now they would enter through the western door, the entrance to the territory of the Longhouse of One Family. The Sonontowa:haka, however, were being pushed farther and farther west, and there were now few left.

Like the other *onkwe:honwe* of the *Rotinonshonni*, their spirits were broken. Many had accepted the deceptive powers of the fire water, which they called the mind changer. Since Sawiskera's Islanders had invaded their country, they could neither live in peace nor go to war. They lived without purpose. The *Otiyaner*, clan matrons, no longer had any land to look after and therefore could no longer grow the three sisters. The men could not hunt, for many of the game animals had been destroyed. Their lands were forcefully given away in treaties by the *Rarontaron*, war chiefs. The *royaner, peace chiefs,* had lost their influence among the people. Sawiskera's Islanders traveled down the ancient pathways of their country, bringing the fiddle, the cards, and the mind changer. The men of Sawiskera's Island would then drink the mind changer and take the *onkwe:honwe* women, knowing that the laws in cases of murder or rape were made to protect them alone.

Next, Christians came and preached against the mind changer, saying that they were the only hope for the *onkwe:honwe* who were suffering from broken spirits. In fact, until they were broken in spirit they had little effect on the *onkwe:honwe*. Once that happened, the Christians would then claim for themselves the land on which the *onkwe:honwe* lived, saying that it was a fair exchange for the gift of Christianity and sobriety.

During this time, the *onkwe:honwe* began to kill one another. They blamed each other for witchcraft. As soon as one fell to the mind changer or to disease, another was accused of witchcraft, blamed, and then sometimes murdered.

Teharonhia:wako saw all this, and he said, "My children are forgetting the things I taught them. My brother has so deceived their minds. Even those that continue my teachings bring the mind changer into their ceremonies. Then, my children commit the worst deeds upon one another from which there is no return once they are committed."

He continued, "I can no longer interfere in the creation. However, I must find a way to direct my children back on the right path so that, when they depart from the world, they may see me again."

He continued, "Before Sawiskera's Islanders arrived, sometimes evil existed but not sin. I had not even seen the need to give the *onkwe:honwe* a word for sin. But from now on those things that pertain to the misdeeds that have come from Sawiskera's island will be called sin."

He continued, "Today, now that they have learned about sin from the Sawiskera Islanders, the *onkwe:honwe* partake in sin. They drink the mind changer, sell land, and murder one another, and that is a sin."

He continued, "If they leave their children alone and beat their wives, that is a sin. If they kill one another in wars that they don't belong in, that is a sin. If they gamble all of their possessions away and then don't feed their children, that is a sin. Those who communicate with the ancient ones now commit witchcraft and use the ancient ones to harm others. That is a sin. They accept the teachings of the ones who brought them and showed them how to sin over the teachings I have given them. That is a sin. Sin will remain with them until they put away those things that they have learned from Sawiskera's Islanders."

Finally, he said, "I will send four messengers to restore the balance that existed from the beginning of time. Because they have lost the territory that belonged to all the Longhouse of One Family by warring against one another, their ceremonial territory will be reduced to a longhouse. That is where I will restore the balance. There, they will continue to be thankful to me and the other beings in the creation until the time when the world will go through another change. If they are vigilant in this, they will see me once again. Those who do not will go to other places, for the order of creation is vast. Those who continue to commit sins and other evil acts will take the road to Sawiskera's, who will be waiting for them as the Punisher. There, they will find acknowledgement of their sins that they believed in and practiced."

Skanyiatar:io Receives the Good Message from the Four Messengers

It was not long after that one of the *royaner* who had become afflicted by the mind changer became sick. For four years he lived with his life spirit outside his body. He was only alive in a physical sense. Except for a spark, his spirit had died years before. This was the power of the mind changer. It made those who drank it spiritless, and, when they finally passed on, their spirits would take the road to the Punisher, wandering aimlessly craving it.

That was because everything was enhanced in the Sky World. Those who lived good lives saw and felt the immensity of its beauty. Those that committed acts against the creation saw and felt the acts of horror that they brought to others in a way that they could not in the Earth World.

For most *onkwe:honwe*, there was still a chance for redemption, even if they had done wrong. However, for some, they could never get beyond the terrible acts that they committed, so they could never see the beauty of the Creator's path. This was the way it was for murderers, witches, and those who harmed others and fell to Sawiskera's powers of deception on the Earth and in the Sky World.

Teharonhia:wako had chosen the *royaner* Skanyiatar:io, because he knew a *royaner* who had fallen to the mind changer would be despised in the worst way by the *onkwe:honwe*. *royaner* were chosen for their qualities of character by the *Otiyaner*, clan matrons. There would be no pity for a *royaner* who had let those qualities lapse. Teharonhia:wako also knew that a *royaner* who redeemed himself could use the title of *royaner* to better the lives of others. However, by continuing to drink the mind changer, he could also destroy the hope of others. Teharonhia:wako hoped that in Skanyiatar:io's case it would be the former and not the latter.

Teharonhia:wako called the four celestial beings and said, "You must go forth to this *royaner* who has fallen and guide him back to me. If that occurs, others will follow him. Remember, Sawiskera will use his power to try to change the things that you show him and teach him. However, the teachings will be so great that he will only be partially successful."

As Skanyiatar:io lay in a state of expectant death in the village of Teyonosata:keh, he pleaded with the Creator, "If you help me, I will never drink the mind changer again."

He had said these words many times before, but each time he said them and meant them, he would drink some more. He had seen many of his people fallen to the mind changer and never recover. It seemed hopeless to him.

However, for four years he remained vigilant in giving thanks to the Creator for another day of life, and he continually asked help for his affliction. He never lost hope that one day he would be free of this illness that destroyed the will of the most powerful of his people.

One day, Skanyiatar:io was lying on his deathbed. His skin had turned yellow and pale. His daughter heard him getting up. She ran into the room as he fell to the ground. It appeared to her that he had died, and so she called her husband.

She said to her husband, "Run quickly and get Skanyiatar:io's nephew."

Her husband ran out the door to retrieve Skanyiatar:io's nephew, Tawanios.

When he arrived, he told Tawanios, "Tell Skanyiatar:io's brother Kaianta:waka that his brother has departed from the earth."

Tawanios looked for Kaianta:waka and, upon seeing him, said, "Your brother has died. They need you at his lodge."

Kaianta:waka replied, "Let me finish planting my field, and I will be there shortly."

Kaianta:waka had no respect for his brother and knew that he would soon depart from the earth. In fact, he was partially happy. For four years, his brother had been a burden to him and the rest of his family. He had told himself that his brother did not deserve the title of *royaner*. He had pleaded with his clan mother to dehorn his brother. She could not as she did not have the heart to do so.

Tawanios went back to where Skanyiatar:io lay and felt his body. He said to the others, "There is still a warm spot near his heart."

Skanyiatar:io, while unconscious, heard a voice call him three times, "Skanyiatar:io, come outside for a while."

Automatically, Skanyiatar:io found himself outside. He saw three men standing in front of him. The men's cheeks were painted red, and they wore only a few feathers in their headdresses. They seemed to be about middle-age, and they looked very much alike. They also carried bows and arrows in one hand, as well as a variety of bushes of berries in the other.

One of the beings said, "The Creator of the world has asked us to come to the Turtle's back once again and visit. That is because we have visited often before and are now returning. He told us to visit the one who is sick from the mind changer and who, in spite of this, continues to give him thanks. We were asked to try and help him. It is you Skanyiatar:io that we have come for, because you have been chosen to deliver a message to the Creator's children the *onkwe:honwe*. He gave us these strawberries to give you to eat. They will give you strength and take away the craving of the mind changer, for they are sweet and will absorb and replace its effects."

Skanyiatar:io then drank the medicine.

The celestial being then said, "Tomorrow, we will arrange it so two people, a man and a woman, will prepare some dried pudding and tobacco dipped in medicine for you. When you are finished these, your craving will be gone and your strength will begin to return. You will then offer the rest of the medicine back to the forests. After that happens, many *onkwe:honwe* will begin to visit you who are also afflicted by the mind changer. When they arrive, you will gather the strawberries and have a feast together. You will drink the juice of the berry and thank the Creator. This will also help them with their craving."

Next, the celestial beings began to tell Skanyiatar:io how things should be on Turtle Island.

One of them said, "Never think that you were chosen because you are special. This happened before, and the one chosen now lies in the valley.

The Creator chooses those who will be given a message, and you should be happy enough with just being alive. There are many who are chosen and begin to think that they are prophets; then they think that they are even the Creator himself. They then go mad and destroy others. The Creator is there for the benefit of all humankind and not just for you alone."

Another said, "It is through your celebrations and the Great Feather Dance that the spirit of your people will be elevated. Then will you and they begin to rebuild your spirits and recover. You will do this during the time when the strawberries are ripe. The juice of the strawberry will be drunk by everyone in order to keep a sober mind. That is because the strawberries are medicine that restores the health of those afflicted by the mind changer." He continued, "We will continue to reveal things to you, and you will then tell the *onkwe:honwe* what we have said. That is because we are four of the ancient ones who were created during the beginning of the world; our duty is to watch over humankind. The reason that you now see three and not four is because the fourth has returned to tell the Creator what has occurred. We will now reveal to you the message that you must give to others."

Just then, Kaianta:waka arrived at Skanyiatar:io's side and also felt a warm spot on his chest. Soon after they noticed it beginning to spread, and then suddenly he opened his eyes.

"How are you feeling, Uncle?" Tawanios asked.

"I am feeling good," answered Skanyiatar:io.

After that, Skanyiatar:io began to spread the Good Message that had come from the three spiritual beings. There were many who believed and others who did not. After he departed from the earth, it was passed on to Skantokawati, and he passed it onto his nephew Shakenjoweneh who also held a Kenienké:haka *royaner* title. As time passed, others heard the message and began to write it down. Sawiskera found a new way to subvert the teachings of Teharonhia:wako. Through the writing system of Sawiskera's Islanders, he would be able to change the meaning of the *Kayeneren:kowa* and the *Kari:wio*. He would make it so that it seemed like Teharonhia:wako had sanctioned warriors and so that the Good Message would appear like the Christian message. In this way many of the *onkwe:honwe* would become divided once again, and some would turn against both.

The first to write it down was John Jackett, who used a system of writing he had learned from a Christian minister Reverend Asher Wright. Wright was one of those who made it his life duty to Christianize *onkwe:honwe*. However, it was Edward Cornplanter who would lose the original writings and then have to rewrite the *Kari:wio*. He would be assisted by a Baptist Christian minister, William Bluesky, who would guide him in his words. This version, along with a written version of the *Kayeneren:kowa* would be used by Arthur Parker. The *Kari:wio*, that Cornplanter had written and taken up by Parker, would be then memorized by the believers in the Good Message.[2]

Parker's work would also be influential in the modern ascendancy of the *rarontaron*, war chiefs, as it would include aspects of Skanawatih's Laws of War and the division between them and the *royaner*, whose position was to always advocate for peaceful resolutions. Both the *Kari:wio* and the *Kayeneren:kowa* would be set down as a set of laws like that of the Sawiskera Islanders. There would be no redemption for those who did wrong in the *Kari:wio*; later, it would seem to sanction the whipping of children and the subservience of women to men. The *Kayeneren:kowa* would be interpreted as giving the war chiefs the prominent position of handing out punishments, such as the clubbing to death of chiefs, as set in Skanawatih's Laws of War.

Skanyiatar:io Relays the Good Message to the *Onkwe:honwe*

In truth, the *Kari:wio* affirmed the traditional culture and the *Kayeneren:kowa*, rather than denying it. They would now work together in the Longhouse tradition. However, the Rotinonshonni should always be governed by the *Kayeneren:kowa*, and the two should not impede one another. That is why there was a place and time for council and a place and time for ceremonies. In fact, up to recent times where the Great Elm stood and where there were multiple onkwe:honwe nations, there were some *royaner* who were baptized as Christian. That is because in order to govern, the *Kayeneren:kowa* had to be for everyone in spite of the differences in belief.

This would change after the Council House was forcibly closed by the Sawiskera Islanders.

The *Kari:wio* was given so that the *onkwe:honwe* would conduct themselves in a manner that the Creator wanted in the first place. The purpose was to have *royaner* and *otiyaner* who were clear minded. With the introduction of sin and the mind changer by the light-skinned beings, the *onkwe:honwe* would need new teachings to alleviate their effects. These are the teachings they were taught that were revealed that fateful day to Skanyiatar:io.

After Skanyiatar:io woke up, he began to relay what he had seen. He said, "When I woke up, I saw three men standing in front of me. They wore paint and each held a bow and arrow in one hand and a shrub in the other." He continued, "They gave me berries to eat to restore my health. They then told me that they had chosen me because of my having given thanks to the Creator. They told me that I should hold a council to explain what I had seen."

At that time when the *onkwe:honwe* met in the council house, Skanyiatar:io revealed the rest that had happened to him.

He began, "I have a message to deliver to you who are gathered. I have been told by the servants of the Creator that I should live upon the earth to teach the *onkwe:honwe* the things that will please the Creator again. The Creator has seen that you have once again transgressed from the things that he taught you. He made you so that you could have good lives and not do harm to others. He sees that you have accepted the sins brought to you by Sawiskera's Islanders. The worst thing that you have done is to take the fire water that you know to be the mind changer. The Creator says that you have to stop this."

He continued, "All this came about because your ancestors first took it from the Light-Skinned Beings. You have suffered ever since because of it. Those that did this have never gotten to the Creator's world in the sky. This was not made for you. It was made for the Light-Skinned Beings as a medicine on Sawiskera's Island just as the *oyonkwa:honwe*, Sacred Tobacco, was made for you. By drinking to excess, they too have violated the will of the Creator who blew life into all of you. The Creator says that to be drunk is forbidden, and he wants you to stop. In fact, he forbids you to continue this evil habit. If you leave it behind, much of your suffering will end, and your children will be happy once again. The Creator is sad that, because of it, there is so much crime and wickedness on the earth. There are some things that were never intended for his Red children."

He continued, "The Creator has withheld from the *onkwe:honwe* the number of days he has on earth. However, he has left a path for the *onkwe:honwe* to follow so that they may tread safely on the earth. This is how you can get on that path."

He continued, "When the Great Spirit made man, he also made woman. He instituted marriage so that they would care for one another and be faithful to each other. The Creator loves to see a man and a woman happy. He asks you to be faithful for your children's sakes and promises to bless them if you do this. Those women who could not have children and want a child should adopt one. There are many who are poor and are orphans that need caring. If you tie up the clothes of an orphan child, you will be rewarded. If an orphan ever crosses your path, be kind to them and treat them with tenderness. It is the parents' responsibility to teach their children reverence for the Creator. They must ensure that children are brought up with good morals. They should also guide their children in having proper marriages by helping to select a good match for them. When both parents have agreed, then the two young persons should be brought together and told of their parents' wishes. If ever they cannot agree with one another or are deemed not to be a good match, they should separate with a good feeling, for there is nothing wrong with this."

He continued, "When a child is born to a man and a woman, they should give thanks to the Creator for the gift of the child. The parents should instruct their children in their duties toward the Creator, their parents, and their fellow men. Children should obey their parents and submit to them. Those who are disobedient are cause of great pain and sadness to their parents. They hurt their feelings and cause them great duress. This will cause them to end up on the road to Sawiskera. Marriage obligations should generate good things for all concerned. If people who are married remain faithful to one another, they will die feeling at peace. Children should not cause suffering to the elderly either, for they should be kind and supportive. The Creator wants all children to love, revere, and obey their parents and elders. This pleases the Creator immensely. If the children show affection for their parents, the parents remain much happier."

He continued, "It is never right for a man to simply abandon his wife or his children. Both a father-in-law and a mother-in-law should always treat their son-in-law or daughter-in-law as their own children. They should not create trouble for them. The mother-in-law is always the next closest to the child after the parents."

He continued, "When parents argue over their children, this is a sin. The children hear their parents fighting and become sad and lonely. The child sees no prospect for happiness in their life and then wants to return to the Creator. If the child dies, the parents then end up weeping, and it is too late. This is a practice that should stop."

He continued, "The Creator never made the earth to be like merchandise. It is there, for everyone to enjoy. The *Rarontaron* and even some *royaner* have violated this ancient trust. Now, all you have are a few small reservations left. They should know that the land is for the generations to come and not for themselves. They should hold the remaining land in trust for their children, as they may be driven from their homes in the future. Those who sell lands will be punished by the Creator, for it goes against what is natural law. There is no price that can buy Mother Earth."

He continued, "Our Creator, when he first made us, designed it so that we could live by hunting. Sometimes, a man would leave on the hunt and would be gone for a long time. His wife would remain in the trust of friends. Upon returning, he finds out she has taken up with another man. The Creator says that this is wrong and should not occur."

He continued, "The four messengers said that it is wrong to punish a child with a rod. In fact, it is almost always wrong to punish someone. Our children should never be punished by a whip or any form of violence. One only needs to use water to punish with. The parent should blow water at the child and if the child doesn't stop, the strictest form of punishment is to plunge them in the water but not hurt them. When the child promises to be better, then the parent should stop."

He continued, "When a person you care for dies, make sure that you put your face close and whisper to them that they will be missed. Tell them that you will live a good life to make sure that you meet again in the future. The dead will hear you and remember what you said."

He continued, "The Creator placed the onkwe:honwe on the earth and gave them rules to live by. The Creator also gave the onkwe:honwe many things to enjoy in life. He made it so that the onkwe:honwe could find everything that they need on the earth. One of these things is berries. The Creator made all of the things that we live upon. When our mother the corn springs from the earth, it is the will of the Creator that we come together for Thanksgiving. It is also his wish that we perform the Great Feather Dance. The feast that we have should consist of the new things that grow from the earth. There should be a four-day festival of thanks. It is also the time to tell any events that are occurring in the future and for those with new names to bring them out."

He continued, "The first day of the festival, is the time for the Great Feather Dance that begins in the early part of the day and ends at noon. The second day is the time for the Thanksgiving Dance. The third day is the time for the performance of the *Atoweh* or the Thanksgiving Song. The fourth day is the time for the Peach Stone Game, which was once the Plum Stone Game. All of these ceremonies should begin during the early part of the day and at noon. The Creator has given us these things many times before, and they became lost. They must continue to be done."

He continued, "During all these times, we must give thanks to the Thunders, our Grandfathers, as well as his assistants. They are assigned the duty of watching over the earth and everything that it produces. It is through the Great Feather Dance, as well as the Thanksgiving Dance that we show our gratitude to the Creator. However, the Thanksgiving Dance belongs specifically to the Grandfathers. During this ceremony we will offer them tobacco. Once again, we must return thanks to our eldest Mother, the Earth, as well as our three mothers who are also referred to as our sisters: corn, beans, and squash. All of these things must be done during daylight and not when the Elder Brother the Sun has hidden himself."

He continued, "During the change of seasons, the cold season begins. This is the time when the men go out and hunt. They see the ancestor hunters in the sky, shoot the Great Bear, and the leaves turn red. Around the fifth day of the new moon, it is time to give the annual thanksgiving to the Creator. We once again partake of all the ceremonies that the Creator has given us."

He continued, "The four messengers have always watched over us and have seen what we have been doing on the earth. They brought me over the earth and told me to look down. What I saw first was a man whose clothes were tattered and torn. He was a drunkard. The mind changer had impoverished him of his body and spirit. I looked down again and saw a woman seated on the ground. She kept gathering every-thing and hoarding it for herself. The messengers said that the woman is selfish and will not leave her worldly goods. Both of these individuals will not be able to make it to the Sky World. The messengers told me to tell the *onkwe:honwe* of these things."

He continued, "Next, they told me to look down again. I saw a man carrying large pieces of meat. He was giving the meat away to many peo-ple who were assembled together. The messengers said that this man is blessed because of his kindness."

He continued, "Next, they told me to look once again. I saw the streams covered with blood. They said that if you don't put away the mind changer, the earth will be covered by the blood of those that are killed while drunk. Brother will kill brother, and friend will kill friend. I then looked and saw the smoke of distilleries rising and shutting out the light of the sun. The messengers then said to me that is where the fire water, the mind changer, is produced."

He continued, "I then saw a large house with whips, ropes, and chains on the inside of it. They told me that this is a house of confinement where those who indulge in the mind changer end up. There they live in bond-age, if they don't stop. That is why the Creator asks us to put this destruc-tive vice away from us."

He continued, "I looked once more and saw many people assembled who were unwilling to be taught anything. They were riotous and took pride in how much they could consume of the mind changer. There were others who wanted to be instructed but were pulled back by the lure of the mind changer. They even seemed to love the smells coming from the mind changer."

He continued, "There were others who listened and obeyed. The Creator loves these persons and is sad that many are becoming divided in their beliefs and taking different paths. The Creator wants us all to live in harmony with one another. The mind changer is one of the causes of division and dissension that exists among the *onkwe:honwe*. The messengers said that it would cause many premature unnatural deaths. Some will freeze in the cold, and others will be burned or drowned. All of this has already happened, just because they used the mind changer."

He continued, "My friends and relatives, is this not the truth? How many of us have suffered unnatural deaths, such as burning or drowning while under the influence of the mind changer? Those who drink the mind changer are already being punished on the earth. There are some that say that the mind changer is simply like food and not wrong to take. Let them then make an experiment. Let everyone who uses the mind changer assemble in a council house. Let those who do not drink the mind changer assemble in another council house. See which house ends up too be riotous and which remains calm. It will be the council house of drunkards that will end in riot and tumult while the other will remain quiet. It is hard to imagine the great harm that this has done to our people. Once again I say, reform and put it away. Some will use the mind changer until near death and then they will repent. By that time, there is little that can be done for them."

He continued, "It is important to know that every person is made equal no matter where they are from. That is because the Creator made a variety of gifts for each to have. Some may be given a beautiful face while others may not be so attractive. Some have nice forms while others may have deformities. Others still may have many worldly goods while others less. However, in the end everyone has the same privileges. That is because you are not the makers of your own fortunes. All the things that we have are gifts of the Creator. It is to him that we must all give thanks, for he is the benefactor of gifts. That is why it is wrong for someone to exalt themselves over another. You must care for one another, because you are all brothers and sisters of the same great family."

He continued, "The Creator asks all of you to offer hospitality and kindness to the needy and helpless. This pleases him very much. If you see a stranger wandering about, use kind words when you speak to them. Welcome him into your home and tell him about the Creator."

He continued, "Each morning, give thanks to the Creator and the Elder Brother the Sun for bringing light and warmth to the day. Each night, renew that thanks for having lived another day without being harmed; then you can rest your body."

He continued, "The four messengers said to me to tell the keepers of the faith to be strong minded and to adhere to the true faith. They said that they feared that the evil-minded will lure them away with temptations. He may bring the fiddle with him or cards and leave them among you. These will cause you to commit sin. The *onkwe:honwe* must be on guard, and it is the duty of the faith keepers to be watchful against these evils. The keepers of the faith are there to preserve the moral conduct of the communities."

He continued, "Whenever there is a meeting to instruct the people on how to live, the evil-minded will be close by. He will try to tempt the *onkwe:honwe* one by one. He will even follow some into the council house to disrupt things so that people will turn away from their traditions. There are many who enter the council house and then never return to it. Others, as they get older, begin to slip away from it. This is a sin and should not occur. It is important that the culture resumes as before."

He continued, "Speak evil of no one. If all you have to say is nothing good, then be quiet. Do not let your tongue carry you toward that which is not right. Instead, you should be cultivating friendships with those who are around you. When this happens, the Creator is pleased."

He continued, "The Creator made it so that there would be those who would ensure that the office and duties of the faith keeper would never end. It is they who have the responsibility of watching over the people and making sure that the culture continues. Those who remain faithful to the teachings the Creator gave will have an easy walk on the path in the Sky World. That is because the duties of the faith keepers continue there as well. Those faith keepers who fail to perform their duties on earth will suffer greatly in the Sky World."

He continued, "It was the Creator's wish that all our feasts of thanksgiving would include the flesh of the deer, since the Peacemaker came and gave us the *Kayeneren:kowa*. However, today we are surrounded by the light-skinned beings from Sawiskera's island. They have destroyed the forests, and there are few, if any, forest animals left. The four messengers said it would be all right if we used the meat of domestic animals in our feasts today. This will no longer be considered wrong."

He continued, "The light-skinned beings are pressing you on every side. You will now have to live as they do in some things in order to survive. You may herd cattle and live in comfortable warm houses such as the light-skinned beings do. The men may now go into the fields and help the women plant and bring in the food. These are the only customs that you should adopt from them, for you cannot be as they are in all things."

He continued, "It still pleases the Creator that you set apart for your lives the three mothers who are also referred to as your sisters - the corn, the beans, and the squash. You should always be thankful for them. Whenever you gather in your harvest, let everyone come together and be thankful as always was done. This will show the Creator that you are still thinking about the things that he gave you."

He continued, "There is a spirit that exists for the medicines. It watches over everyone and assists the needy when called. The Creator made it so that there are some who possess the gift of the medicines. However, it pains him to see some of them charge high prices that people can't pay for medicines that the sick need."

He continued, "The Creator also gave us the tobacco plant. This is important when medicines are administered. When people who are sick recover, they must return thanks to the Creator by using the tobacco plant. That is because it is through the kindness of the Creator that people regain their health. In this way, the medicines are blessed. The medicine person should be rewarded only what the sick person can afford to give to him. There are some who have nothing to give and a thank you should suffice as payment. The medicine person will be rewarded by seeing the sick person, a member of the extended family of relations, get well."

He continued, "The Creator said he has given every people their own teachings to satisfy their needs. They should try not to mingle the blood of the different peoples who exist, because they may then forget the original instructions that each of them have been given. A blue bird and robin don't mix; yet, they still remain a part of the family of birds, and each follows their original instructions."

Skanyiatar:io Explains What Happened
When He Was Taken to the Sky World

He continued, "The four messengers then said to me. You will now see the place where people are tormented by the deeds they have done. They took me on a path that traveled through the sky. There the path divided with one turning toward the right and the other toward the left. To the right was the road toward the Creator's abode. To the left was the road that turned toward the place of torment. At the fork in the road were two gate keepers. If the person had lived a life of evil, the keeper of the evil-minded's path would point in that direction. Automatically, the person ended up on the road toward the evil-minded's place. If the person lived a life of virtue, the gate keepers of the path to the Creator's place pointed to the other road. The person then ended up on the road toward the Creator. This is the way Teharonhia:wako made it, so that his brother Sawiskera would have his own place away from his."

He continued, "It is true that the path toward the Creator has not been used very much in recent years, and the other path has been well-trodden. There are also times when it is difficult to balance individuals' acts in life as to whether they were more good than bad. This is why those who take the path to the evil-minded may only be there for a day, a month, or a year. Others may be there longer. The evil-minded can only hold people for so long, and then, when they have made their penance, they can take the road to the Creator. However, there are certain actions that one may commit that will prevent that person from ever reaching the place of the Creator. They are the using of witchcraft to try and destroy the spirit of others and the committing of a murder. Finally, the third thing is the killing of children both born and unborn. Those who commit these acts may never reach the Creator's place."

He continued, "The four messengers then took me to a house of many rooms. One of the messengers pointed his staff to the roof of the house, whereupon it disappeared and we were on top looking down at the rooms."

He continued, "The first thing that I saw was a man who was haggard. His eyes were sunken and his body was half-consumed by everything he had been through. This man was a drunkard. The evil-minded one then called him by name. The man obeyed and was given a cauldron of red-hot liquid and commanded to drink it. The man drank from it, and one could see the steam rise out of his mouth. He then cried for help. He was then tormented to sing and dance, just as he had done while drunk on the earth. The messengers said, 'Let drunkards take warning from this. Everything is enhanced in the Sky World, and Sawiskera's deception is even greater there than on the earth.'"

He continued, "Others were then summoned, a husband and a wife. Sawiskera told them to act toward each other as they have done on the earth. The couple then began to quarrel with one another. They were so angry with each other that they got to the point where their words made no sense, and they seemed blinded to the other person. This is the way that Sawiskera uses the conduct of those on earth to punish them. In fact, they are only doing the same thing that they did on earth. The messengers said, 'Be warned and live together in peace and harmony with one another.'"

He continued, "Next, the evil-minded called upon a woman who had been a witch. She was plunged in a cauldron of boiling liquid and then a freezing one. The messenger said that this woman will suffer from eternal punishment, for she has used her power on earth to unnatural extremes."

He continued, "The evil-minded then called up a man who beat his wife. In front of him was a red-hot statue of a woman. He was then told to beat the statue. As he struck the statue, sparks flew in all directions, and his arm was consumed. This is the punishment in store for wife-beaters, the messengers said."

He continued, "I looked again and saw a woman who was skin and bones. She had been a seller of fire water, the mind changer, to the people. The flesh on her hands had rotted away. The messengers said that this is the fate of those who sell the mind changer."

He continued, "Then I looked and saw Farmers Brother, a former friend of mine. He was removing a heap of sand, grain by grain. Even though he continually worked, the heap of sand would not diminish in size. This is what happens to those who sell their first Mother, the Earth."

He continued, "Next, I saw a field of corn beside the house of torment. There was a woman cutting down the corn, and as she cut them more grew in their place. This is what happens to those women who work the lands and are lazy."

He continued, "These are some of the things that I saw taking place. There is much more, and I have given you some examples. There are things that are more important to learn than dwelling on punishments."

He continued, "The Creator made it so that the *onkwe:honwe* would need to depend on one another. He made it so that they should be sociable toward one another. That means when a person visits you, set food out for them. If it is your next door neighbors, you should feed them. They will leave from your place feeling good, and will thank you."

He continued, "The messengers told me that stealing was wrong. The Creator will meet all your needs, and you only have to tell him what they are and they will be supplied. Children sometimes take things that are not their own. Let the parents be the teachers so that they may learn not to steal."

He continued, "Our old people have lived a long time. It is important that they be given the proper respect and are treated with reverence. They have witnessed and felt much pain in their lives. Always be kind to the oldest and most helpless. Wash their hands and their face and nurse them with care. This is the wish of the Creator for the elders."

He continued, "It has always been the custom to mourn a person for a full year. This is wrong, because during the time of mourning, the children are neglected from being cared for. Only mourn a person for ten days. Address the body and tell the deceased how much you cared for them. Respect for the departed is extremely important."

He continued, "The four messengers then took me to see the Town Destroyer. Upon the road leading to the Creator's place, there was a light ahead that shone brilliantly. To the side was a cold water spring where we took a break. Then, there was a pleasant ground that spread itself out everywhere. Finally, we reached the abode of the Creator. To the side of the path grew berries of every kind. Their fragrance was so great that you could smell them in the air wherever you went. Just the taste of one was enough to fill one's appetite. There were also fruits of every kind growing."

He continued, "The persons who resided here spent their time amusing themselves and enjoying their surroundings. They were extremely content. Here, families were reunited and lived together in harmony. They possessed a bodily form and retained all their senses and remembered their life on earth. None of the light-skinned people ever entered here. They had their own place to be with their relations."

He continued, "Just then I looked and saw a small hut near the entrance to the spirit world. It looked like a fort and within it was the Town Destroyer walking back and forth. By the way he held himself he appeared to be a good man. During the wars between the great Crown and the Americans, he decided not to completely destroy us after the great Crown deserted us to the Americans. For this act, he is the only light-skinned being to make it this far to our spirit world. However, he can go no farther, for he has killed many and given much of the *onkwe:honwe* lands away. Instead he is to walk alone and, there, live his life in contentment. It is also a reminder to you as you walk to the spirit world of the Creator to remember who now controls your lands. You took sides against one another, and now most of your lands are lost. Those *onkwe:honwe* who pass by the Town Destroyer see him but pass him in silence, as he never speaks to anyone. Always remember that he could have destroyed you completely but chose not to do so. If he had done so there would be none of you left, and so he is left to wander in peace."

He continued, "The four messengers then said that unless the *onkwe:honwe* do what the Creator has ordained for them, he will lose his patience with you. Then, he will be angry with you, and he won't help you to continue to exist. If you *onkwe:honwe* do not do as he asks of you, then how can you go on as *onkwe:honwe*? You will be the cause of your own demise. You have been given your own belief system and language. If you fail in these, then there is no place for you left as *onkwe:honwe* on Earth or in the Sky World. You will have to go somewhere else, perhaps with the light-skinned beings."

He continued, "The Creator made both the light and the darkness. He asked our Elder Brother the Sun to give us heat and light in the day. He asked our Grandmother the Moon to shine at night and to cool the Earth when it becomes too hot. If we stop giving thanks to the Creator for the things he has given us, the clouds will be still. The spirit of the waters of the springs and brooks will no longer look after them for our benefit. The Sun will go dim and then darkness will cover the earth. A great smoke will arise in the air and cover all the earth. Then the poisonous monsters created by Sawiskera will appear, and the evil-minded will perish from the earth."

He continued, "However, before this terrible event occurs, Teharonhia:wako will visit one last time and bring the good-minded back with him. First, they will lie down to sleep and when they awake they will rise and go home with the Creator."

This was all that Shakenjoweneh could remember of what he had been told about what Skanyiatar:io revealed about the Good Message. He said that there was more, but that he could not relate it all in the allotted time. All of what he said was a Good Message. It would be up to others to decide what should be added. If they are to add to the message, let them do so in the spirit of the Rotinonshonni. Remember that Sawiskera is close by listening and waiting to subvert the meaning of the Good Message.

Notes

Select Bibliography

Notes

Introduction

1. Rotinonshonni means the People of the Longhouse. They include the Kenienké:haka (Mohawk), the Oneota:haka (Oneida), the Onontaka:haka (Onondaga), the Kaokwa:haka (Cayuga) and the Sonontowa:haka (Seneca).

2. Brian Rice, "A Methodology Based on Rotinonshonni Traditions." In *Native Voices in Research* (Winnipeg: Univ. of Manitoba Aboriginal Issues Press, 2003), 177–180.

3. The Tanakh is the Old Testament of the Jewish People. Kenneth Davis, *Don't Know Much About the Bible: Everything You Need to Know About the Good Book but Never Learned* (New York: Eagle Brook, 1998).

4. *On the Origin of Species by Means of Natural Selection, or the Preservation of Favoured Races in the Struggle of Life*, discussed in Robert Berkhofer, *The Whiteman's Indian* (New York: Vintage Books, 1979), 50.

5. According to Berkhofer (*Whiteman*, 53), Morgan in his work *Ancient Society, or Researches in the Lines of Human Progress from Savagery through Barbarism to Civilization* (1877) divided human kin as passing through seven stages of evolution, lower, middle, and upper savagery; lower, middle, and upper barbarism; and civilization. The Indians living in villages of North and South America were said to be in the middle barbaric stage.

6. George E. Sioui, *For an Amerindian Autohistory* (Montreal: McGill-Queen's Univ. Press, 1992).

7. William Fenton, *The Great Law and the Longhouse: A Political History of the Iroquois Confederacy* (Norman: Univ. of Oklahoma Press, 1998).

8. The speech of Kiasaton, in Thomas Grassmann's (1969:97–99) work, *The Mohawk Indians and Their Valley: Being a Chronology Documentary Record of the End of 1693*, offers an example of a Native expression of culture that has been useful to the writer.

9. Another author's work that has been helpful to the writer is William Fenton's work, *The Great Law and the Longhouse*. There is a story that from Fenton use that the writer added to the oral tradition of the Great Law concerning Atotarhoh and his abuse of women.

10. The Great Law, also known as the *Kayeneren:kowa,* came to the Iroquoian peoples around 1300 AD according to oral traditions by Tekana:wita (the Peacemaker) and unified what were then the five Iroquois Nations.

11. According to archeologist Dean R. Snow, *The Peoples of America: The Iroquois* (Cambridge: Blackwell Publishers, 1996), 12, artifacts place Point Peninsula culture anywhere from England to southern Ontario and Quebec to north of the Canadian Shield. This would be in line with the migration of the Anishnaabe, according to their oral traditions from the east coast to northern Ontario.

12. Richard Acquila, *The Iroquois Restoration: Iroquois Diplomacy on the Colonial Frontier 1704–1754* (Detroit: Wayne State Univ. Press, 1997), 170; Barbara Graymont, *The Iroquois in the American Revolution* (Syracuse: Syracuse Univ. Press, 1972), 45.

13. J. N. B. Hewitt, "The Myth of the Earth-Grasper of De'haen'hiyawa'khon," *Bureau of American Ethnology,* 43, 21st annual report (1900).

14. The *Kari:wio* is also known as the Good Message of Skanyiatar:io and is more commonly known as the Code of Handsome Lake. The message was brought to the Iroquois around 1800 AD after Skanyiatar:io received his revelations from four angelic beings.

15. Lewis Henry Morgan, *League of the Iroquois* (New York: Citadel Press, 1962, 232–259).

16. Isabel Thompson Kelsey, *Joseph Brant 1743–1807: Man of Two Worlds* (Syracuse: Syracuse Univ. Press, 1984, 611). Note that the Creator's game, mentioned in this paragraph, refers to lacrosse.

1. The Creation Story

Note: For chapter 1, I have used as my main sources of reference: J. N. B. Hewitt, "The Myth of the Earth-Grasper of De'haen'hiyawa'khon,'" *Bureau of American Ethnology,* 43, 21st Annual Report (1900): 1–55. Jacob Thomas, *The Great Law of Peace,* Twelve Day Oral Recital, June 26–July 7, 1994, days one and two of which I attended.

1. *Orenta* is the life-giving energy that inhabits all things. Some people are able to enhance their *orenta* through spiritual practices. *Orenta* has influence over events and things (Herrick 1995, 14).

2. I was first made aware of *otkon* during a Mohawk cultural class in *Kahnawake,* defined as being the transference of *orenta* into *otkon* by using it for malevolent purposes. They are in fact two sides of the same coin. Christianized Mohawks use the term *otkon* in reference to the devil (*Traditional Teachings,*Mohawk Culture Class, Kanawake, Quebec 1991).

3. Jacob Thomas was said to have been born with in a caul. According to tradition, this meant that a person was destined for some important duty (Jacob Thomas, *Traditional Teachings*: Personal Correspondence Jake Thomas Learning Centre, 1992).

4. Jacob Thomas, 1992 *Great Law* recital. In his recitation of the *Great Law,* Jacob Thomas mentions that the Peacemaker was also hidden under the husk. This was a rite of passage for all Iroquois children at one time.

5. This has been the custom of the Rotinonshonni until recent years, when they began living in nuclear families. According to tradition, this was to ensure that the children would never become bitter toward their mothers. A common punishment would be to squirt water in the face of children rather than hit them (*Traditional Teachings, Mohawk Cultural Course, Kahnawake, Quebec,* 1991).

6. According to Jacob Thomas (1992, *Great Law* Recital, Jake Thomas Learning Centre, Oshweken), the Great White Pine is the most important tree for the Rotinonshonni. Its boughs are used for purification, and the pine needles represent the five original Rotinonshonni Nations.

7. The Tree of Life is a cross-cultural teaching that can be found within many traditional societies. In fact, it is considered a universal symbol for the passageway that is at the center of the different spirit worlds in the universe. Campbell (1989, p. 157) and Halifax (1979, p. 17) say that fledgling shamans are nurtured in nests on top of a tree where they receive their visions.

8. Three is a sacred number among the Rotinonshonni. In fact, those who were accused of witchcraft were given three warnings to denounce it, whereupon if they did, they were let go free (Newell, 1965, 49).

9. According to Jacob Thomas (1994, *Great Law* recital), the heart is where the life spirit resides.

10. The Ancient Uncle, or Dew Eagle of the Sky World, had been replaced by the Eagle by the time of the Peacemaker. He is said to be the brother of Hato:i, *whose distorted face is associated with* the thunders(Thomas, 1992, *Great Law* recital, Jake Thomas Learning Centre, Oshwegen).

11. The Elm Tree is of great importance to the Rotinonshonni, as it is from the Elm that they would construct their Longhouses and their canoes; it is also used as a medicine. This was the tree that provided for their everyday needs (Herrick, 1995, 18).

12. According to Jacob Thomas (1992, *Great Law* recital, Jake Thomas Learning Centre, Osheweken), at one time the dead were placed above the ground on scaffolds and kept in the lodge. This changed with the story of the vampire skeleton (Cornplanter, 1986, 147).

13. Dreams signified messages from a higher order, and they needed to be deciphered, as they could produce sickness if not taken care of. If they weren't interpreted properly, the messages they brought remained unsettled and unresolved in a person's soul. The acting out and interpreting of a dream helped to bring into balance the inner conscience of a person and result in healing (Wallace, 1969, 59).

14. Halifax (1979, p. 153) shows that shamans have to go through extensive ordeals in order to become shamans. First, the body has to be broken down so that one can be reborn into the spirit. Often this means that the flesh is destroyed and the bones are cleansed. Then the shaman is remade whole, with their new added sight. Among the Rotinonshonni, when they moved their villages, the bones of the departed were cleaned and taken to a common burial place where the community of ancestors would continue to exist. The most noted

example of this in Rotinonshonni culture is seen in the story, *A Traditional Journal of an Expedition to the Skyland* (J. N. B. Hewitt, 1899).

15. The last white dog sacrifice was held in 1934 at Six Nations reserve in Ontario (Hale, 1989, 322). The white dogs were messengers to the Sky World and keepers of the Tree of Light (Thomas, 1992, *Traditional Teachings: Personal Correspondence, Jake Thomas Learning Centre, Oshweken*).

16. Lacrosse is known as the great game of war. It represents the duality in the world and is played to keep the balance of the world's energy intact. Opposing nations could resolve disputes by playing a game of lacrosse (Thomas, 1992, *Traditional Teachings: Personal Correspondence: Jake Thomas Learning Centre, Oshweken*).

17. Jacob Thomas (1992, *Traditional Teachings: Personal Correspondence: Jake Thomas Learning Centre, Osheweken*) says that you are married only one time in Rotinonshonni society.

18. In contemporary Rotinonshonni society, the boy to be betrothed will move in with the girl, unlike what occurs in the Sky World. That could be because things are done opposite in the Sky World than the Earth World. Dancers dance clockwise in the Sky World, while they dance counterclockwise in the Earth World (Jacob Thomas, 1992, *Traditional Teachings: Personal Correspondence, Jake Thomas Learning Centre, Oshweken*).

19. In every shamanic spiritual experience, one faces obstacles that try to distract the person having the experience. They may appear in human form and test a person to see if he or she is worthy of going on. Halifax (1979) gives some examples of shamanic experiences and the obstacles shamans faced when entering the spirit world.

20. This is a common tradition among many ancient cultures. The comet's appearance is a sign that a great change is about to take place. In fact some Native cultures such as the Ojibwe believe that a comet once destroyed the world (Williamson and Farrer, 1992, 43).

21. Mature Flowers's essence lies with the water that pours down from the birth canal of the Sky World. She then fertilizes the Earth World with her life-giving powers.

22. These are the sacred plants of the Rotinonshonni.

23. Thomas, 1994, *The Creation Story and Recital of the Great Law of Peace, Oshweken*.

24. The Turtle is among the first of creation to begin the process of life. He is considered the oldest of the clans in many Native cultures, including those of the Rotinonshonni.

25. Her mother, bringing in the fertile producing rains, begins the process of the growing of the plant life.

26. There is a Rotinonshonni tradition that humanity had its beginnings from two arrows that sprang from the earth (Thomas, 1992, *Traditional Teachings: Personal Correspondence, Jake Thomas Learning Centre, Oshweken*).

27. This teaching was first presented to me by Kevin Deer (1991, Mohawk Cultural Course). I have elaborated on the teaching.

28. Ten days is also the traditional time for mourning the dead since Skanyiatar:io's reforms. After ten days a feast and giveaway occurs. According to Jacob Thomas (1992,

Traditional Teachings: Personal Correspondence, Jake Thomas Learning Centre, Oshweken), this final part had been reduced from a year. The Yearafter Feast is still done by other Native societies in the Northeast such as the Ojibwe. The author was a participant in a traditional Midewiwin Yearafter Ceremony.

29. Jacob Thomas (1994, *The Creation Story and the Recital of the Great Law of Peace, Jake Thomas Learning Centre, Oshweken*) was always adamant about the wrongs of killing and pointed to this story when reciting the creation story, which preceded his reciting of the Great Law.

30. At one time, the sunflower was a much more important source of nourishment than it is today (Herrick, 1995:20).

31. The red willow is one of the foremost medicine plants in use. It is second only to tobacco in its medicinal properties. It is considered a blood cleanser (Thomas, 1992, *Traditional Teachings, Jake Thomas Learning Centre, Oshweken*).

32. The Strawberries are a medicine plant and were one of the few medicines that Skanyiatar:io sanctioned when he reformed the traditions. It is the first plant that is seen on the spirit road (1991, *Traditional Teachings: Mohawk Cultural Course, Kahnawake, Quebec*).

33. Sawiskera's power lies with the winter cold. The root of the word *awisé* means ice in Mohawk. By taking some of Sawiskera's power away from him, Teharonhia:wako was able to end the ice age but not all of Sawiskera's power. That is why we still have winter.

34. Corn, along with squash and beans, are the three sisters that were referred to as mothers by the *onkwe:honwe* and helped to sustain the lives of the Rotinonshonni (1991, *Traditional Teachings: Mohawk Cultural Course, Kahnawake, Quebec*).

35. *Oskenonto* means "first to the spirit world." This reflects the importance of the deer, as a messenger to the Sky World (1992 , *Traditional Teachings: Personal Correspondance: Jake Thomas Learning Centre, Oshewken*).

36. This is an important aspect of Star Knowledge and praying to the ancestors. Pam Colorado (1994) has incorporated this in her course in the Traditional Knowledge Program at the California Institute of Integral Studies. What passes from this world travels back to the Sky World and becomes recognizable as the star constellations. They then help human beings to know when to fulfill their life duties by their position in the sky. Goodman (1992) has written extensively on Lacota Star Knowledge and how the movements of the stars help to inform the Lacota about their life duties.

37. It is my presumption that the horns of the deer are the lightning bolts that accompany the spring rains and help break up the ice in lakes and rivers.

38. Many of the animals still return to hibernate in caves in the winter, showing that Sawiskera still exerts some control over their lives. In fact, it is control over the creation that Sawiskera most desires.

39. Hoarding is one of the things that traditional societies least respect. While living in the community of Winneway, the Algonquins of that community referred to the freezer as

the stingy box. The same can be said for the Rotinonshonni. In fact, their leaders gave away much of their possessions as a sign to their people that they did not consider themselves to be above them (Newell, 1965, 21).

40. The male human beings, born later, would learn to always provide for their grand-mothers and others of their community when they came of age, no matter how they were treated (Thomas, 1992, *Great Law* recital, Jake Thomas Learning Centre, Oshweken).

41. Among traditionalists, Sawiskera's creations are considered to be vile in compari-son to Teharonhia:wako's. Nonetheless, they still have a purpose.

42. This was one of the most important medicines for cleansing and purifying the blood (Thomas, 1992, *Traditional Teachings: Personal Correspondence, Jake Thomas Learning Centre, Oshweken*).

43. *Onkwe:honwe* refers to real human being.

44. The writer believes this to be the Neanderthals. There are many traditional stories about the hairy-breasted humans that the *onkwe:honwe* and other Indigenous peoples of the Americas battled against. The *onkwe:honwe* referred to them as Stone Giants (Parker, 1989, 340).

45. This story represents the importance of sharing in Rotinonshonni society (Thomas, 1992, *Traditional Teachings: Personal Correspondence, Jake Thomas Learning Centre, Oshweken*).

46. The writer believes that this could represent the eruption of a volcano.

47. I have changed this element of the story and have mixed the earth with snow to make Sawiskera's human beings. Some stories have the earth mixed with water. This has to do with the coldness that the Rotinonshonni felt that the white people had toward them. The snow is also a manifestation of Sawiskera's power of control over the creation; I use it both as a metaphor and as a reflection of the Rotinonshonni view of their relationship with the Europeans.

48. This has to do with the Euro-Western society's belief that the creation has to be controlled rather than lived within a relationship.

49. This shows that there is a connection that exists in all the creation.

50. Those that practice traditions believe that some of these creatures are uranium ore and disease. Traditionalists believe that if the earth is disrupted and they are let out, they could destroy the world. Traditional Teachings 1991, Mohawk Cultural Course, Kahn-awake, Quebec.

51. The great bowl game is still played in the Longhouse ceremonies of the *onkwe:honwe* during midwinter and harvest. This is in remembrance of the battle over who would con-trol the creation as well as in remembrance of the great change in the weather about to take place. It was first played with plum pits but later peaches were introduced in the area and they were used as well.

52. The Hato:i society, known by some as the "False Face" Society, still exists in some communities. It is said that to mock the society while it is performing a ritual will result

in a twisted deformed face (1991, *Traditional Teachings: Mohawk Cultural Course, Kahnawake, Quebec*).

53. That was because it was Beaver who held the Grandmother's power, which was water, so that he could allow the others to escape the flooding from the rain.

54. Traditionally, an *onkwe:honwe* family consisted of three children. With the population disappearing rapidly due to disease, warfare, and alcohol in the nineteenth century, Skanyiatar:io would change it to twelve children (Thomas, 1992, *Traditional Teachings: Personal Correspondence, Jake Thomas Learning Centre, Oshweken*).

55. This is in reference to the coming of Christianity, Western science, and technology.

56. Jacob Thomas (1992, *Great Law* recital) was adamant against the killing of another human being.

57. This may show that the Rotinonshonni were aware of the Rocky Mountains, as there are various references to them in traditional stories.

58. These stories were given to me by Jacob Thomas (1995) at the University of Sudbury.

59. This is reflected in the Two Row Wampum Belt, which the Rotinonshonni would use with the coming of the Dutch (Thomas, 1992, *Great Law of Peace* recital, Jake Thomas Learning Centre, Oshweken).

60. Beauchamp (1888, 48). I have included this old Seneca story.

61. This is in reference to the Harvest Ceremony, part of the yearly ceremonial festivals still performed in the Longhouse.

62. The Midwinter ceremony is still done in the Longhouse around mid-February.

63. The matrilineal clan system did not come into effect until the clan system is developed by the great young man (See chapter 2, *The Clan System and Migration*).

64. The giving of the thanks is still an essential part of the Rotinonshonni culture. It is now the first thing done at gatherings and ceremonies.

65. Strawberry juice is still drunk during the early summer during the ceremonial cycle. The author has participated in it. The Rotinonshonni also believed it could be used to quell the desire of alcohol (see chapter 5).

66. The author has never witnessed a Mulberry or a Raspberry Ceremony in the ceremonial Longhouse.

67. The author has participated in the Maple Ceremony in the Mohawk Trail Longhouse at Kahnawake.

68. There is much debate over whether the sky trail that forks right and left mentioned in the Code of Handsome Lake that travels to the Creator's and the Punisher's is a new innovation influenced by Christianity. In fact, as reflected in the Creation story, the sky trail fits nicely with the renewal of the cosmology when things begin to die in the Earth World and are reborn into the Sky World.

69. There are still influential herbalists in many of the Rotinonshonni communities.

70. These are still referred to as the three sisters by contemporary *onkwe:honwe*.

2. The Clan System and the Migration of the
Rotinonshonni to Their Traditional Territory

Note: For chapter 2, I have used as my main sources of reference: J. N. B. Hewitt, "De'haen'hiyawa'khon,'" *Bureau of American Ethnology*, 43, 21st Annual Report (1900): 116–130. Jacob Thomas, *The Great Law of Peace*, Twelve Day Oral Recital, June 26–July 7, 1994, days one and two of which I attended.

1. I am basing this on the traditional *Lenni Lenape* story cited by John Heckwelder in his *An Account of the History, Manners, and Customs of the Indian Nations* as mentioned in Wesslager, *The Delaware Indians* (New Jersey: Rutgers Univ. Press, 88)

2. This is a story found in Gerald R. Alfred, *Heeding the Voices of the Ancestors* (Detroit: Wayne State Univ. Press 1995), 28.

3. I have based this story on Rotinonshonni tradition found in Beauchamp, *Iroquois Folk Lore*, 10–11.

3. *The Kayeneren:kowa* (Great Way of Peace)

Note: For chapter 3, I have used Jacob Thomas, *The Great Law of Peace*, Twelve Day Oral Recital, June 26–July 7, 1994, days three through twelve of which I attended. To help with some of the more obscure Mohawk terms I have used Seth Newhouse, 1887, *The Constitution of the Confederacy by the Peacemaker*, revised by Jacob Thomas, February 1989. The Sandpiper Press c/o The Jacob Thomas Learning Centre, index 1–10.)

1. Beauchamp, *Iroquois Folk Lore*, 137–143.

2. *Duda* is a term for Grandmother in Mohawk.

3. *Atotarhoh* was said to have a large phallus that he used as part of his self-indulgent behavior (Fenton, 1998, 82).

4. I have added the moon cycle here to explain the Rotinonshonni seasonal cycles; Bernice Loft Winslow, *Iroquois Fires: The Six Nations Lyrics and Lore of Dawendine* (Ottawa: Penumbra Press, 1995).

4. Sawiskera Gains Control

1. Edward Benton-Banai, *The Mishomis Book: The Voice of the Ojibwa* (St. Paul: The Red Schoolhouse, 1988, 95). The Anishnaabe have an oral tradition about seven prophets who forecasted disaster if the people didn't leave the Atlantic coastal region.

2. This great white wind was predicted in the great law (Thomas, 1994, *Great Law* recital).

3. Ruth Holmes, *The Old Man Told Us: Excerpts from Micmac History Whitehead 1500–1950* (Halifax: Nimbus Publishing, 1991, 8). This is a traditional Micmac story of the coming of the white man.

4. John Gilmary Shea, *History and General Description of New France by Reverend P. F. X. de Charlevoix, S.J.*, vol. 1 (Reprinted, Chicago: Chicago Univ. Press, 116–123). I have taken this

story written by Pierre de Charlevoix (1870) and inserted it as the first meeting between the Rotinonshonni and the Europeans.

5. William W. Warren, *History of the Ojibwa People* (St. Paul: Minnesota Historical Society, 1984, 77–80). This oral tradition of the migration was first written down in 1885 by William Warren, and it follows the same plot as contemporary versions by Anishnaabe traditionalist Benton-Banai.

6. Cadwallender Coldon, *The History of the Five Indian Nations: Depending on the Provinces of New York in America*, 1980, 4). This story was also first told by Pierre de Charlevoix in his *History of New France 1744*, vol. 1, and then written down by the governor of New York, Cadwallader Colden, in 1747.

7. Morgan, *League*, 5. Although Morgan says they lived in the vicinity of Montreal, his story is similar to the oral tradition of the Rotinonshonni and their dispersal from Montreal Island.

8. Tehanetorens, *Tales of the Iroquois*, vols. 1 and 2 (Ohseweken, Ontario: Iroqrafts Ltd., 1992, 113–124). This is another story that confirms the migration of some of the Rotinonshonni from the Montreal area.

9. This would later be called the Ottawa.

10. Grassmann, *The Mohawk Indians*, 61. There is an Anishnaabe tradition that states that the Martin warrior clan was made of Rotinonshonni captives (Benton-Banai, *Mishomis*, 96).

11. Biggar 1922–1936, 99–100; this story was written down in Henry Percival Biggar, ed., *Works of Samuel De Champlain: Reprinted, Translated and Annotated by Six Canadian Scholars under the General Editorship of H. P. Biggar* (Toronto: Champlain Society, 1922–1936), 65–107.

12. Daniel K. Richter, *The Ordeal of the Longhouse: The Peoples of the Iroquois League in the Era of European Colonization*, Chapel Hill: Univ. of North Carolina Press, 1992), 51. The year 1609 was when Henry Hudson sailed up the river later named after him and met the Mohawk.

13. This is referred as the Two Row Wampum by traditionalists. (1992, *Traditional Teachings*, Jacob Thomas, 1992, *Great Law* recital).

14. Richter, *The Ordeal*, 24. It was said that Arent van Curler drowned in Lake Champlain after laughing at the beliefs of his hosts, the *Mohawk*.

15. Ibid., 88. There is a good chance that Elkens may have been involved in the Two Row Wampum agreement, as 1614 is one of the dates given for the treaty by the Rotinonshonni.

16. Biggar, *Works*, 253–254. I believe that this event was pivotal and resulted in a realignment of the confederacy in favor of the war chiefs.

17. I have based this on the oral tradition that Skanawatih was the first *royaner* to take up the war club since the coming of the Great Peace. According to Cayuga *Royaner* Jacob Thomas, he also took the name Rosehraha:hons (Jacob Thomas, 1992, *Great Law* recital).

18. There is an oral tradition that the Oneida had to borrow Mohawk men to fill their clans so devastating had the losses become to Wendat attacks (Thomas, 1992, *Great Law*

recital). I have also found a story in the *Jesuit Relations* that corroborates this (Grassmann, 1969, 105).

19. I have based this on what was told to Morgan (*League*, 99). The Pine Tree and warrior chiefs were a later innovation in the confederacy. It may be why Snow and others believe the league may have originated in the early seventeenth century (Dean R. Snow, *The Peoples of America: The Iroquois*, Cambridge: Blackwell Publishers, 1996).

20. Parker's work on the Great Law has led to confusion among some contemporary *onkwe:honwe* who believe the Great Law sanctions a warrior society. Arthur C. Parker, *Seneca Myths and Folktales* (Lincoln: Univ. of Nebraska Press, 1989).

21. Bruce Trigger, *Natives and Newcomers: Canada's Heroic Age Reconsidered* (Montreal: McGill-Queen's Univ. Press, 1985), 242–251, has pointed out the effects of disease on Iroquoian populations.

22. Isaac Jogues was a Jesuit priest who had come to minister to the Kenienké:haka. He was first held captive by them and then adopted into a Kenienké:haka village in 1645. He escaped and then returned only to be killed in 1646. The Kenienké:haka believed that he had brought smallpox to them (Grassman, *The Mohawk Indians*, 118).

23. Ibid., 97–99.

24. Ibid., 115.

25. Ibid., 118–119.

26. *Traditional Teachings*, 1992, *Great Law* recital, Jake Thomas
Learning Centre, Oshweken

27. Beauchamp, *Iroquois*, 142.

28. I have based this on the fact that Tsakonsasé's lodge was said to be near present-day Lewiston, New York, and near Pete Jemmison, who looks after the seventeenth-century Seneca site Ganondagon.

29. Grassman, *The Mohawk Indians*, 250.

30. Ibid., 276.

31. Ibid., 290.

32. Fenton, *The Great Law*, 253; I have based this on the reason that *Tekarihokenh* left with his family for the settlement at Laprairie. In fact the title of *Tekarihokenh* is still used in one of the Longhouses at *Kahnawake*.

33. Henri S. J. Bechard, *The Original Caughnawaga Indians* (Montreal: International Publishers), 30.

34. This is based on the oral traditions of the Rotinonshonni as told to the writer, attending *Traditional Teachings*, 1992, *Great Law* recital. Richter and Merrell have it occurring between 1675 and 1677. Daniel Richter and James Merrell, *Beyond the Covenant Chain: The Iroquois and Their Neighbors in Indian North America 1600–1800* (Syracuse: Syracuse Univ. Press, 1987).

35. Seneca traditionalist Pete Jemmison told me this story while I visited him on my journey.

36. Grassmann, *The Mohawk Indians*, 443.

37. There has been a long simmering dispute between some Kahnawake Mohawk and the Onondaga. Alfred, *Heeding the Voices*, 47, mentions in passing about this dispute.

38. Richter, *The Ordeal*, 175.

39. Fenton, *The Great Law*, 348

40. Shirley Hill Witt, *The Tuscaroras* (New York: Cromwell Collier Press, 1972), 10.

41. Jacob Thomas (1992, *Great Law* recital) says that the Tuscarora were let in the back door for a period of four years to see whether they would accept the Great Law. They never accepted it; many fought on the American side during the American Revolutionary War.

42. Aquila, *The Iroquois*, 170.

43. Venables, *Founding*, 80.

44. The Seven Nation Confederacy were Christianized Natives that included Iroquois from Kahnawake, Kanesetake, Akwesasne, and Oswegatchie. In addition, it included the Abenaki from Odanak and Becancour, the Algonquin and Nipissing of Kanesetake, and the Huron of Lorrette.

45. James Thomas Flexner, *Mohawk Baronet: A Biography of Sir William Johnson* (Norman: Univ. of Oklahoma Press, 1979), 145–146.

46. Ibid.

47. Graymont, *The Iroquois*, 45.

48. I have based this section on the selling of lands by the Rotinonshonni on the Treaty of Fort Stanwix (Flexner, *Mohawk*, 328) as well as on the bitterness that the Lenni Lenape and other Native groups south of them felt about the treaty. C. A. Weslager, *The Delaware Indians: A History* (New Jersey: Rutgers Univ. Press, 1991), 252.

49. Weslager, *The Delaware*, 191.

50. Kelsey, *Joseph Brant*, 90.

51. Graymont, *The Iroquois*, 48.

52. Ibid., 52.

53. Ibid., 58.

54. Ibid., 51.

55. Ibid., 61.

56. Ibid., 98.

57. Ibid., 99.

58. Ibid., 113.

59. Ibid., 120.

60. Ibid., 112.

61. Ibid., 135.

62. Ibid., 163.

5. The *Kari:wio* of Skanyiatar:io

Note: For chapter 5 I have used Lewis Henry Morgan, 1962, *League of the Iroquois* (New York: Citadel Press), 234–259.

1. I have amalgamated the story of the Kenienké:haka man who had the first visions (Kelsey, *Joseph Brant*, 611), and the traditional story of the man whose steam could be seen from the valley and who lost his visions and his life (Parker, *Seneca Myths*, 26).

2. Parker, *Seneca Myths*, 18–19.

Select Bibliography

Primary Sources

Published Primary Sources

Hewitt, J. N. B. "The Myth of the Earth-Grasper of De'haen'hiyawa'khon." *Bureau of American Ethnology* 43, 21st Annual Report (1900): 1–130.

Morgan, Lewis Henry. *League of the Iroquois.* New York: Citadel Press, 1962.

Oral Recitations

Colorado, Pamela. *Star Knowledge.* Californian Institute of Integral Studies: The Shadows, San Francisco, Oct. 19–27, 1994.

Traditional Teachings. Mohawk Cultural Course, Kahnawake, July 1–30, 1991.

Thomas, Jacob. *Star Stories.* Univ. of Sudbury, Nov. 11, 1995.

———. *The Creation Story.* Oral Recital, Jacob Thomas Learning Centre, Ohsweken, June 26–July 7, 1994.

———. *The Great Law of Peace.* Nine Day Oral Recital, Jacob Thomas Learning Centre, Ohsweken, Sept. 19–27, 1992.

———. *The Great Law of Peace.* Twelve Day Oral Recital, Jacob Thomas Learning Centre, Ohsweken, June 26–July 7, 1994.

———. *Traditional Teachings.* Jacob Thomas Learning Centre, Ohsweken, Sept. 19–27, 1992.

———. *Traditional Teachings.* Mohawk Cultural Course, Kahnawake, July 1–30, 1991.

Secondary Sources

Acquila, Richard. *The Iroquois Restoration: Iroquois Diplomacy on the Colonial Frontier, 1704–1754.* Detroit: Wayne State Univ. Press, 1997.

Alfred, Gerald R. *Heeding the Voices of Our Ancestors: Kahnawake Mohawk Politics and the Rise of Native Nationalism.* Toronto: Oxford Univ. Press, 1995.

Beauchamp, W. M. *Iroquois Folk Lore: Gathered from the Six Nations of New York*. Port Washington, N.Y.: Empire State Historical Publication, 31, 1888.

———. *The Iroquois Trail: Or Footprints of the Six Nations in Customs, Traditions, and History*. Fayetteville, N.Y.: Recorder Office, 1892.

Bechard, Henri S. J. *The Original Caughnawaga Indians*. Montreal: International Publishers, 1976.

Benton-Banai, Edward. *The Mishomis Book: The Voice of the Ojibwa*. St. Paul: Red School House, 1988.

Berkhofer, Robert F. *The Whiteman's Indian*. New York: Vintage Books, 1979.

Biggar, Henry Percival. *The Works of Samuel De Champlain: Reprinted, Translated and Annotated by Six Canadian Scholars under the General Editorship of H. P. Biggar*. Toronto: Champlain Society, 1922–1936.

Campbell, Joseph. *Historical Atlas of the World Mythology: The Way of the Seeded Earth*, part 2, vol. 2, *Mythologies of the Primitive Planters: The Northern America*. New York: Harper & Row, 1989.

Coldon, Cadwallender. *The History of the Five Indian Nations: Depending on the Provinces of New York in America*. Ithaca: Cornell Univ. Press, 1980.

Cornplanter, J. J. *Legends of the Longhouse*. Ohsweken: Iroqrafts Ltd., 1986.

Davis, Kenneth. *Don't Know Much about the Bible: Everything You Need to Know about the Good Book but Never Learned*. New York: Eagle Brook, 1998.

Fenton, William. *The Great Law and the Longhouse: A Political History of the Iroquois Confederacy*. Norman: Univ. of Oklahoma Press, 1998.

Flexner, James Thomas. *Mohawk Baronet: A Biography of Sir William Johnson*. Syracuse: Syracuse Univ. Press, 1979.

Goodman, Ronald. *Lacota Star Knowledge: Studies in Lakota Stellar Theology*. Rosebud, S. Dak.: Sinte Gleska Univ., 1992.

Grassmann, Thomas. *The Mohawk Indians and Their Valley: Being a Chronology Documentary Record to the End of 1693*. Schenectady, N.Y.: Hugo Photography and Printing Co., 1969.

Graymont, Barbara. *The Iroquois in the American Revolution*. Syracuse: Syracuse Univ. Press, 1972.

Hale, H. E. *The Iroquois Book of Rites: And Hale on the Iroquois*. Ohsweken: Iroqrafts Ltd., 1989.

Halifax, Joan. *Shamanic Voices: A Survey of Visionary Narratives*. New York: Penguin Group, 1979.

Hall, Louis. *Karoniaktajeh: Rebuilding the Iroquois Confederacy*. Self-Publication, 1990.

Heckwelder, John. "An Account of the History, Manners, and Customs of the Indian Nations, 1819." In *The Delaware Indians: A History*, edited by C. A. Wesslager, 88. New Jersey: Rutgers Univ. Press, 1991.

Herrick, James W. *Iroquois Medical Botany*. Syracuse: Syracuse Univ. Press, 1995.

Hewitt, J. N. B. *A Traditional Journal of an Expedition to the Skyland: by Chief John Arthur Gibson, 1899*. Library of Yvonne and Jacob Thomas. Ohsweken: The Jacob Thomas Learning Centre.

Kelsey, Isabel Thompson. *Joseph Brant 1743–1807: Man of Two Worlds*. Syracuse: Syracuse Univ. Press, 1984.

Newell, William B. *Crime and Justice among the Iroquois Nations*. Montreal: Caughnawaka Historical Society, 1965.

Newhouse, Seth. *The Constitution of the Confederacy by the Peacemaker, 1887*. Revised by Jacob Thomas, February 1989. Wilsonville, Ontario : The Sandpiper Press c/o The Jacob Thomas Learning Centre, 1989.

Parker, Arthur C. *Seneca Myths and Folk Tales*. Lincoln: Univ. of Nebraska Press, 1989.

———. *The Code of Handsome Lake: The Seneca Prophet*. Ohsweken: Iroqrafts Ltd., 1990.

Rice, Brian. "A Methodology Based on Rotinonshonni Traditions." In *Native Voices in Research*, edited by Jill Oakes, Rick Riewe, Kimberley Wilde, Alison Edmunds, and Alison Dubois, 177–180. Winnipeg: Univ. of Manitoba Aboriginal Issues Press, 2003.

Richter, Daniel K. *The Ordeal of the Longhouse: The Peoples of the Iroquois League in the Era of European Colonization*. Chapel Hill: Univ. of North Carolina Press, 1992.

Richter, Daniel K., and Merrell, James H. *Beyond the Covenant Chain: The Iroquois and Their Neighbors in Indian North America, 1600–1800*. Syracuse: Syracuse Univ. Press, 1987.

Shea, John Gilmary. *History and General Description of New France by Rev. P. F. X. De Charlevoix, S.J.*, vol. 1. Reprinted, Chicago: Chicago Univ. Press 1866.

Sioui, George E. *For an Amerindian Autohistory*. Montreal: McGill–Queen's Univ. Press, 1992.

Snow, Dean R. *The Peoples of America: The Iroquois*. Cambridge: Blackwell Publishers, 1996.

Tehanetorens. *Tales of the Iroquois*, vols. 1 and 2. Ohsweken: Iroqrafts Ltd., 1992.

Trigger, Bruce. *Natives and Newcomers: Canada's Heroic Age Reconsidered*. Montreal: McGill-Queen's Univ. Press, 1989.

Venables, Robert W. "The Founding Fathers: Choosing to be the Romans." edited by J. Barreiro, 30–55 vol. 6, no 4, winter North East Quarterly, Ithaca: Cornell Univ., 1989.

Wallace, Anthony F. C. *The Death and Rebirth of the Seneca*. New York: Vintage Books, 1969.

Warren, William W. *History of the Ojibwa People*. St. Paul: Minnesota Historical Society, 1984.

Wesslager, C. A. *The Delaware Indians: A History*. New Jersey: Rutgers Univ. Press, 1991.

Whitehead, Ruth Holmes. *The Old Man Told Us: Excerpts from Micmac History 1500–1950*. Halifax: Nimbus Publishing, 1991.

Williamson, Ray A., and Farrer, Claire R. *Earth & Sky: Visions of the Cosmos in Native American Folklore*. Albuquerque: Univ. of New Mexico Press, 1992.

Winslow, Bernice Loft. *Iroquois Fires: The Six Nations Lyrics and Lore of Dawendine*. Ottawa: Penumbra Press, 1995.

Witt, Shirley Hill. *The Tuscaroras*. New York: Cromwell-Collier Press, 1972.